# THE ONLY WAY TO...
# LEARN ABOUT
# RELATIONSHIPS

# THE ONLY WAY TO . . .
# LEARN ABOUT
# RELATIONSHIPS

## VOLUME V

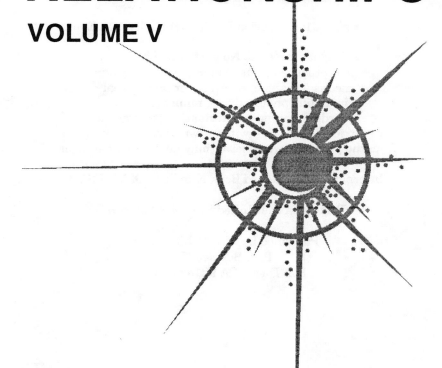

## SYNASTRY TECHNIQUES

## by MARION D. MARCH & JOAN McEVERS

International Standard Book Number 0-935127-21-6

Printed in the United States of America

Published by ACS Publications
P.O. Box 34487
San Diego, CA 92163-4487

# DEDICATION

We dedicate this book to our enchanting grandchildren
Marina and Sebastiano Andina
Heather McEvers Gray and Devin McEvers
Tia Rose, Chelsea and Caleb McEvers
Trevor McEvers
Watching them grow has helped us learn more
about how astrology works.

# TABLE OF CONTENTS

Page

# PART IV  PUTTING IT ALL TOGETHER

# APPENDIX

# HOROSCOPES USED IN "THE ONLY WAY TO... LEARN ABOUT RELATIONSHIPS"

All data according to Rodden System etc.

We thank Lois M. Rodden and Edwin Steinbrecher for generously sharing data with us.

# INDEX OF HOROSCOPES IN VOLUMES I, II, III AND IV

# INTRODUCTION

In our *The Only Way to...Learn Astrology* series, we have taken you from the very beginning, when you knew nothing about astrology, through the planets, signs, houses and aspects, into all kinds of refinements as well as different methods for erecting horoscopes. In Volume III we explained how rulers work and introduced you to various methods of chart interpretation. These first three books only involved the natal chart, the exact moment frozen in space when **you** were born.

In Volume IV, *The Only Way to...Learn About Tomorrow*, we taught you how to move the static horoscope forward by progression, direction, transit and solar as well as lunar returns. For the first time you realized that you can look at two or even three charts and compare one to another. Of course, it was always the horoscope of the same person, just projected forward by different methods— but it demonstrated how you can find aspects to the natal from the progressions or directions and the transits for the year— in other words the interaction of one horoscope to another.

In this book, *The Only Way to...Learn About Relationships*, we will continue the interaction between charts, but we will view two different charts, those of two lovers, or husband and wife, parent and child, siblings, business partners or any other combination of people. This method of comparing one horoscope to another is called **synastry** or **chart comparison**. We will also address a fairly new but most effective way of discovering compatibility between people, namely **composite charts**.

As John Donne said so eloquently: "No man is an island entire of itself," thus all forms of relating assume enormous importance in chart interpretation. How you feel about contact with others can be seen in more ways than synastry or chart comparison. Your attitude toward relating can be found mainly in the natal chart. How you feel about your siblings and what you need from them is quite obvious when you examine the 3rd house; how you relate to your parents can be determined by studying the 4th and 10th houses; your attitude toward your children is indicated by your 5th house, and so on around the wheel. All of this and more will be included in this book.

There are, of course, many other significant and revealing approaches to astrology, but none more so than any and all forms of relating. So sit back, relax and join us in learning a fun way to explore comparison astrology.

# PART ONE: THE FOUNDATION
## LESSON 1

# THE NATAL CHART: WHAT YOU NEED FROM ANOTHER PERSON

You've probably heard it a million times— but, before you can analyze or compare two charts, you must first grasp the real needs of each individual in question; in other words, you must understand each natal chart. Before you can diagnose how well you will like (or not like) someone else, you must realize what you need or want from this other person, and that can only be found in the natal horoscope.

## The Overview

Astrological language never changes; the keywords and key phrases stay the same whether you are interpreting a natal chart, moving it forward or comparing it to another horoscope, therefore the same rules apply and you must understand the synthesis of the whole before you take it apart; we call this **the overview.** (See Volume II, Chapter 20, "Steps to Delineation.")

A predominance (seven to ten) of **planets above the horizon** suggests that you have an outgoing personality and probably wish to rise above your status at birth. If that is so, you like to surround yourself with people who are also ambitious and can understand your needs. If you have more **planets below the horizon** (seven to ten), you may be introspective, or less anxious to be recognized out in the world, therefore you may prefer the company of people with similar needs.

A preponderance of planets **east of the Meridian** (seven to ten) usually indicates that you are self-motivated and do not depend on others to get you started. If you do not need too many people, those you do associate with should be willing to let you be the leader- a role you probably enjoy.

With a majority of **planets on the west side of the chart** (seven to ten), your destiny is often caught up with others and you need to have an audience or someone to bounce your ideas off on. Happiest among pacesetters, you frequently prefer others to be the initiators while you enjoy finishing what they start.

**Chart patterns** should be observed, but they really have more meaning in comparing two charts than in actually indicating your own needs as seen in your natal horoscope.

The same applies to **configurations** which assume great importance in synastry, but in the natal horoscope just indicate where the action may take place, as well as how easy or difficult planetary integration could be, rather than revealing what you need from somebody else.

House emphasis, dignities, exaltations, detriments, fall, planetary high focus, interceptions, retrogrades and any other areas that you consider before you take the chart apart, should be studied in order to assess the individual and her/his general needs, but cannot really help determine what you specifically desire from another.

**Lacks** in the natal chart can be very revealing, especially in examining one-to-one relationships. The natural tendency is to seek what you lack in someone else. Unfortunately once you find this missing quality or element in another, you don't always know what to do with it. If, for example, you have **no planets in Earth signs** in your natal chart, you may seek people with many Earth planets. They can provide the practicality, organizational qualities and down-to-earth attitudes that you feel you lack, but it may be difficult for you to adapt to such regimentation. The same principle applies if a **quality** is missing or a **house** is unoccupied. If you have an **isolated planet**, one not connected by major aspects to the rest of the horoscope, you may seek someone who brings aspects to that planet, so that it is easier for you to integrate the basics of the planet through interaction with the other person.

A predominance of **qualities** and **elements**, which results in what we call the **signature** can also be very revealing. In our practice we have found that the signature acts very much like a second Ascendant. Not necessarily the way you look, but most certainly the way you express and act. For example, one of our students with an Aries signature is almost always taken for an Aries, yet she has Sagittarius rising and a Taurus Sun with only Uranus in Aries. If the signature is in the same sign as the Sun, Moon or Ascendant, it merely accentuates your ego (Sun), emotional expression (Moon) or persona (Ascendant). The signature is most revealing when it is in a different sign because it adds another dimension to your self-expression.

## LESSON 2
# HOUSE POSITIONS: 1ST AND 7TH

## The 1st House
Most important in understanding relationships and what you, as an individual, desire from others, is to comprehend the houses and their meaning in the horoscope. The 1st house always depicts your persona, the way you package yourself and want others to see you. Of course, you must look at the entire chart in order to really define your total personality, but the rising sign or Ascendant, as well as the signature can give many clues.

## The 7th House
Since this book is all about relating, the 7th house assumes a double role. Astrologically speaking, just as the 1st house is "you," the 7th house represents the partner: marital, business or any other face-to-face committed relationship. The Ascendant illustrates your abilities, traits and talents and the 7th mirrors what you seek from others. The kind of person who can fulfill your intimate needs is depicted by the 7th house and the sign on the cusp and its ruler, as well as any planets in the house.

Psychologically speaking, the 7th house symbolizes what Carl Jung called "the shadow." Some people call it your alter ego. By any name it represents the other, often unknown side of the Ascendant. The 1st house, Aries/Mars, fiery and positive says: "I am strong; I don't need anybody." The 7th, Libra/Venus in airily detached fashion thinks: "Wait until Aries wakes up and realizes what happens when my air stops feeding his fire." Until you become consciously aware of the other side or opposition and make use of the polarity, you not only fail to understand "the other," you also fail to understand yourself.

The glyph for Venus (♀) symbolizes the mirror Aphrodite/Venus is so often identified with. It also becomes the mirror the Ascendant (the I) uses in order to see the Descendant (you); but all you see is the reflected, sometimes blurred and always reversed image of your Self.

The 7th house represents all you yearn for because you do not as yet possess or understand it. It reveals what you lack and though you are not consciously aware of what is missing, you instinctively recognize it when you find it in another person. Then, of course, comes the hard part of integrating it into your personality, rather than resisting the new and unknown and returning to your own status quo.

Relationships are very complicated and the 1st/7th axis reflects this complexity. Truly relating to another human being, seeing them and accepting them as they are and not as you wish them to be can be the task of a lifetime.

## Aries on the 1st House Cusp

Assertive and energetic, you usually know very well what you want to do and when you want to do it, therefore you prefer not to associate with bullies who try to tell you how to live or when to do what. With your innate independence you are happiest among people who let you compete or indulge your impulsiveness and who realize why you don't always have time to think before you speak or act.

Princess Margaret, sister of Queen Elizabeth II, has Aries rising, just about the most difficult Ascendant for one raised with the concept of obeying the rules and regulations that apply to English royalty. Yet Margaret revealed her impulsive and assertive self by falling in love with "unsuitable" war hero, Group Captain Peter Townsend, whom she was not allowed to marry, then divorcing her husband and father of her two children, the Earl of Snowdon.

Do not deduce that Aries rising and Libra on the 7th *per se* indicate divorce. In this chart the Descendant ruler, Venus in the 7th house, opposes Uranus in the 1st and squares Jupiter, forming a tough T-square; some astrologers may even consider this a Grand Cross by including Saturn. The challenges denoted by these kinds of aspects, unless properly handled, can lead to divorce, disappointment or dissatisfaction in one-to-one relationships.

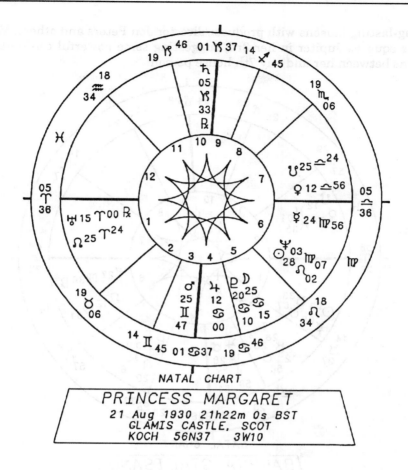

NATAL CHART

PRINCESS MARGARET
21 Aug 1930 21h22m 0s BST
GLAMIS CASTLE, SCOT
KOCH   56N37   3W10

## Libra on the 7th House Cusp

With Aries rising, Libra represents what you need from others, so you seek social outlets through partners and hope to find someone who is companionable, balanced, friendly and agreeable. Since you are a forceful, active person, you look for a partner who is somewhat passive and lets you decide the social calendar and vacation plans, but occasionally you need challenges to stimulate you. Much, of course, depends upon the placement of Venus, ruler of Libra. Your Aries Ascendant desires feedback therefore you really enjoy interacting with someone who confronts you. Singer/actress Barbara Streisand relates best to someone who is willing to remain in the background and let her shine. Venus, ruler of her Libra 7th, is in the 12th house in gentle, empathetic Pisces. She invariably chooses a lover who is in a behind-the-scenes profession (12th house) and who is not bowled over by her energy, drive and bossiness. Her only legal partner was actor Elliott Gould, but she has had long-lasting liaisons with producer/director Jon Peters and others. Venus squares Jupiter in her 3rd, suggesting some powerful confrontations between her and any 7th house person.

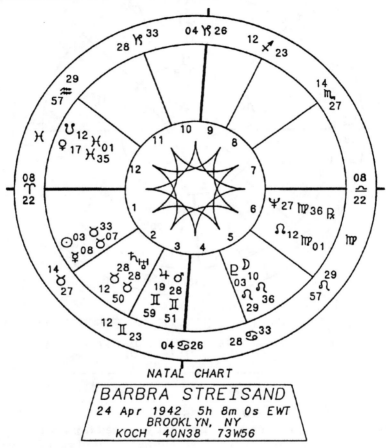

NATAL CHART

BARBRA STREISAND
24 Apr 1942   5h 8m 0s EWT
BROOKLYN, NY
KOCH   40N38   73W56

With Libra on the Descendant, you really enjoy partnering, but the partnership fares best if you maintain the control so dear to your Aries Ascendant.

## Taurus on the 1st House Cusp

You are quite determined in all you do and like to plan your activities. You look forward to tangible accomplishments, therefore wishy-washy or goalless people tend to annoy you. On the other hand, since you can be quite stubborn, you need friends and partners who know how to give in occasionally, else you may become quite frustrated when you don't get your way. This behavior might surprise casual acquaintances who most likely see you as warm, charming, calm and in control. With

Taurus rising it is particularly important to pick the right marriage or business partner. Scorpio rules your 7th house and unless the rulers Pluto and Mars are very challenged, you prefer a strong person as mate or associate, yet too much strength or dominance will go against your fixed nature. Therefore many other factors need to be weighed.

Liza Minelli has a Taurus Ascendant and the chart ruler, Venus, is in Aries in her 12th House. This is a fairly difficult placement because the Taurean need to plan well and natural inclination to be in control, is hampered by Aries' wish to do everything right here and now. Her calm and collected Taurus side is contradicted by the 12th house tendency to be shy and afraid of rejection.

Add to this a sensitive Pisces Sun as well as an empathetic Cancer Moon, Mars, IC and Saturn— this much water denotes a very sensitive nature— and we must assume that whatever composure she displays, is a great front to hide her true nature. Cancer on the 4th cusp certainly verifies a strong tie with her mother, Judy Garland, who had Cancer rising.

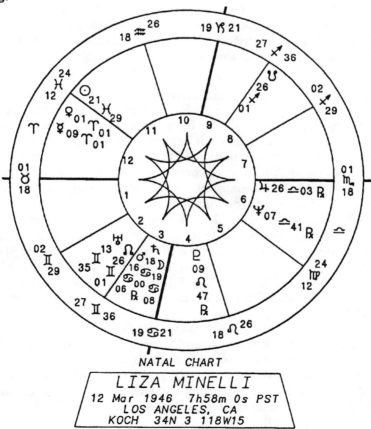

NATAL CHART

LIZA MINELLI
12 Mar 1946    7h58m 0s PST
LOS ANGELES, CA
KOCH    34N 3  118W15

## Scorpio on the 7th House Cusp

When you commit to any alliance, you put your heart, soul and considerable persistence into it. No matter how the relationship works, you toil to make the best of it. You desire someone who is totally devoted to you and in turn you try to remain devoted to your partner. Much depends on the placement of Mars and Pluto, but with the strong fixity embodied in Taurus/Scorpio, you are often dedicated to the concept of marriage with a capital M.

Robert Kennedy, though rumored to be unfaithful to his wife, Ethel, nonetheless received unwavering devotion from her (as well as 11 children). (See his chart on page 123.) Mars is in Scorpio and has very challenging aspects, so certainly the relationship had its ups and downs, but Pluto trines Saturn, representative of time and endurance. There are many aspects that depict the stormy seas encountered in being committed to one person: Pluto opposes Jupiter and Venus suggesting a tendency to self-indulgence when it comes to others; Mars opposes the Ascendant and squares the Moon, a rather formidable T-square, implying a lack of self-confidence when dealing with other people on a one-to-one basis. This could have been very disruptive in intimate relationships and these kind of aspects can lead to divorce if you do not have a strong religious or spiritual commitment or this stubbornly fixed polarity.

## Gemini on the 1st House Cusp

Variety is the spice of your life. You may fear boredom more than the loss of money or prestige and your friends and lovers had better understand that, or the relationship will be short-lived. You relish those who can provide mental stimulation; pedantic perfectionists are not for you (nor you for them). All forms of communication are important to you and you delight in social engagements as long as you can participate and are not expected to idly sit and watch the world go by.

You have Sagittarius on the 7th house cusp which, according to some astrologers, may not augur too well for intimate attachments, as you can be considered fickle and too independent. This is not always the case; it depends on how the rulers, Mercury and Jupiter, are placed in the chart. You can be as loyal or faithful as anyone else, as long as you and your partner share common ideas, ideals or new avenues to study and discuss.

Henry Kissinger has Gemini rising. His Sun and Mercury are conjunct in Gemini in the 12th house and Mars is also in Gemini, but in the 1st. This very cerebral and intellectual man surely displays many of the typical Gemini characteristics. His life is fascinating as well as diversified. Communicating by spoken and written word is the essence of his existence, whether as Harvard professor, Secretary of State or author. Even now Henry Kissinger is interviewed whenever something happens on the international front.

Jupiter, ruler of his Descendant, is in Scorpio in the 5th house. His one-to-one needs are intense; his desire to love and be loved is strong. Since Jupiter opposes Venus and squares Neptune, his understanding of what he wants from a woman may not always be clear, which is difficult for a man used to thinking in a concise and succinct manner. His first marriage, which produced two children, lasted 15 years. He spent the next ten years active in politics and was very busy as a "ladies man." In 1974 he married a second time and is still married to Nancy.

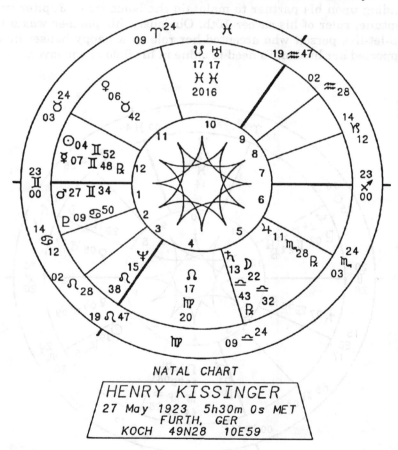

NATAL CHART

HENRY KISSINGER
27 May 1923   5h30m 0s MET
FURTH, GER
KOCH   49N28   10E59

## Sagittarius on the 7th House Cusp

You need plenty of elbow room in any intimate union. Jupiter, planet of expansion, rules your house of partnership and pairing is important to you, but usually on your terms which are spelled out quite openly (Gemini rising). Freedom is your keyword and this latitude, which is so important to you, should also be freely given to your partner. Whether you choose to do this depends on the placement of Jupiter and the Moon (indicator of your emotional nature). You want a spouse who shares your philosophy of life and who will discuss any and all subjects with you. Often you are attracted to someone from a totally different background, which enables you to expand your horizons through your interaction with that person.

With Jupiter, ruler of his Sagittarius 7th cusp in Virgo in the 4th house, General George Patton exhibited his need for freedom and doing his own thing by choosing a military career, going off to war and depending upon his partner to maintain the home front. Jupiter trines Neptune, ruler of his career 10th. Obviously, his partner was a live-and-let-live person who accepted her role as a happy housewife and supported her husband's need to shine in his field of endeavor.

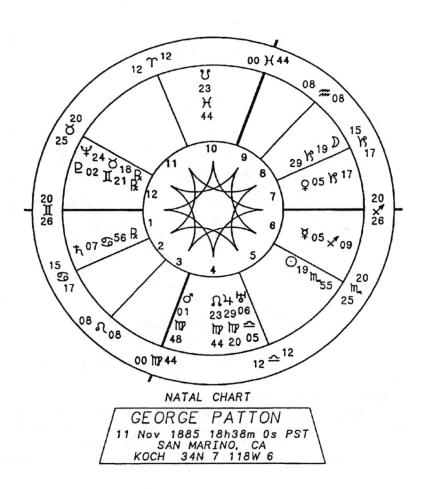

NATAL CHART

GEORGE PATTON
11 Nov 1885  18h38m 0s PST
SAN MARINO, CA
KOCH  34N 7  118W 6

If Jupiter has tension-producing aspects, this can depict a partner who is very demanding, presumptuous, even self-indulgent. This kind of behavior on the part of the other person may not sit well with you and you may soon leave the relationship, in spirit, if not in actuality.

## Cancer on the 1st House Cusp

This Ascendant often denotes a sensitive nature and feelings of vulnerability. Unless Uranus is prominent (elevated, angular or heavily aspected), you do not wish to call too much attention to yourself and prefer to retreat into your protective shell. You choose to be with others who are responsive to your insecurities and do not threaten you. Though life may bring many changes, including home moves, you always treasure your childhood memories. Hearth and home are significant in your life and you can even turn a hotel room into a homey atmosphere. You may find it difficult to accept criticism and often misunderstand even well-meant remarks, whether from loved ones, friends or foes. You take all one-to-one relationships very seriously and separations or divorce, if you experience them, take a lot out of you.

Judy Garland (See her chart on page 100.) had Cancer rising and the Moon, her chart ruler, was in the 6th house in Sagittarius. This may look less vulnerable than our Cancer rising description, especially since Judy has a fun-loving Gemini Sun. But look a bit closer; her Sun is in the 12th house, perfect for an actress who does not want to show her insecurities and instead hides behind her roles, but this was difficult to live with, since the Sun opposed Mars and squared Uranus, forming a demanding T-square. Even more troublesome was the Moon opposed Mercury and square Saturn in the 4th house, forming a second T-square. The feeling of lack of love from her parents (Moon square Saturn) influenced her partnership needs (Capricorn on the 7th), by reinforcing her constant hunger for being loved and cherished. None of her five husbands seems to have fulfilled her deep cravings or stilled her sense of inadequacy.

## Capricorn on the 7th House Cusp

You seek a partner who can provide security, organization and strong bonding. With Cancer rising, you rely on your perception and intuition to get you where you want to go, so it helps to have a mate who channels your intuitiveness into productive avenues. How this works out depends upon the Moon and Saturn, your Ascendant and Descendant rulers, and their aspects. Sometimes you seek someone who is older and more settled than you are (the parent image) and occasionally you will attract a younger person (you wish to do the parenting), but one who is steadfast, down-to-earth and practical. These are qualities that often go undeveloped in your personality until you find your match.

The first time around entertainer Cher married Sonny Bono* who was much older. She had a quick marriage to Greg Allman, but has been attracted to much younger men as she grows older. This is often typical of a Saturn-ruled 7th house. Her Saturn is in the 1st house in Cancer, so she is looking for her own security through partnership. Having a mate is important to her sense of self with Saturn here, but it opposes the Moon and squares Jupiter, suggesting her judgment is not always the best when choosing a partner. Saturn's sextile to Mercury helps reflect her ability to attract people.

When the ruler of the 7th house is in the 1st, you need to identify strongly with your partner and vice versa. The characteristics represented by that planet and its aspects show how the relationship will enhance your life. When it is Saturn, you may rekindle an early romance later in your life.

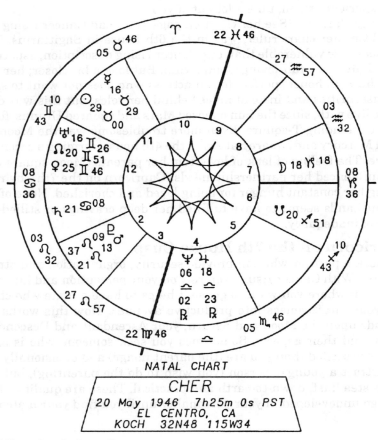

NATAL CHART

CHER
20 May 1946   7h25m 0s PST
EL CENTRO, CA
KOCH   32N48  115W34

*Chart data in Appendix.

## Leo on the 1st House Cusp

You are anything but shy, and contrary to the Cancer persona, you love to draw attention to yourself, often with hair that you toss around like a lion's mane, by shaving your head as Yul Brynner did, or by using your often dramatic voice. Proud of being "somebody," you like to impress others; in fact, you will camouflage loss of status or money, even hurt feelings, in order to make the impression you desire. Since you must shine, you favor the company of admirers over competitors, but you can hold your own with almost everybody.

As selfish as you may appear at times, you are really a romantic softy and appreciate the opposite sex, especially in love affairs (Sagittarius on the 5th house cusp). In marriage (Aquarius on the 7th) you need an independent and detached mate, one who does not feel put down or out of sorts, regardless of the role you may play. You desire occasional applause and a pat on the back.

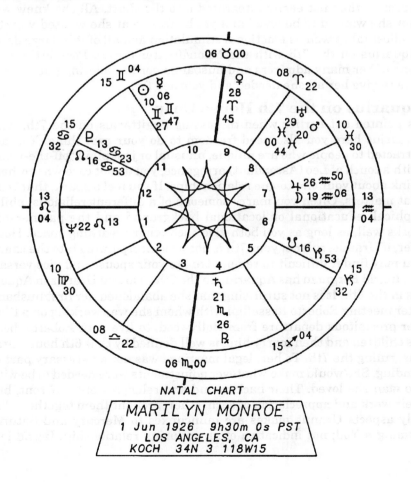

NATAL CHART

MARILYN MONROE
1 Jun 1926   9h30m 0s PST
LOS ANGELES, CA
KOCH   34N 3  118W15

Actress Marilyn Monroe incorporated many of the typical Leo rising qualities. Being "somebody" was imperative to her, especially since she had a very unhappy youth, product of an unstable and unwed mother who ended her life in a mental institution. Money and fame were Marilyn's two goals—with the rulers of the 1st and 2nd houses conjunct in the 10th and unaspected to any other planets in her chart. She accomplished her mission, but it did not bring her the happiness she dreamt of.

Neptune in the 1st indicates allure, glamor and magnetism in her public persona, but also denotes Marilyn's inability to see herself and her role in life clearly. A tight T-square involving Neptune opposed to the Moon and Jupiter, with all three planets square Saturn in the 4th house, implies she lacked feelings of stability, of a rightful place in the hearts of her parents and subsequently in her intimate relationships, whether husbands or lovers. Uranus which rules her 7th house is unaspected, thus not easily integrated into the chart. All she knew was that she wanted to be loved and yet be free; that she wanted variety, intellectual as well as emotional stimulation and all of it in large doses (Aquarius on the 7th with the Moon/Jupiter there). Poor little waif, none of her many admirers and husbands nor her adoring public were able to give her all she needed and yearned for.

## Aquarius on the 7th House Cusp

As pointed out earlier when discussing Sagittarius on the 7th, with Aquarius here you also need freedom to do your own thing. You are attracted to people who are unique, unusual or just plain "off-the-wall." With a touch of Leo (Ascendant) arrogance, you do not care what others think about your one-to-one relationships. If you feel a spark, that is all that matters. Often you marry someone of a different religious, philosophical, educational or locational background and the partnership works well, as long as you both give each other breathing space. However, if Uranus, ruler of your 7th is not well incorporated into the chart, you may find it difficult to remain true to your spouse and vice versa.

Ingrid Bergman has Aquarius on the 7th cusp and Uranus in Aquarius in the 6th. It is not surprising that she abandoned her first husband after meeting Roberto Rossellini with whom she was working on a film. Her precipitous departure from Hollywood, to live with Roberto, bear his children and then marry him, is well defined by that 6th house Uranus, ruling the 7th. To her, legal marriage was not a necessary part of bonding. She would make whatever adjustments were needed to be with the man she loved. Their background and religion were different, but their work and appreciation of each other, brought them together. The only aspects Uranus makes are quincunxes to Mercury and Saturn, forming a Yod; not indicative of an enduring relationship. Ingrid left

Rossellini and subsequently married and divorced again. (See chart on page 122.)

Though the 7th house always pictures what you are looking for from a partner, when dealing with a second marriage, the 9th house must also be considered. It adds information about the type of partner sought. Bergman has Mars in Cancer ruling the 9th in a stellium with Pluto and Saturn. This suggests that she expected an ardent, yet home oriented, sensitive and intuitive partner the second-time-around. Looking at Roberto's chart on page 122, not much shows this kind of response from him. Ingrid's Mars is the Midpoint between her Sun/MC and sextiles both, and her Moon in the 9th trines her Venus all signalling quick, easy attractions to men. While the relationship lasted, it was wonderful. But fireworks were obvious with the Cancer stellium, and underlying all partnerships for Ingrid is Uranus in those adjustment (yod) aspects to Mercury and Saturn. At best, all intimate relations were difficult and needed much effort and adaptability on her part.

## Virgo on the 1st House Cusp

You may suffer from an inferiority complex, because your innate sense of perfection applies its critique not only to others, but also to yourself. Actor Henry Fonda, unassuming and quiet, is a rather typical example of Virgo rising. (See page 16.) Chart ruler Mercury in Taurus conjunct Venus (his Sun ruler), added to his gentle demeanor; the opposition to the Moon often denotes a tendency to repressed feelings and some emotionally painful ups-and-downs, but in the case of an actor this is often helpful in getting to the depth of certain demanding roles.

If you have trouble overcoming your sense of insecurity, you may overcompensate and become loud, boisterous and a show-off like writer Ernest Hemingway (See his chart on page 154.) According to all biographical material available on Hemingway, his strong mother emasculated his father who committed suicide, and she tried to do the same with Ernest. According to him, she did not succeed...but Saturn square Mars and opposed to Pluto/Neptune sends a slightly different message. This type of configuration in a male chart can symbolize a fear of possible failure of male performance. The typical reaction is to overcompensate and be very macho. This was Hemingway's approach; watch the blood run at the bullfights, participate in boxing matches, shoot the biggest and most dangerous animal on a safari, love as many women as possible.

With Virgo rising you like to see concrete results for the hard work you put out. With Pisces on the 7th you seek a mate who is sensitive, gentle and understanding; in other words, one who displays some Piscean traits.

## Pisces on the 7th House Cusp

You are looking for someone you can bolster up and help through the crises of life; someone who will lean on you and expect a lot from you; but you may end up with a mate who appears to suffer through and with all you have to offer, the typical martyr. Much depends on where Neptune is and how it is aspected. With Virgo rising, to cover up your innate insecurity, you often look for someone who will let you be in control and so you are happiest with a partner who lets you take over.

Film director Roberto Rossellini is a perfect example. (See chart on page 122.) He needs someone who will look up to him and be a friend (Neptune in the 11th), who is maternal and sensitive (Neptune in Cancer), yet someone who is stable and practical (Saturn in the 7th house). Bergman fulfilled many of his 7th house needs, but she was not weak and certainly not always willing to let him assume control. His 9th house (this was his second marriage) is ruled by Mars which squares Saturn and quincunxes Uranus, suggesting that perhaps he felt restricted by

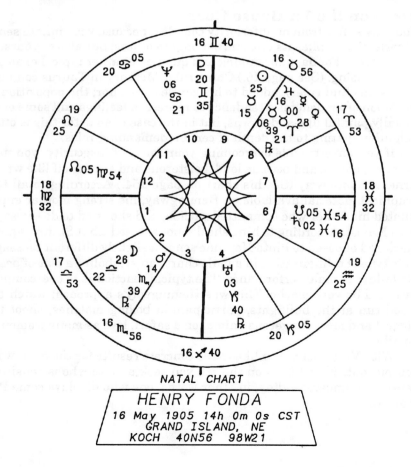

NATAL CHART

HENRY FONDA
16 May 1905  14h 0m 0s  CST
GRAND ISLAND, NE
KOCH   40N56   98W21

her and their three children. His Sun is also in this house and opposes the Moon; obviously he needed to work on his own concept of *anima/animus*. Neptune, the ruler of his marital house opposes Uranus, often, but not always justly, termed the "divorce" planet.

Pisces on the 7th can be very disconcerting. Though you seek understanding from others, your Virgo Ascendant may lead you to fault-finding ways that your sensitive mate cannot contend with.

## Libra on the 1st House Cusp

This sign of harmony and balance rising often suggests that you are charming and therefore can, figuratively speaking, get away with murder. What would bring enmity when said by anyone else, will be accepted from a Libran who puts it so smoothly that no one gets ruffled or angry. Because of your refined and urbane ways, you usually are very popular and much in demand on the social circuit. In order to feel complete, you need a partner, a sounding board for your ideas, as well as a

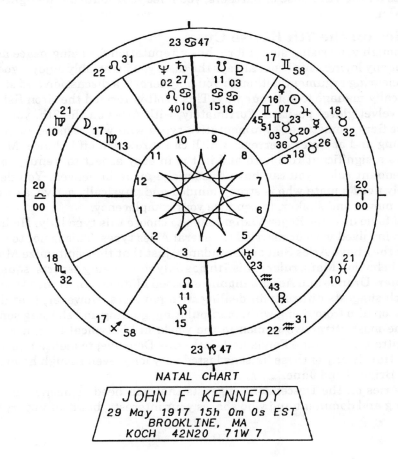

NATAL CHART

JOHN F KENNEDY
29 May 1917  15h 0m 0s EST
BROOKLINE, MA
KOCH  42N20  71W 7

recipient for your outpouring of love. Love with a capital L is essential to Venus-ruled Libra.

John F. Kennedy is a prime example of a Libra Ascendant. His charm and charisma were legend; so was his need to make love, though not necessarily just to his wife. Ascendant ruler Venus, in the sexual 8th was conjunct his Sun. Descendant ruler Mars conjuncted expansive Jupiter in sensual, tactile Taurus from the 7th/8th houses. Both squared Uranus in the fun and excitement-loving 5th.

More often than not, with Libra rising, you have Aquarius on the 5th house of love affairs and being faithful is not always your strong suit. Unless Venus is aspected to Saturn, you're in love with love, or like Jimmy Carter, who had a Libra Sun and Ascendant, the latter conjunct Saturn, you just "lust in your heart." You have a great need to be liked, therefore you may find it difficult to be unpleasant and would rather walk away from a situation than face chaos or ugliness. With Aries on the 7th house of partners, you'll let your mate do the fighting for you.

## Aries on the 7th House Cusp

Although your rising sign, Libra, has a reputation for being peace and harmony loving, this is not always the case; you invariably enjoy a good, air-clearing argument, although you may term it a discussion and strategically manage to get your way. This is often termed the "iron fist in the velvet glove" position. Fortunately, with Aries on the 7th, you attract fiery, sometimes argumentative types who will respond to your baiting and at times overreact which can throw you off balance. Mars plays a significant role here and if it is in easy aspect to Venus, your Ascendant ruler, you can have a marriage made in heaven. You definitely need a mate who is strong minded and physically active, as well as a mover and shaker, to equalize your complacency.

Movie director Roger Vadim tends to choose this type lady. He has been involved with or married to several Aries types. This is not to say that they have Aries Sun or Ascendants, just that they epitomize Martian behavior. Mars, ruler of his 7th has only challenging aspects: square Jupiter, Uranus and Ascendant and opposed Midheaven, a tense set-up which suggests difficulty in dealing with partners. However, that did not stop him from living with, manipulating, guiding and shaping some of the most attractive women in the world in his typical Libran way: Brigitte Bardot, Jane Fonda and Catherine Deneuve, to mention just a few. Hardly any of these liaisons lasted very long, even though he married Brigitte and Jane.

Aries on the Descendant suggests that you need someone who is strong and dominant and who shares your interests, but does not try to

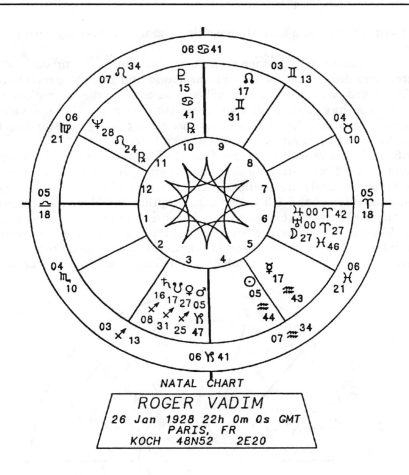

NATAL CHART

ROGER VADIM
26 Jan 1928 22h 0m 0s GMT
PARIS, FR
KOCH   48N52   2E20

eclipse you. The placement of Mars will point out the kind of interests. For instance, if Mars is in the 11th, perhaps you will both enjoy some kind of group activity; with Mars in the 5th, sports or some sort of creative endeavor may help bond you.

## Scorpio on the 1st House Cusp

What you see is not necessarily what you get with this rising sign or signature. You are able to package yourself in enough layers of personality that you can easily hide your true feelings. You do this out of strength, not weakness, as well as your tremendous need for privacy. According to your principles, who you really are is no one's business but your own. Obviously you are very careful in your choice of associates, every bit as discriminating as Virgo, the sign on your 11th house of friends. Once you choose a friend or lover, you are very loyal, and like all fixed signs, have a hard time making changes, especially with partners.

With Scorpio rising you may come across as calm and composed...still waters run deep. Your feelings are profound and you will protect and defend loved ones, but when provoked, you can become an implacable enemy. You have a difficult time associating with weak or indecisive people, yet you may lock horns with those strong enough to stand up to you. As a result you are often considered a loner.

Scorpio rising well describes Camille Claudel, a young lady well ahead of her time both in independence and guts. Born to an upper middle class family, her sculpting talent was visible at an early age. Neptune, ruler of the 5th in the 5th, conjunct the Moon, is not only artistic, but to use the creative juices becomes an emotional need. Neptune T-squares Uranus and Mercury implying a definite push toward individuality. Neptune's trine to Jupiter and sextile to chart ruler Mars indicates easy access to her talents. Her father believed in her as a

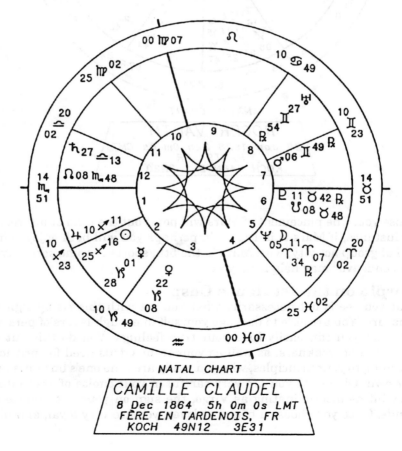

NATAL CHART

CAMILLE CLAUDEL
8 Dec 1864    5h 0m 0s LMT
FÈRE EN TARDENOIS, FR
KOCH    49N12    3E31

sculptress and helped her go to Paris to study. Her mother wanted a "normal" life for her little girl and did everything she could to convince Camille to take a different path.

Quietly determined (Scorpio rising) Camille did exactly as she wanted, finagled her way into then already famous Auguste Rodin's studio to become one of his students and later his mistress. What to her was a deep and meaningful commitment, one she was sure would end up in marriage since she believed that Rodin* would divorce his rather simplistic wife, was but one of many love affairs to him. Camille's chart ruler Pluto is conjunct the Descendant and co-ruler Mars is in the 7th house—to Camille giving of herself meant a full involvement. The difficult aspects of Pluto to the Sun, Jupiter and the Ascendant reflect this relationship that was too hot to handle from the beginning. Her love for Rodin turned into hatred. Even those who believed in her talent had a hard time dealing with her as her moods became violent and she totally withdrew from people. Though she was living like an animal, her brother whom she adored and trusted, managed to take her to an insane asylum for help. She stayed there for the rest of her life, 30 years, longing for her parental home. Her brother, Paul Claudel, a well known poet, felt guilty for the rest of his life for having had Camille confined.

## Taurus on the 7th House Cusp

With Taurus on the cusp of the partnership house, you look for someone who is tactile, who likes to be caressed, fondled, patted, hugged and held and who will do the same for you; also a person who values beautiful things and who is, in your eyes, beautiful or handsome, who dresses well and is sociable as well as steadfast. This description is modified by the placement of Venus. If it is in the 2nd house, you may prefer that your partner be financially independent; if in the 10th, you could be attracted to public figures, or a person who is well established in a career, or one willing to help you with yours. Not for you a homebody, unless Venus is in the 4th or Cancer. This placement is much like Scorpio on the 7th; you like things to stay as they are and will try your mightiest to keep the relationship going, so no one can point a finger and say you didn't try hard enough.

Benito Mussolini, the ill-fated Italian dictator, had Taurus on the 7th and he was married to Rachele* until the end of his life.

Venus is in Cancer and his home and children were very important to him. However, Venus conjuncts Jupiter and excess was the name of the game. For years Claretta Petacci was his mistress, and it was she who was with him when they were shot by Italian partisans and hung in infamy in the public square. True to their European background and religious beliefs, the Mussolinis maintained their home and marriage until the end.

* See chart data in Appendix.

Claretta had Taurus rising and her sensuousness was what Il Duce needed. Rachele was a strong Aries and with Capricorn rising, much more demanding than his Leo Sun cared to compete with. He had Neptune, Pluto, Saturn, Moon and Mars in the 7th so partnership was always significant in his life; including his ill-fated affiliation with Hitler.

## Sagittarius on the 1st House Cusp

Honest, gregarious and outgoing, your naivete can be touching when based on ideas and ideals you strive for, annoying to friends and relatives when you misplace your trust, or put your foot in your mouth by blurting out anything and everything that comes to mind. Depending on Jupiter's placement and aspects, you can be a philosopher, zealous missionary or super salesperson. You love to talk and influence others, especially partners and loved ones, but without necessarily running their lives; how you do this depends on other placements than just the Ascendant.

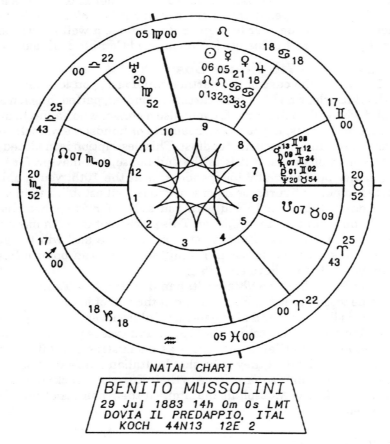

NATAL CHART

BENITO MUSSOLINI
29 Jul 1883 14h 0m 0s LMT
DOVIA IL PREDAPPIO, ITAL
KOCH 44N13 12E 2

Shrewd businessman, master sailor and founder of the worldwide 24-hour TV news station CNN, Ted Turner has Sagittarius on the Ascendant.

Chart ruler Jupiter is in Aquarius in his 3rd house of communication; it squares the Sun and Venus, trines the Moon and quincunxes Neptune, enough challenges and creative flow to utilize the best inherent in Jupiter. He most certainly has managed to influence others without personally directing or dictating their lives. In fact he has managed to change the way the nation—nay the world, receives news.

People around you have to understand where you come from and that you basically mean well. Otherwise they'll have a hard time living with you. With Sagittarius rising and Gemini on the 7th house, you want to be free, flexible and stimulated. If your partner tries to tell you what to do, or even worse, bores you, the relationship will be of very short duration. Ted Turner has been divorced twice so far.

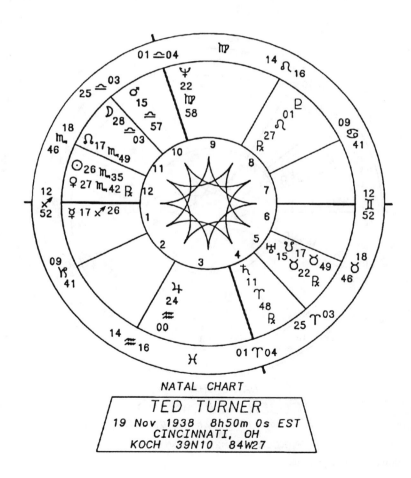

NATAL CHART

TED TURNER
19 Nov 1938   8h50m 0s EST
CINCINNATI, OH
KOCH   39N10   84W27

## Gemini on the 7th House Cusp

When you have Gemini here, you need to be partners with someone who will keep you enthralled, entertained, amused and informed. Exchange of ideas is imperative to keep things from getting dull. If there is anything that Gemini on the 7th can't stand, it is boredom. Since you have a Sagittarian Ascendant, discussions on philosophy, travel, world affairs and religion can keep you intrigued. Much depends on where Mercury and Jupiter are, if they aspect each other, and how.

One of the most enduring love stories of all time is that of Elizabeth Barrett* and Robert Browning. She was a sickly, reclusive writer who defied her tyrannical father to marry an almost penniless poet. They decamped to Italy where they wrote beautiful poetry and lived happily ever after.

He has Gemini on the 7th and the ruler, Mercury conjuncts his Sun in Taurus in the 5th, the house of love and creativity. Each fueled the

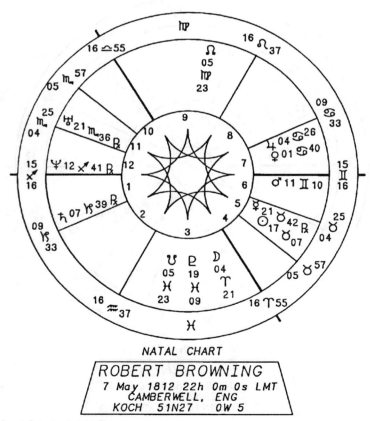

NATAL CHART

ROBERT BROWNING
7 May 1812 22h 0m 0s LMT
CAMBERWELL, ENG
KOCH 51N27 0W 5

* See chart data in Appendix.

other's self-expression and between them, they created enduring literary works.

Unless the ruler of your 7th house is in a fixed sign in the 5th like Robert Browning's, variety is the spice of your life and when you seek a partner, it is a person who is lively, informed and adaptable. If Mercury has difficult aspects, you may try more than once to establish a successful union.

## Capricorn on the 1st House Cusp

Down-to-earth and dependable, usually driven to achieve, you feel best about yourself after you've attained some concrete and tangible success. To have a partner or loved one who is understanding, nurturing and helpful is very important to Cancer on the 7th, yet you will only overcome feelings of inadequacy after you've succeeded on your own.

When young, you appear very serious and capable of taking on many responsibilities at an early age. The surer you feel, the more your *Puer* or youthful nature can come through. This calls for a careful choice of spouse or one-to-one relationship. If your partner is drawn to you for your adult, reliable and steady behavior, he or she may have a hard time adjusting to the "youthful" you. Joanne Woodward and Paul Newman who share a Capricorn Ascendant are not likely to face this problem; they both expect the same behavior with Cancer on the 7th house.

Queen Elizabeth II and Prince Philip also share a Capricorn Ascendant/Cancer Descendant (see page 26). Whereas Newman and Woodward both have almost the same wheel, Elizabeth has a Pisces/Virgo interception in the 2nd/8th houses while Philip's interception is Aries/Libra in the 3rd/9th. Though they share the same angles, 2nd/8th, and 6th/12th axes, their 3rd/9th and 5th/11th house cusps are different, changing their outlooks and approaches in those areas. Though interesting and stimulating, this can also produce the need for adjustments to each other, maybe even some concessions since her 11th and 3rd house rulers, Jupiter and Mars square her Ascendant ruler Saturn and oppose her Neptune (T-square) which conjuncts his Moon.

As serious and reserved as you may appear, you can be a surprisingly ardent and expressive lover if you have an interception and Aries is on the 5th and Leo on the 8th house cusps. Another good way to understand the need of the Capricorn rising personality, is to have the opposite horizon line: Cancer rising, Capricorn setting.

## Cancer on the 7th House Cusp

Home, family and children often play a significant role in your choice of a spouse. You need someone who softens and ameliorates your sometimes austere attitudes (Capricorn rising); someone who understands and eases your fears and trepidations; someone who is always there for you.

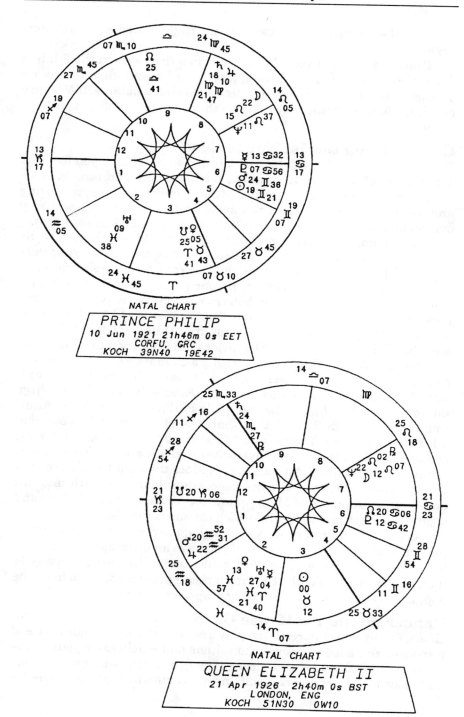

NATAL CHART

PRINCE PHILIP
10 Jun 1921 21h46m 0s EET
CORFU, GRC
KOCH   39N40   19E42

NATAL CHART

QUEEN ELIZABETH II
21 Apr 1926  2h40m 0s BST
LONDON, ENG
KOCH   51N30   0W10

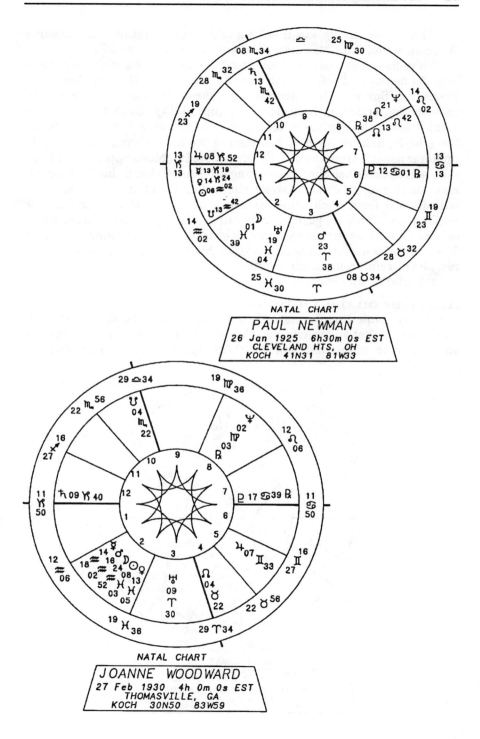

NATAL CHART

PAUL NEWMAN
26 Jan 1925   6h30m 0s EST
CLEVELAND HTS, OH
KOCH   41N31   81W33

NATAL CHART

JOANNE WOODWARD
27 Feb 1930   4h 0m 0s EST
THOMASVILLE, GA
KOCH   30N50   83W59

The classic example of this kind of liaison is that of actors Joanne Woodward and Paul Newman (See both charts on page 27).

They have been married for over 30 years and have three daughters. As mentioned before, both have Cancer on the 7th; his Moon is in Pisces, her Sun sign; her Moon is in Aquarius, his Sun sign. Those are very strong, enduring indicators of compatibility. Each of them have what it takes to keep the other absorbed, comforted and nurtured. Interestingly, neither Moon is aspected in the natal chart, but both pick up lunar aspects from the other's horoscope. His Moon opposes her Neptune and squares her Jupiter, creating a T-square that indicates a strong emotional energy flow between them, but could mirror emotional withdrawal from each other in times of stress. It also trines her Midheaven, which suggests that he can give her good career advice and be emotionally supportive when career issues are not going well. Her Moon opposes his Neptune and sextiles his Mars and widely conjuncts his Moon, reinforcing their emotional (Moon), artistic (Neptune) and sexual (Mars) rapport.

## Aquarius on the 1st House Cusp

You enjoy coming across as different and unique. To disappear in a crowd is not what you relish. You cherish new experiences and are wide open to fresh ideas and original thinking. The Aquarian nature is

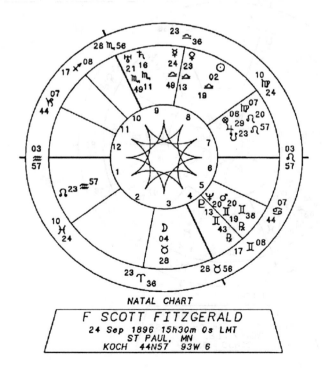

NATAL CHART

F SCOTT FITZGERALD
24 Sep 1896 15h30m 0s LMT
ST PAUL, MN
KOCH  44N57  93W 6

always intrigued by societal problems and you would as soon comfort a needy person or animal, as worry about money, home or investments. That does not mean that you do not want a family— just that your way of raising them may be distinctive and your way of showing love and emotion is unusual.

Yet with Leo on the Descendant, the one-to-one relationships that really appeal to you are with those who can openly and warmly show their love, who may not care about the welfare of whales, the homeless or the ozone layer. This can lead to great love matches like that of F. Scott Fitzgerald and his wife Zelda* with her Leo Ascendant—much love but also much fighting about whose values should be followed.

Like all fixed signs, once you decide on something, it is difficult for you to change your mind. In order to stand a chance, others should appeal to your good sense of logic and clear-thinking, rather than tell you what to do, else the rebel in you will awaken and try to rule.

Dyan Cannon has Aquarius rising. She may not be a particularly unusual actress, but she surely occupies a unique position as the wife who finally gave Cary Grant a much desired child, daughter Jennifer.

Whether Grant was able to give her all the personal love she wished for is questionable, but the marriage to him most certainly enhanced her reputation and exposed her to the public applause and approval that Leo on the Descendant thrives on.

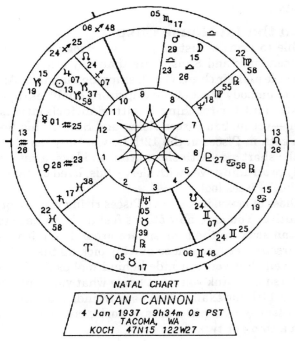

NATAL CHART

DYAN CANNON
4 Jan 1937   9h34m 0s PST
TACOMA,   WA
KOCH   47N15   122W27

* See chart data in index

## Leo on the 7th House Cusp

Dramatic, outspoken, friendly people attract you. Not for you a shrinking violet, unless your Sun, ruler of your 7th, is in a passive sign or does not have very exciting aspects. With Aquarius rising, you tend to march to your own drummer and thus often prefer to deal with others who are willing to experiment and challenge your concepts and ideas.

Writer George Sand epitomizes this position. Her many romantic involvements led to only one early marriage which was devastating; it took her five years to obtain a divorce (Sun square Uranus). In the 19th century, women did not divorce. Only men did. (See chart on page 94.) Many misconceptions abound about her relationship with Chopin; with her 7th house ruler, the Sun in Cancer in the 5th, it is easy to see why she cared for, supported, nurtured, pampered and encouraged him. A free thinker, though profligate, she was totally devoted to the man of the moment. Another misconception about George Sand is that she wore men's clothes and changed her birth name (Amandine Dupin) because of lesbian tendencies...she wore men's clothing because it was comfortable and she changed her name so her writing would be accepted in an era when women were supposed to marry, bear children and keep house, not be creative and famous. But Sand, with Aquarius rising and Uranus square the Sun, did her own thing, long before the phrase became popular. Leo on the 7th generally needs a strong love partner, who is willing to be patient with the sometimes outrageous behavior of the Aquarian Ascendant.

## Pisces on the 1st House Cusp

You are able to express just about any persona you wish to portray. Piscean Ascendants and Suns, more than any other sign can hide behind the facade of their chart. Greek shipping magnate, Aristotle Onassis*, seems to embody most of the Capricorn qualities (his Sun) as well as optimistic and far-reaching Sagittarian inclinations (Moon and Midheaven)—yet he had Pisces rising and Saturn (his Sun ruler) and Mars were both in Pisces in the 12th house. Only his physical appearance—on the short side with short arms and legs, a rather fleshy body and slightly protruding eyes with sleepy lids, lived up to the description of the "typical" Pisces looks.

Regardless of looks, if you have Pisces rising you are quite emotional and intuitive. You care how others feel and you hate to hurt them. Since you can soak up the atmosphere around you, it is wise to avoid negative persons, because you so quickly pick up their vibrations. This Neptunian veil that you can hide behind makes all forms of relating tricky. Others may think you don't know what you want, yet with Capricorn on the 11th for example, as your friends may soon find out, you are not necessarily living in a dream world, but you can ably lead and teach them a thing or two.

* See chart data in Appendix.

With a Pisces Ascendant or signature, your often gentle and help-less appearance can be deceiving to others— they forget that the con-stant drip-drip of water can create holes in even the hardest rock! Mary Welsh Hemingway, fourth wife and widow of author Ernest Heming-way, stayed with him through thick and thin. Here is another example of the attraction of opposites. He had a Virgo Ascendant, she had Pisces rising, but in the end it was he who gave up (committed suicide) while she survived. (See charts on page 154.)

## Virgo on the 7th House Cusp

With Pisces rising, you tend to be quite visionary and creative and some-times careless of details, so you often seek a partner who is dedicated to organization and who will bring you back down to earth from your flights of fancy. The positions of Mercury and Neptune may show if this is true or if you are attracted to a different type of person. A client with Mercu-ry/Sun in Aquarius opposed chart ruler Neptune in Leo, married an actress with Sun/Mercury in Pisces. He manages her career.

Often your spouse is the one who handles the finances, keeps track of social engagements and is generally the household manager. If you are of the generation with Neptune in Virgo, you are probably well able to handle your own affairs and if Neptune and Mercury are in tension-producing aspect to each other, you may experience a tug-of-war with your partner over the details of everyday life.

Dancer Gwen Verdon has Pisces rising with Uranus conjunct the Ascendant; Virgo is on her 7th cusp and Mercury is in the 10th conjunct Venus and Jupiter, trine the Moon in the 6th and widely trine Neptune there. (See chart on page 32.) She was crippled as a child and rather than have her legs broken and reset, her mother insisted on dance les-sons at age two. She appeared publicly at age 6 and has had an ac-claimed career on stage and in the movies. Marriage for her certainly looks like a wonderful experience if you only regard the 7th house. How-ever, as we constantly remind our students, you must judge the whole chart, not just one part, if you are to understand how the person is acting it out.

In Verdon's chart, Mercury not only rules the 7th house, it also governs the 4th, representative of the background she came from. With Mercury's benign aspects, it appears that she had a positive relation-ship with her 4th house parent and that she would look for similar behavior from her partner. Gemini there suggests an atmosphere of intellectuality and with Mercury in the 10th in Sagittarius, a parent who was successful, philosophical and aspiring. Pluto is in the 4th house opposed to Jupiter in the 10th and square Mars in the 1st. These are provocative aspects which are best worked out in some kind of physical activity (Mars is in Aries).

Her parents may not always have seen eye-to-eye (Jupiter in the 10th in Capricorn opposed Pluto in Cancer in the 4th), but the favorable aspects flowing from Saturn and Uranus to Pluto and Jupiter's trine to the Moon suggest that Gwen would be optimistic and hopeful in a committed relationship, based on what she experienced at home.

At age 17, she interrupted her dancing career to marry a writer and have a son, James. This early marriage ended in divorce five years later.

With Mercury, the ruler of her 7th house in the 10th, it is not surprising she married someone who was career oriented. Mercury's conjunction to Venus suggests that she enters partnerships with a deeply loving commitment. Its trine to the Moon in Virgo in the 6th, reinforces her ability and need to work with her partner, which was the case with her second husband Bob Fosse. Virgo on the 7th often seeks a partner who is a perfectionist. We don't know about her first husband, but Fosse was painstakingly so. Her Mercury in the 10th wants someone to look

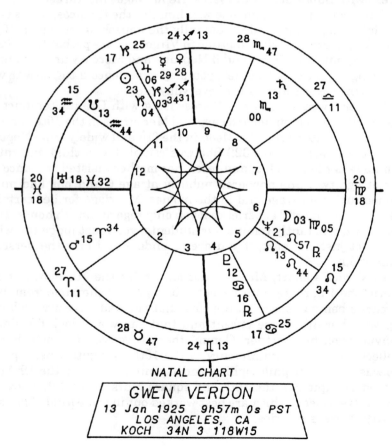

NATAL CHART

GWEN VERDON
13 Jan 1925   9h57m 0s PST
LOS ANGELES, CA
KOCH  34N 3  118W15

up to and the conjunction to Jupiter in and ruling the 10th indicates a partner who was capable of great achievements.

At age 35 she married fellow dancer and choreographer, Bob Fosse. Their commitment lasted 12 years, and though they divorced, she still worked with him, dancing and choreographing.

With all the favorable 7th house aspects, why two divorces? Verdon has Uranus, significator of the unexpected, opposing her 7th house cusp (Descendant). With the two male archetypes, the Sun and Mars squaring each other and the Sun quincunx Neptune, she does not always see male relationships clearly or handle them wisely or well.

To gain further understanding of her relationship with her second husband, you must look at her 9th house. Mars and Pluto rule it and Mars is in Aries in the 1st house quincunx Saturn in the 8th, trine Neptune in the 6th and square the other 9th house ruler, Pluto in Cancer in the 4th, as well as the Sun. She and Fosse certainly danced beautifully together (Neptune); she identified strongly with him (Mars in the 1st), but perhaps their sexual needs were not finely attuned (Saturn in the 8th). The Mars/Pluto square is a tough one to work through and obviously she had much to learn from this relationship about values, money and, above all, self-worth (Mars also rules the 2nd house).

But to really understand the circumstances of this partnership, we have to compare the charts and consider the compatibility and longevity factors, as well as their composite chart which we will do in Part 4.

# LESSON 3

# HOUSE POSITIONS:
# THE 4TH AND 10TH HOUSES

The 4th house illustrates your roots, the home base that your parents, usually your mother, established for you, so what you really want, expect or need from others is found in this house more often than anywhere else. This is where you received your first nurturing, or lack of it. Parents set the tone for deep relationship prerequisites and the archetypes by which they are represented astrologically can help you recognize some of the patterns. Did your mother/father/4th house/Cancer/Moon give you all the love and affection you felt entitled to or yearned for? Was your childhood happy or sad? Were you carefree or did you assume early responsibility for siblings or an ailing relative? Did you feel protected or neglected? Stimulated or held back? The 4th house illustrates these as well as other possible tendencies and potential developments. Through an understanding of your roots and childhood background, it is easier to grasp what you require from others, especially in intimate relationships.

Just as the 4th house depicts your background, the home you came from, the opposite house, the 10th, illustrates the pinnacle or highest point you reach for—not in a spiritual or religious (9th house) sense, but in a very practical and tangible (Capricorn) way. The 4th house Cancer/Moon represents parental protection and support; the Capricorn/Saturn/10th house portrays parental discipline and authority, the limitations imposed to keep you within the family rules and regulations, to teach you what in later years translates into laws and policies. Traditionally the child visualized the father as the money earner and authority figure, the 10th house.

The 10th house cusp is the ego point in the horoscope and your ego development comes as a result of how you deal with the authority figure in your life. As you learn to abide by the family decrees and directives, you learn and grow to know and understand who you are as an individual.

At this point we must again stress what we teach over and over: **The natal chart is a road map; which road you take is up to you; it's your choice!**

Free will as well as life circumstances usually determine which parent is represented by either the 4th or 10th house. Astrologers have diverse opinions as to which house represents which parent. Some insist that the 4th house always mirrors the mother and the 10th the father; others are sure it is the reverse; yet another group states that in a woman's chart the 4th symbolizes the father, while it describes the mother in a man's horoscope!

We try not to assign a particular house to a specific parent; instead we feel you should understand the basic meaning of the 4th and 10th houses by referring to the flat chart with Aries rising and Cancer on the 4th. The sign Cancer typifies nurturing and caring, even the glyph depicts a protective design, protective to self as well as others. This disposition is usually attributed to the female or mother, but life does not always follow textbook descriptions. Often the father is warmer and more loving than the mother, who may be the disciplinarian (10th house) in the family. In today's modern household, father may not only change diapers, but take on the homemaker role, while mother may be out in the working world, supporting the family (10th). In that case who do you, the child, perceive as the nurturing 4th and as the authoritarian 10th house? When you are young both parents may be represented by the 4th house, because you tend to view them as a unit, both exemplifying home and family.

As we have repeatedly stated, each horoscope is unique and though you may correctly assume which house reflects which parent, it is best to ask your clients, friends or family how they feel about their parental significators before drawing any final conclusions.

Here is a typical example of what can happen: A student has Cancer on the 4th with the Moon in Virgo in the 6th house; it trines the Sun, Venus and Mercury in Taurus in the 2nd house; Saturn, ruler of her 10th house, is in Scorpio and opposes her Taurus cluster. This looks like a nice mother (Moon has three trines, two sextiles and an opposition to Uranus), maybe a bit picky (Moon in Virgo) and probably insistent on good work ethics (6th house). Father might seem quite demanding (Saturn opposite Sun/Mercury/Venus).

As she tells it: "My father was the most loving, gentle man you ever want to meet. He would hurry home after a full day's work and take us, my brother and me, to buy ice cream or play ball or some fun thing we could do together. He would hug and kiss us, encourage all our endeavors, reward good school work and teach us something new every day. My mother was very artistic; she had a lovely singing voice and spent 90% of her time singing scales, taking lessons, participating in any and all activities that involved her career and had very little time for us. She was quite beautiful, but she rarely embraced us for fear it might muss her hair or make-up. Very strict, she insisted on her children being seen and not heard, that we keep our rooms as well as our persons clean and neat. Both my parents contributed to the family finances, but my father definitely had all the Cancer 4th house attributes whereas mother is well described by my Capricorn 10th house."

Moral of this story: Ask your clients/friends/relatives to tell you how they perceive their parents before you make any decisions.

It is especially important to remember that the parental, or male/female archetypes are not only found in the 4th/10th axis, but also in the planets, significantly the Sun and Saturn (male) and the Moon and Venus (female). Sometimes even Mars (male) and Pluto (female) can prove enlightening.

As always in astrology, keep the whole chart in mind regardless of what house you are interpreting. Don't jump to any conclusions; there are no absolutes.

## Aries on the 4th House - Libra on the 10th House

With Aries on the cusp of the 4th house, you probably hail from an active home, but contrary to what many astrological books assert, there does not have to be strife in the home, even if Mars is in that house. There definitely is a lot of coming and going. If your 4th house ruler, Mars, is very challenged, you may shy away from intimate relations, for fear they will be disrupted as your early environment could have been.

If the 4th house typifies your mother, she may have been a dynamo, quick to love you, but just as quick to reprimand. Aries is the sign of self—thus your mother may have been more involved in her own affairs than yours. Despite some psychological inhibitions brought on through mother's benign neglect, eventually you will want to have some say-so in what happens in your home. If your mate is very strong and opinionated (as was mother), it could lead to the kind of fights the textbooks often ascribe to Mars.

Libra on the 10th does not necessarily mean that your father, or the authority figure in the home, is just and balanced—a lot depends on where the ruler, Venus, is placed, what aspects it makes and what other planets are located in the house. Generally speaking, this placement denotes someone you can reason with, who will listen to your side of the story, who hands out orders or restrictions with tact and diplomacy.

Unless Venus is very stressed, you will learn to accept limits without resentment.

Caroline Kennedy Schlossberg, daughter of President John F. Kennedy and Jacqueline Kennedy Onassis, has Aries on her 4th house cusp and Libra on the 10th. Mars, ruler of the 4th, which probably represents her mother, is involved in a challenging T-Square with her Moon (mother again) and Uranus. Although she appears to get along with her mother (Moon trine Midheaven, sextile Ascendant) and accepts her mother's discipline and authority (Moon sextile Saturn), she must also have had a few run-ins or blow-ups (Mars square Uranus) with her, and may have even experienced a bit of female jealousy while growing up.

Father, on the other hand, partially described by Libra on the 10th, ruler Venus in Capricorn in the 2nd square Jupiter in the 10th and Neptune also there, looms larger than life (Jupiter expands, Neptune veils). Caroline probably overidealized him, as children are wont to do,

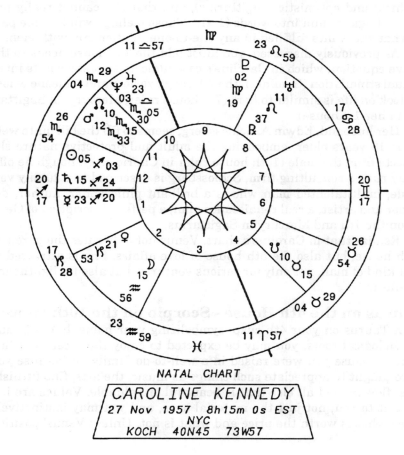

NATAL CHART

CAROLINE KENNEDY
27 Nov 1957    8h15m 0s EST
NYC
KOCH    40N45    73W57

when a beloved parent, especially one as much in the public eye as Jack Kennedy, is taken away in their early years of development.

Remember, unless you can ask people to describe their parents, you can only guess which house symbolizes whom, and very often the child sees the parents as a unit—"my parents" made me do this or that; "my parents" set the rules, loved me, abandoned me or whatever. Since JFK was assassinated when Caroline was only six years old, she may have changed her perception and switched her mother from her 4th house representation to the 10th.

What influence could this have on her expectations later in life? The two female archetypes, Moon and Venus, are both in the 2nd house, in Capricorn and Aquarius respectively. Caroline obviously was taught from early on what it meant to be a Kennedy; the values expected of her and the status (Venus rules the 10th) appropriate for her. The male or *anima* archetypes, Sun and Saturn, are both in her 12th house in Sagittarius, indicating that she most likely thinks of her father as philosophical and optimistic (Sagittarius), and that she cannot really put her feelings for him into words (12th). These feelings will become part of what she wants fulfilled in any one-to-one relationship with men.

As previously discussed, you must add the 7th house needs to the above equation, which in Caroline's case indicate that she wants intellectual stimulation (Gemini on the 7th cusp), variety and someone whose outlook on life is similar to hers (7th house ruler, Mercury, in Sagittarius in her 1st house).

Her husband, Edwin A. Schlossberg, seems to fill the bill quite well. He is 13 years older, embodying the adult and protective nature she expects from the male (10th house ruler in Capricorn). Though he officially runs a consulting firm, Schlossberg is described as a totally versatile, multitalented man who is a brilliant philosopher, author, designer and artist, a real renaissance man, a perfect description of Gemini on the 7th and Mercury in Sagittarius.

Realize that in Caroline's chart, Venus not only rules the parental 10th house, but also the 5th house of love affairs. She is attracted to that kind of man, not only for serious ventures, but also for lighthearted affairs.

## Taurus on the 4th House - Scorpio on the 10th House

With Taurus on your 4th cusp, symbolizing your home, heredity and psychological roots, you may be expected to enjoy the niceties of life, either because you were raised in a well-to-do family, or because you were taught to appreciate such things as music, the arts, fine furnishings, flowers and all else that is beautiful or valuable. Values are important to you, not just the material ones, and you may instinctively know what is worth the price and what is not. Unless Venus' position denies this, you are loyal by nature and prefer a steady life to the comings and goings that Aries on the 4th savors.

Scorpio on the 10th often indicates a domineering parent who sets the rules without much regard to what you, as a child, say or want. This "take charge" type of parent can serve as a negative role model especially if Pluto or co-ruler Mars have challenging aspects. We have quite a few examples in our files of Scorpio MCs who rebelled time and time again first in their youth by not doing what the parent asked, then in later years by not being able to sustain one-to-one relationships.

Beautiful Italian actress Sophia Loren well illustrates how early childhood trauma, as well as parental lacks, can influence future relationship needs. Venus, ruler of her 4th house, is in Virgo in the 8th, conjunct Neptune and trine the Ascendant. In her eyes, mother was glamorous, yet she may not have seen her clearly (Neptune); she was picky, as well as demanding (Virgo) and fairly possessive (8th house), but Sophia knew that she meant well (Venus trines the Ascendant). To

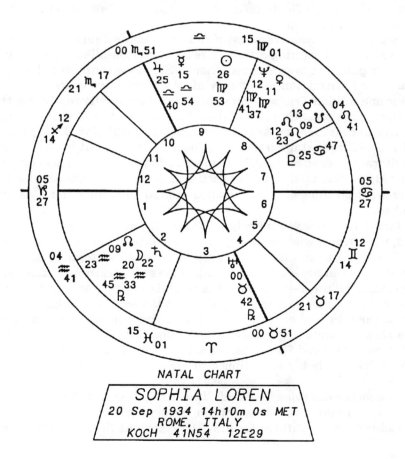

NATAL CHART

SOPHIA LOREN
20 Sep 1934  14h10m 0s MET
ROME,  ITALY
KOCH   41N54   12E29

add excitement and a bit of the unusual to their relationship, Uranus exactly conjuncts the cusp of the 4th house. Sophia's transformation from "illegitimate scarecrow of a girl buried in poverty" as she describes herself, to one of the world's most beautiful, famous and rich women could be termed very Uranian.

Scorpio on the 10th house is primarily ruled by Pluto in Cancer in the 7th, forming a troublesome T-square with the MC, which it rules, Jupiter and Uranus. Sophia's perception of the male archetype, as personified by her father in her youth, certainly was not the happiest. Pluto square Jupiter in the 9th might depict an early yearning for male guidance, square the Midheaven, a challenge to father and authorities. The square to Uranus could indicate an innately rebellious nature, but all of this immediately denotes the strong will of a survivor. Since Pluto is the focal planet in the 7th, a future marriage partner would necessarily reflect many of Sophia's feelings toward her father. The two male archetypes, the Sun and Saturn, quincunx each other are another indication of the many adjustments she had to make before she could reconcile the *animus* part of her nature.

Sophia Loren was the eldest of two illegitimate daughters of Ricardo Scicolone and aspiring actress, Greta Garbo look-alike, Romilda Villani. Her parents never married, though Sophia was granted the right to use her father's name, but only after she, in later years, paid her father one million lire, was younger sister, Maria, allowed to use the surname Scicolone. (Co-ruler of the 10th, Mars in Leo in the 8th). She admires her mother and asserts that during World War II, "My sister and I would have starved if my mother hadn't gone out in the streets and literally begged for food," but on a less happy note, she also reveals that, "My mother pushed me into acting. I never had a real childhood. I never went on the beach and strolled around with the other kids and laughed."

Memories of her youth are bittersweet; "If you live a very hard childhood, you become wise because you have to face the facts of life so early." Of her father she states: "His rejection of us was total...I saw him only six times in my life...yet he shaped me as a person more than any other man." (Pluto T-square) Sophia reminisced, "I often wonder what he was thinking as he saw me up there on the screen," having learned that toward the end of his life, her father spent many hours in darkened theaters watching his daughter's films. "With all the grandiose gifts I have received," she once confided, "one of my greatest possessions was the only toy my father ever gave me, a little blue auto with my name on it."

In another interview she said: "It was the dream of my life to have a father, and that is why I sought him everywhere. I spent much of my life looking for substitutes for him." One obvious father figure is her husband, Carlo Ponti, 21 years her senior. She became his protege at age 15 and he groomed her for international stardom. A married man at that time, Carlo was accused of bigamy when his Mexican divorce and subsequent marriage to Sophia were not recognized in Italy. It took 15 years and becoming French citizens to get the marriage recognized. It took Sophia five more years and four miscarriages to finally bear two healthy sons.

The Moon which rules Sophia's 7th house is conjunct Saturn, indicating that for marriage she prefers a responsible, possibly older man; with both planets in Aquarius, she would not settle for a run-of-the-mill type; he, or the circumstances surrounding him, must be distinctive and unusual.

That Sophia would seek a "father replacement" in any of her serious love commitments is pretty obvious. Any astrologer or psychologist can figure that out. Why she chose Carlo Ponti rather than film idol Cary Grant*, also many years her senior and certainly very desirable, is easier to find in chart comparison than in her natal chart, though both men have tremendous contact points with her. Love, trust (important for a Virgo Sun/Capricorn Ascendant), loyalty and even habit all play a role. Ponti was a father replacement at an age when she needed one desperately. He guided her through the intricacies and intrigues of film life, no less entangled in Rome than Hollywood, to become an enduring star, winner of an Oscar as well as many other awards and glories.

## Gemini on the 4th House - Sagittarius on the 10th

Mercurial Gemini on the 4th frequently portrays a home where conversation is cherished and reading held dear. Just as often it represents a homemaking parent who is quick, ingenious and interested and who therefore raised you to be curious, to ask questions and take nothing for granted. Even with a fairly difficult Mercury, you enjoy cerebral pursuits whether in the form of games, books or stimulating discussions.

The Sagittarius/Gemini axis, depending, of course, on Mercury/Jupiter placements, reflects parents who live and let live, who try to instill certain ideals and concepts to guide their children rather than force them into a preset mold. Many times religion and philosophy play a significant role in your attitudes. Unless you have an interception, Gemini on the 4th house results in Virgo on the 7th, both ruled by Mercury. Your parental home and early upbringing will greatly influence the partner you choose.

Princess Caroline of Monaco has Gemini on the 4th house; the ruler Mercury is in Capricorn in the 11th, conjunct Venus and sextile the Moon. Jupiter, ruler of her 10th house is in the 7th in Libra, trine the Sun, sextile Uranus, quincunx Mars and the Ascendant. Except for a few adjustments expected from her in order to live up to her royal stand-

* See chart data in Appendix.

ing, she would seem to have no major problems with either parent. Yet the Sun/Moon placements contradict this by T-squaring Uranus. A fixed Aquarius Sun opposed its ruler, Uranus, and both square the Moon/Neptune conjunction in Scorpio augur many challenges with her parents. This configuration symbolizes her need to learn to understand and work with her own *anima/animus.* Her basic childhood and home influence was solid (Mercury in Capricorn) and she felt loved (Mercury conjunct Venus), both important factors to help overcome difficulties in later years.

Those difficulties stem from her stubborn Sun which loves to rebel (Sun opposed its ruler Uranus) but cannot, or will not explain or talk about the reasons for rebellion (Sun in the 12th square Moon in Scorpio), yet she can be very emotional about the situation. In her teens she may have felt that sex was the solution (Moon/Neptune in the 8th); not only because of the fun it represents, but also because this would get back at mother (Moon) and father (Sun).

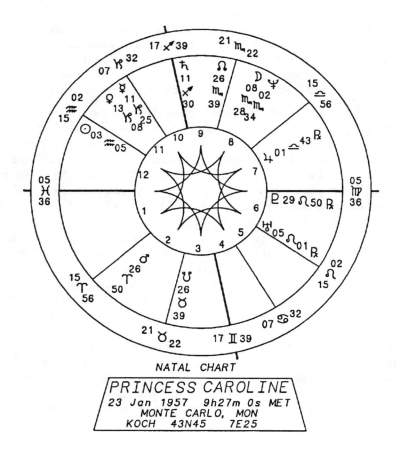

NATAL CHART

PRINCESS CAROLINE
23 Jan 1957   9h27m 0s MET
MONTE CARLO, MON
KOCH   43N45   7E25

Steven Englund, in his book *Grace of Monaco* (Doubleday 1984) gives an interesting description of Caroline, especially the period in the 70s when she graduated from a protected, strict Catholic school near Ascot, England with the equivalent of a high school diploma. She was only 16 and not academically prepared to enter her father's alma mater in Paris.

Caroline was adamant about preparing for her baccalaureat in a Parisian lycee, and her parents, especially her father, did not feel they should oppose her. Always overprotective, her mother, Princess Grace, felt that Caroline was very naive and decided that she and her younger sister Stephanie would accompany her to Paris. Grace's fears about Caroline's lack of sophistication turned out to be right. Beautiful and now eligible Caroline was surrounded by reporters, writers and the ever present paparazzi who staked out the townhouse day and night, headlining pictures with ridiculous captions.

Grace became an ever hovering presence and was viewed by Caroline more as an adversary than an ally. She entered the Ecole Libre that fall, but she also acquired a taste for "*la vie mondaine.*" By now the resentment between mother and daughter was quite obvious. Caroline stressed her resemblance to her father, emphasizing qualities she felt were lacking in Grace. "Even when my father is busy, he still finds time to sit in an armchair and listen to me. I hope I'll find a man like my father..." (Jupiter, ruler of the 10th, father, is in the 7th house). But even her indulgent father became worried when Caroline's gay Parisian life got out of hand and for the first time she failed an exam. Rainier convinced her to apply to Princeton, which he considered the ideal place for a "driving intellectual student like his daughter." Caroline was accepted and agreed to go there, not for herself, but to please her parents.

However, during the summer of 1976 she met Philippe Junot*. Self-assured, he had charm and style; 17 years her senior, he could show her how to live...the romance blossomed...they were seen everywhere together, spending a lot of time in Philippe's apartment. "Philippe has given me the first freedom I've ever known in my life," she said, "His apartment helped me to have some independence and provided me with an escape from my normal routine," (Moon, ruler of the 5th in the 8th, squares the Sun and Uranus). She refused to go to Princeton.

The Grimaldis considered Junot a seducer and fortune hunter. However, both parents kept the door open for their daughter. The wedding of Caroline and Junot was a rather subdued affair; her illusion that Philippe would be another Rainier quickly faded. Her husband basically believed that "staying single was the natural condition for a man." Indiscreet extramarital affairs, a round of parties and nightlife became his lifestyle.

* See chart data in Appendix.

Despite their Catholic background, behind the scenes Grace and Rainier tacitly let Caroline know that they would not be scandalized by a separation or divorce. It took a long time for Caroline to recover; it took even longer for the Vatican to grant an annulment of her marriage to Junot, which is why she married her second husband, Stefano Casiraghi in 1983 in a civil ceremony.

It is doubtful that astrology could foresee that Caroline would marry and divorce a playboy. With the ruler of the 7th house, Mercury, in Capricorn, Caroline definitely preferred an older mate, someone she could rely on. Philippe was older and most certainly more experienced than Caroline, which she may have mistaken for adult behavior; his lavish lifestyle could have impressed her and probably fulfilled her need for a generous partner (Jupiter in the 7th). Theirs was a great love affair (his Sun/Jupiter conjuncts her Mars) but a difficult marriage (his Mars/Venus square Moon becomes a T-Square with Caroline's Saturn/MC).

## Cancer on the 4th House - Capricorn on the 10th House

Cancer on the 4th is the so-called natural position for this Moon ruled sign. It often indicates that you love your home and are always eager to have a place to hang your proverbial hat. It does not imply that you want to stay put all the time; in fact, many facets in your horoscope may indicate a love of travel; you just need a place to come back to.

Depending upon the placement and aspects of the Moon, you may be quite patriotic, hang the flag whenever possible, volunteer for civic duties and be interested in genealogy. You may also be a collector, especially of antiques, or just a "pack rat." All these potential traits are important in your relationships, but not every mate or spouse will be agreeable to these needs, which can be deeply rooted. In most cases your mother plays a very important role; whether positively or negatively depends on the Moon and Saturn's (ruler of the MC) location and aspects.

Saturn ruling the 10th house denotes that one of the parents (often the father) was quite authoritarian and instilled a sense of responsibility in you. Rules and regulations were probably important in your childhood home and you may even have felt that limitations were imposed. Yet, in later years, you no doubt appreciated the discipline ingrained in you from early on, therefore making it easier for you to adapt to school procedures as well as work demands. If Saturn has many tense aspects, especially to the Moon or Venus in a female chart and to the Sun or Mars in a male one, you may have felt that one or both parents did not love you as much as you felt you deserved, nor did they give you enough warmth or tenderness.

Lorna Luft, second daughter of Judy Garland, half-sister to and six years younger than Liza Minelli, is an actress and singer who has this Cancer/Capricorn axis. Her father was Sid Luft, Judy's third husband; the press referred to the marriage as alternately stormy and sublime. According to most accounts brother Joey, born two years after Lorna, became the apple of Judy's eye. "He was the prince," says Lorna, "so I became the classic second child, fighting for love and survival."

Her Moon, ruler of the 4th is in the 9th in Capricorn, conjunct the MC and Mars, square the Saturn/Neptune conjunction and quincunx Pluto in the 4th. This is a very stressed Moon with only one easy outlet, the sextile to the Sun. If Lorna's 4th house represents her mother, Judy Garland, (and from all the biographical material we have seen, this seems to be so) theirs was a very difficult relationship. The Moon is not too happy in Capricorn, the sign of its detriment. The square to Saturn describes the rather classic "you don't love me enough" syndrome. Moon square Neptune portrays Lorna's unrealistic expectations as well as her overidealization of mother and also father (Saturn) and reflects a very sensitive, easily hurt nature.

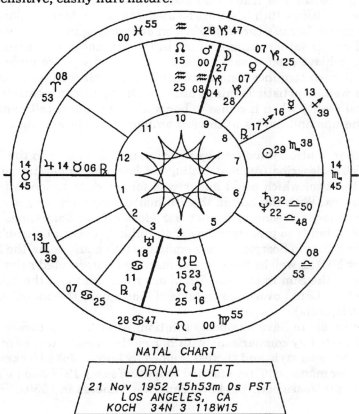

NATAL CHART

LORNA LUFT
21 Nov 1952 15h53m 0s PST
LOS ANGELES, CA
KOCH 34N 3 118W15

The Moon's conjunction to Mars, though typifying a tendency to a hot temper, is basically healthy, since it reflects Lorna's ability to stand up for what she wants and fight back when it is necessary. The Moon's quincunx to Pluto in the 4th illustrates the adjustments necessary to live up to what she thought her parents expected of her, to be as good as or better than her mother (Moon conjunct the MC) and to get away from mother's domination over her (Pluto in the 4th). "Almost nothing in our life was normal, we grew up in hotels; my favorite words are still 'taxi' and 'room service'" Lorna jokes. "What I remember so much about being a kid was moving. Mother always took the three of us wherever she went. I'd be in some school and a note to the teacher would say, 'Please excuse Lorna as we are flying to London tonight.' As a kid I never had any friends, because we never stayed in one place long enough..." How difficult for someone with Cancer on the 4th. Only 16 when Judy died from an overdose of barbiturates (June 22, 1969), Lorna was devastated and finished high school with a D average. "Those were tough times," she says, "I experimented with drugs. But when things got better, the drugs went away."

The ambitious 10th (Capricorn ruled, Moon and Mars conjunct the MC) portrays Lorna's career/profession or standing in the community, as well as her father. Ruler Saturn in the 6th not only denotes hard work to achieve professional goals, but also hard work to understand father. Saturn conjunct Neptune describes unclear feelings regarding Dad as well as artistic leanings and the ability to put creativity into practical reality when it comes to her work. The square to Uranus depicts the ups and downs in the father/daughter relationship or work habits.

Father is also symbolized by the Sun, and its sextile to the Moon/Mars could describe frequent feelings of love and understanding between the two, which could augur well for intimate unions with the opposite sex. With the Sun in the 7th house, Lorna feels a great need for a partner, someone to bounce her ideas off on. Sometimes a 7th house Sun tends to give itself away, an unlikely event in Lorna's case since the Sun is in Scorpio. Career eminence (4th house ruler, the Moon, conjunct MC) as well as a successful marriage (intercepted ruler of the 4th house, the Sun in the 7th; 7th house ruler, Pluto, in the 4th) will greatly help Lorna overcome feelings of inadequacy (Moon/MC square Saturn/Neptune).

She seems to have found the solution. After a rocky career start, being haunted by comparisons with her mother and sister, Lorna discovered her own style and success, helped by hubby, Jake Hooker, who became her manager. They married Valentine's Day 1977 and have two children, son Jesse born 1984 and daughter Vanessa in 1990.

## Leo on the 4th House - Aquarius on the 10th House

When proud and showy Leo is found on the house of home and family, you may, depending on the Sun's position and aspects, hail from a splendid, splashy or illustrious background. A client with Leo on the 4th has the Sun in Cancer conjunct Jupiter in the 3rd and is one of triplets. With the Sun ruling your 4th and Uranus your 10th house, both so-called masculine symbols, it becomes particularly important to discuss your feelings about your parents, in order to decide which house represents which parent.

The Leo parent, more often than not, will have certain dramatic qualities, be sympathetic to your feelings and even condone and understand your emotional outbursts. Being fairly self-involved, s/he may not always have time for you, but makes up for it by giving you a double dose of love. Of course, a problematic Sun can reflect a parent who, conversely, has no time for you and difficulty in displaying love and caring.

The Aquarius/Uranus parent in your perception will always be different than other people's parents; maybe having an unusual business or occupation; possibly being absent a lot of the time; perhaps just having unique looks, mannerisms or a foreign accent...As a result, you too, may strive to be distinctive, to do something noteworthy or extraordinary. Leo and Aquarius are both fixed and unless the Sun and/or Uranus are in mutable signs, your parents may have been autocratic and bossy, bringing out the rebellious side of your nature and only at your first Saturn return (age 28 to 30) will you be willing to seriously face the consequences as well as your future.

Anthony West, illegitimate son of writers Dame Rebecca West* and H.G. Wells*, has Leo on his 4th house with the Sun which rules it on the 3rd house side of the IC. Uranus, ruler of the 10th house, conjuncts the Aquarian MC from the 9th; the two planets closely oppose each other. West, personified by the 4th house, according to Victoria Glendinning's biography *Rebecca West, This is What Matters,* "was a formidable figure, a passionate lover, an ambivalent mother and a devoted wife." Nee Cicely Isabel Fairfield, she took the pen name Rebecca West in order not to embarrass her mother by her unladylike language in a book review. West was an instant sensation in literary London. "Looking like a schoolgirl in pastel frocks and garden party hats, she delivered outrageous statements in a mellifluous voice trained for the stage." She desperately wanted to be an actress, as she herself states in her posthumously published novel, *Sunflower.* Writing was second choice.

H.G. Wells, seen by Anthony as Uranus in Aquarius, closely conjunct the Midheaven and widely conjunct Jupiter, was very popular in England in Anthony's childhood years and to him his father loomed larger than life. Author of such predictive novels as *War of the Worlds,*

* Chart data in Appendix.

*The Time Machine* and *The First Men on the Moon*, Wells was a highly sexual man who married twice and according to biographer, Gordan Ray, "sated his lust elsewhere." Apparently he fathered a number of children while engaged in these extramarital affairs. His main affair, however, was with Rebecca, 26 years his junior, lasting for ten years. States biographer Gollancz, "She had the duty of assuaging the physical itch that would otherwise distract him from writing." Wells was 48 years old when Anthony was born and had little or no time for him.

Yet both parents had an indelible influence on Anthony (Saturn conjunct Pluto in the 1st), who is recognized as a master craftsman in his own writing career. His autobiographical novel *Heritage* is a biting account of his agonizing relationship with his illustrious parents. It is of more than passing interest that his father's Ascendant at 12 Aquarius is Anthony's Midheaven and that his mother's Ascendant at 22 Sagittarius is his Descendant.

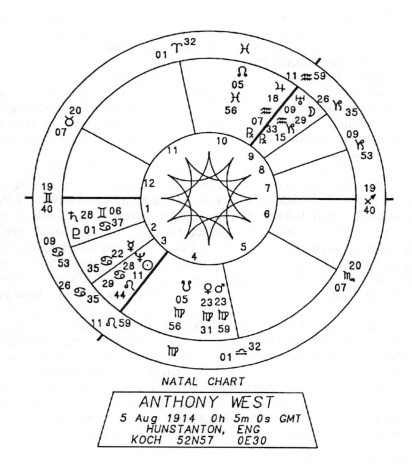

NATAL CHART

ANTHONY WEST

5 Aug 1914   0h 5m 0s GMT
HUNSTANTON,   ENG
KOCH   52N57   0E30

Does a painful relationship with your parents, such as Anthony experienced, influence your future, your wish to marry or have children of your own? Of course it does. Astrology cannot, and astrologers should not try to predict what a person will or will not do. But to help someone recognize potential parental problems is a very important task for the astrologer.

Anthony West came to the United States in 1950; he married in 1958 and has 11 children, seven daughters and four sons. He calls himself a good father!

## Virgo on the 4th House - Pisces on the 10th House

You may not always see your 10th house (Pisces) parent as s/he really is, either because of overidealization, through misunderstandings and sometimes simply because s/he is absent. If glamorous, occasionally mysterious and always charismatic Pisces personifies one parent, then discriminating and often nit-picking Virgo represents the other one. If Mercury, ruler of the 4th, has flowing aspects, you may find it fairly easy to live up to that parent's expectations. A client with this axis has Neptune, ruler of the 10th in Libra in the 4th square Mars in Capricorn in the 8th, and Mercury, ruler of the 4th is in the 4th in Virgo conjunct Saturn. The Sun is in Leo in the 3rd conjunct Pluto. His parents divorced and mother married an alcoholic, while father wed a glamorous movie star. They had joint custody and he spent his developing years shuttling between these two totally divergent backgrounds. Though successful in business, his marital record (3 times) leaves a lot to be desired.

If the Virgo 4th house depicts your mother, she may strike you as too demanding, especially compared to your Neptunian, often nebulous father. On the other hand, she may be the parent who provides a home where learning is important. She is the one to teach you about hygiene, how to keep an intelligent schedule, how to maintain a healthy body by eating healthful foods. Father, contrarily, may excel in telling wonderful fairy tales and showing you the difference between a Rubens and a Renoir, Wolfgang Amadeus Mozart and Henry Mancini.

Successful actor, writer, director and producer, Peter Fonda, son of Henry, brother of Jane, has this Virgo/Pisces axis. Mercury, which rules his 4th house, is in Pisces in the 10th; it opposes Neptune, ruler of the 10th which is in Virgo in the 4th. Mercury and Neptune form a T-Square with his Gemini Ascendant which is also Mercury ruled. As if this role reversal was not challenging enough, Fonda's Sun in Pisces in the 10th, conjunct the MC, opposes his Moon in Virgo in the 4th house.

His mother, Frances Seymour Brokaw Fonda, second wife of Henry, committed suicide, but Peter, who was only ten when it happened, was not told, and in fact, only found out about it by chance at age 15.

According to an interview with Michael Leahy (*TV Guide* 10/20/84), Fonda describes the family's decision to hide the truth from him as a conspiracy for which he's never forgiven them. For years he carried the hidden guilt that his dreams about his mother dying had brought on her death. Though he concedes that Jane might have wanted to shelter him when she found out the truth through an indiscreet friend, he did not credit his father with the same consideration when he confronted him. "I think it just blew him away so badly and made him feel so guilty..."

In fact, Henry never talked to his son about his mother's death. He never faced the source of Peter's anger or worries or the violent incidents that happened at boarding school. (Neptune, ruler of the 10th opposed Mercury, ruler of the 4th, both square Ascendant.) According to Peter, "Henry didn't talk about much of anything. He got along best with other reticent people, like Jimmy Stewart. I was never sure who he was. He wouldn't reveal himself...he was a perfectionist, always on

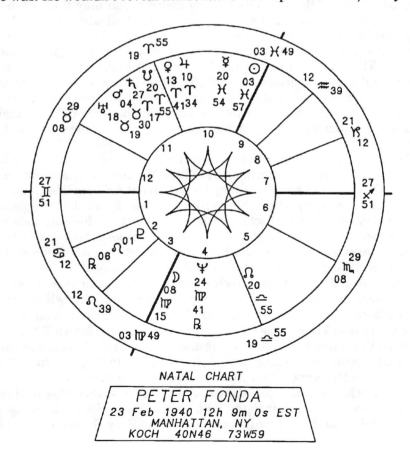

NATAL CHART

PETER FONDA
23 Feb 1940 12h 9m 0s EST
MANHATTAN, NY
KOCH  40N46  73W59

my case for something. He wanted me to be what he was not." And saddest of all according to Peter, his father never said, "I love you." Only toward the end, shortly before Henry Fonda's death, did father and son come to an understanding and tell each other, "I love you."

It seems pretty obvious that Peter's mother was represented by the 4th house with the Moon there. The Sun in Pisces in the 10th, fits the image Peter had of his father: glamorous, famous, vague, nebulous and more interested in his career and his quest for the perfect partner (five wives in total), than he was in taking on the nurturing parent role with either of his children.

## Libra on the 4th House - Aries on the 10th House

Libra on the 4th cusp suggests that you come from a home where peace and harmony prevail, where discussions rarely become arguments, and you enjoy an active social life with educational opportunities. Of course, much depends upon the placement of Venus, the ruler of Libra. If it is not in positive cosmic placement, the opposite may apply: there is little peace and harmony; many arguments between parents, possibly involving you; your parents may shun social activity and feel that an education is unimportant.

Your mother, in this case represented by a feminine planet, Venus, may reflect many of the positive traits of this lovely Evening Star: beauty, musical or artistic talent, pleasing etiquette and warm expression of love. Unless Venus' aspects are most challenging, she bestows all this upon you and you bask in her warmth.

With Libra on the 4th, Aries is naturally on the 10th and indicates that you deal with authority with great energy, often arguing with or contradicting the source of power. Again, much depends on the placement of Mars, ruler of Aries. If Mars is in a passive sign (earth or water) and has mild aspects, you may find it easy to respect those who have influence over you; thus your relationship with your father could be an easy one. If, however, Mars is stressful in your chart, this could be a bone of contention and you have much to learn about respect for authority. If you are a male with Mars in hard aspect to Saturn, you could have problems with your father as a role model to the point of mistrusting your own masculinity.

Prince Charles of England has this axis; Venus, ruler of his 4th is in Libra in this house, as are Neptune, Mercury and the Sun. Since the Sun is an indicator of the father, Charles undoubtedly sees his parents as a unit; charming and gracious (Venus), at times stern and unyielding (Mercury and Sun in Scorpio), and occasionally confusing (Neptune). Venus sextiles Mars, his 10th house ruler and Pluto in his 1st, so he most likely identifies strongly with his mother. This is doubly confirmed by comparing his (page 131) and Queen Elizabeth's charts (page 26). His Moon, the other indicator of mother, exactly conjuncts her Sun. It also trines Saturn in his 2nd, so he tends to value what she values. The Moon elevated verifies her prominent position in his life. With this angular Moon and so many planets in the 4th house, it is most intriguing that his wife, Princess Diana has the Sun in Cancer.

Prince Philip, his father, is described by Mars in the 5th, ruler of his 10th, and the Sun in Scorpio in the 4th. Mars has excellent aspects (trine Pluto, sextile Venus), so Charles' relationship with his father appears to flow smoothly. With such an active 4th house, home and family are a focal point for him, which becomes his status as heir to the British Royal throne. As Prince Regent, Charles is very careful in how he refers to his parents, especially his mother, the Queen. According to Stephen P. Barry's *Royal Service* son and mother "are very close, yet they conduct themselves formally. Charles visits 'Mummy' in the Queen's Chambers, never the other way around."

## Scorpio on the 4th House -Taurus on the 10th House

Scorpio on the 4th house can suggest an early childhood in which there may be some skeletons in the closet, a very intense atmosphere and often an extremely dominant or manipulative parent (usually mother, if the Moon's or Venus' placement supports this). The generation with Pluto in Leo expected a great deal from their parents. Those of that group with these signs on the parental axis, may have learned their grandiose expectations at their parent's knee.

Of course, as we have reiterated so often in the past, so much depends upon the placement of Pluto and Mars, the rulers of Scorpio and in determining the characteristics of the mother, the Moon, too, plays a significant role. A 40-year-old client with Scorpio on the 4th, Moon in the 4th square a Leo Ascendant conjunct Pluto has a very manipulative mother; sweet, charming, but nonetheless manipulative. He has found it difficult to cut the umbilical cord and has never married; every time he is on the verge, Mommy needs him for one reason or another.

This sign on the 4th often indicates a strong, determined, iron hand in the velvet glove, parental relationship. Sometimes you mirror these traits as you grow up; other times you seek these qualities in your partner. Mars' position is quite revealing as to how you work out your parental interaction.

With Taurus on the 10th, much attention must be given to your Venus to see how you respond to the authoritative parent. In this combination, many times the parental roles reverse, with the stronger influence coming from the 4th house parent. If Venus has some challenging aspects, you may find it easier to identify with authority, than to rebel against it.

It is important to remember that your 10th house cusp is your ego point, and reflects your status, prestige and achievement potential. So a thorough analysis of this house is very significant in examining the potential of the partnership relationship, since the 10th signifies the ultimate outcome of the marriage 7th.

Natalie Cole, daughter of the legendary Nat King Cole, has Taurus on the Midheaven with the ruler, Venus, in the 6th house, so it is not unusual that she followed in her father's footsteps as far as her career goes. Venus trines the Moon and Mars (co-ruler of her 4th) suggesting that her parents were a positive influence in her childhood and teenage years. Her Sun, also representative of her father, opposes Pluto and squares her MC, symbolizing the early loss of his presence. He died shortly after her fifteenth birthday and the parental role reversal took effect. She feels that his name hurt as much as it helped her and found it difficult to live up to his image. However, she had great early success with her singing career.

In 1982 her mother petitioned the L.A. Supreme Court for conservatorship of Natalie, because of health problems and severe drug addic-

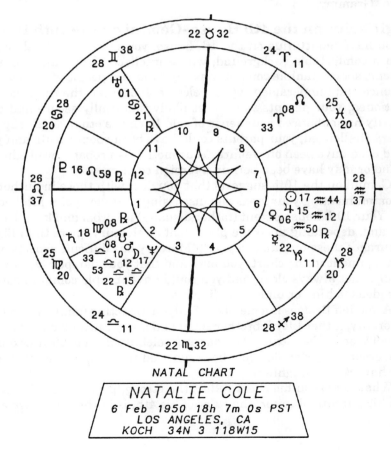

NATAL CHART

NATALIE COLE
6 Feb 1950 18h 7m 0s PST
LOS ANGELES, CA
KOCH 34N 3 118W15

tion. Her mother is represented by Pluto, ruler of the 4th, which opposes her Sun/Jupiter conjunction and squares her MC, a most difficult T-Square. Her resentment of her mother seemed justified to her (the empty leg of the T-Square is in the 4th house) and it was not until several years later that she was able to kick her addiction and get her career started in a new direction. Her Moon in Libra in the 2nd house has excellent, flowing aspects, so while there have been ups and downs in her relationship with her mother, the love they feel for each other has seen them through it.

Obviously Natalie looks for a paternal type partner who can also be her friend; Uranus, ruler of her 7th is in Cancer in the 11th. Aquarius on the 7th often seeks someone unique and distinctive. Pluto and Mars ruling the 4th, indicate that she is drawn to strong and powerful people. Her marriage to her father's producer ended in divorce... she feels due to her health and drug breakdown. Currently she, her second husband and teenage son are enjoying "good times" and great success with more "Grammys."

## Sagittarius on the 4th House -Gemini on the 10th House

If you have Sagittarius on the 4th house, you more than likely come from a comfortable background, where intellectual pursuits were *de rigueur*, sportsmanlike conduct was expected and people of various experience and temperament were welcome. If Jupiter, the ruler, is well positioned, your parents were most likely financially secure and this security has enhanced your sense of self. If, on the other hand, Jupiter is very challenged, your parents could have been spendthrifts and you could even have been on welfare. Your mother is probably well educated and/or may have been born in a foreign country.

Gemini on the 10th suggests that you deal with those in authority by communicating your ideas and discussing your viewpoint intellectually. Your 10th house parent (father, usually) is verbal and knowledgeable and, depending upon the placement of Mercury, more than likely encourages these qualities in you. If Mercury has difficult aspects or is not prominent in the chart, you may find that your perspective of your father is not always clear, and you could have trouble communicating your ideas to him, or understanding his.

Actor Jeff Bridges is a member of a dynastic acting family. His mother Dorothy, father Lloyd, brother Beau and sister Lucinda have all acted on TV or in the movies. His parents celebrated their 50th wedding anniversary in 1989. Jeff has been married to Susan since 1977 and they have three daughters.

What factors in his chart reflect the strong, positive relationships with his parents? Jupiter, the ruler of his 4th, is in the 5th house conjunct Venus and quincunx Uranus; his Moon is in Gemini in the 9th house opposing his Sun and trine Neptune. Jeff likes women and views his mother as the glue that held the family together while his father was traveling for his career. Even though Dorothy was an actress, when the children arrived, she took pleasure from her role as mother. Jeff's Sun/Moon opposition may suggest that his parents had problems, but he denies this. Gemini/Sagittarius can indicate nothing more than philosophical, intellectual discussion. "My mother was wonderfully fanatical about dedicating an entire hour to each kid every day...Mom called it our time, and during those three hours each day, she took no phone calls and harbored no distractions—it was just intense kid time." About what you might expect from your mom with Mercury in the 4th.

When we look at the father factor in Bridges' chart, the ruler of the 10th is in the 4th and has many aspects, both easy and challenging. The Sun widely conjuncts Mercury which rules the Midheaven, so it is not difficult to understand why he followed in his father's footsteps. He

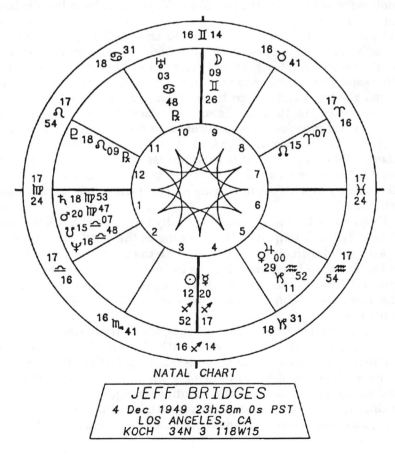

NATAL CHART

JEFF BRIDGES
4 Dec 1949  23h58m 0s  PST
LOS ANGELES, CA
KOCH   34N 3  118W15

gave his first performance at six months and then retired until age eight, when he appeared on his father's TV show "Sea Hunt." After high school, Jeff studied acting at New York's Berghof Studios and made his feature debut in "Halls of Anger."

According to Bridges, his relationship with his family is "totally normal," the usual disagreements, but also lots of love and fun. With the Moon in Gemini trining Neptune, ruler of the 7th, he truly enjoys women and is happily married to one with whom he can communicate. He worried about getting married, because before he met Susan he was quite a womanizer (Sun opposition Moon, Venus conjunct Jupiter in the 5th, and Mars, ruler of the 8th square Mercury). However, once settled down, his marriage appears to be as sound as that of his parents.

## Capricorn on the 4th House - Cancer on the 10th House

Saturn ruling the 4th house can denote the single parent home, or a childhood of poverty; on the positive side, you may have been raised on a farm or in a country home and you are comfortable with earth-related concepts. If Saturn is well placed in the chart, your parents may have started with little and gradually have become successful. Discipline is usually meted out by mother, but you pay heed to both parents and are quite respectful of authority and maturity. Many times a grandparent or older relative lived in your home when you were young.

Cancer on the 10th can be an indication that the mother fulfills both parental roles; or it may indicate that father plays a strong paternal role in the family much like Leon Ames role in the movie *Meet Me in St Louis*. When you have this axis, you learn early on that security is important to your well-being, thus you generally seek a partner who will provide you with the nurturing and protection you became used to in childhood.

Ex-president Jimmy Carter generally remembers his childhood as sunny—idyllic, fishing, hunting, running in the woods, but his memories are tinged with defiance, at odds with the major themes of love and caring. "I worked hard when I was a little child," he once said, "but I'm proud of it." Mostly raised by black women, because his mother, an R.N., nursed day and night; though he was proud of his mother, he missed her presence.

In almost all accounts of his parents, his mother is described as the "liberal" counterweight to his "conservative" father. James Earl Carter, Sr. represented authority and ambition. Miss Lillian, the nurse, was the "caring" parent, devoted to helping the poor and weak. His father was complex, often contradictory. Exuding strength, he was timid; hard-working, yet fun-loving; ambitious, yet satisfied. In public, he appeared hard; in private, he was compassionate. Carter writes that his father "was a stern disciplinarian and punished me severely when I misbehaved..."

This description seems much more in keeping with Carter's 4th house than his 10th. Saturn rules it and is in powerful, manipulative Scorpio in Jimmy's 1st house and squares the Midheaven. Mars is in Aquarius in the 4th. The Sun in Libra in the 12th house squares Pluto, repeating the power theme. This Sun placement also reinforces the comments about his father's timidity. With both Mars and Saturn involved with this house it is easy to see why his relationship with his father was somewhat tenuous. In spite of that, Carter's great wish was to emulate his father.

In this case with the 4th house representing father, the 10th depicts his mother. The Moon that rules it is in Scorpio in the 1st suggesting a strong, at times manipulative, occasionally remote and private person, but Jimmy had a great attachment to her since the Moon is in a Grand Trine with Pluto and Uranus. This configuration indicates an

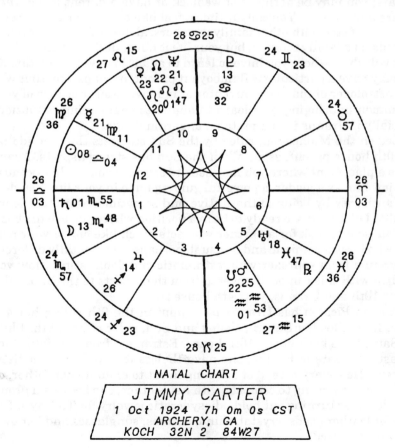

NATAL CHART

JIMMY CARTER
1 Oct 1924   7h 0m 0s CST
ARCHERY, GA
KOCH   32N 2   84W27

easy flow of emotions as well as an ability to relate well to the women in his life. With Venus conjunct Neptune in the 10th, he tends to idealize women and recognized his mother as the culture bearer in the home. She also offered her children religious inspiration, often a function of Neptune.

His choice of a wife reflects his country upbringing. He chose a woman with many of the qualities of both parents. Rosalyn comes from the same type background and morality that he does. Mars in his 4th house rules his 7th and trines the 4th house ruler, Saturn. He loves and venerates his wife with the same zeal, love and respect that he felt for his father and mother.

## Aquarius on the 4th House - Leo on the 10th House

With Uranus ruling your background and heredity, your early home life may be fraught with change and upset. Your parents could move a lot and you may have to adjust to a different environment every couple of years; you may be born out of wedlock or have a parent leave when you are quite young. You can, at times, feel like a stranger in your own home, out of step with other family members, alone and solitary even in the midst of a family reunion, but your life is never dull... Uranus' placement will show where you have to learn to adapt to new circumstances. You may have a particularly flamboyant parent; perhaps a mother who is an astrologer or maybe an inventor or mud wrestler. Because of your uncommon upbringing, you learn to adjust to challenging  situations especially if Uranus is in a mutable or cardinal sign.

Leo on the Midheaven, ruled by the Sun suggests that you idolize the 10th house parent, especially if the Sun has strong aspects. Again, this is a placement where you may seek to emulate your father because you view him as a leader, a powerful guiding force in your life. You deal with authority by being authoritative and sometimes you must learn humility before you are ready to be in a position where you are the boss.

You tend to look for a partner who acts much like one of your parents, who is either unique and unusual, perhaps from a totally different background from yours; or who is dramatic and dominating. How you will deal with this can be discovered from the aspects to the Sun, ruler of your 10th and Uranus, your 4th house ruler.

Paloma Picasso has Uranus in Gemini in the 9th ruling her 4th house. It sextiles her Saturn, Venus and Sun, ruler of her 10th. Pluto and Saturn are both in the 10th house. Estranged from her father for the last ten years of his life, she nevertheless followed in his artistic footsteps. However, instead of dabbling in art to emulate her father, or in painting or writing to compete with her mother, she became a prominent designer turning out bold, idiosyncratic jewelry for Tiffany's. Designs for leather goods, crystal, china, scarves, sunglasses and her own fragrance followed.

Her father, artist Pablo Picasso, is well defined by her 10th house, with Pluto and Saturn there suggesting his need to control, either by dictating her lifestyle or ignoring her altogether. Yet there was a lot of love. "He was not your usual father," she remembers. "He was very playful (Sun conjunct Venus). Once he took my white canvas espadrille shoes and did drawings all over them." Her Sun in Aries exactly opposes her Ascendant, reinforcing the break with her father. Notwithstanding Pluto's relatively "good" aspects, this break caused her creative juices to dry up. In spite of the debacle, she slowly worked her way back to productivity and is well known as a top achiever in her field.

Francoise Gilot, her mother, is depicted by the Uranian ruled 4th house. Francoise and Pablo never married; Paloma was born out of wedlock to a very strong minded woman, a painter and writer who was the one woman Picasso could never subdue. The Moon is in Capricorn suggesting that Paloma's mother presented a cool, businesslike demeanor, yet with

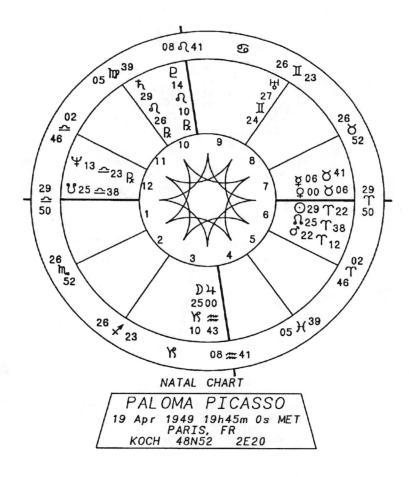

NATAL CHART

PALOMA PICASSO
19 Apr 1949 19h45m 0s MET
PARIS, FR
KOCH 48N52 2E20

Uranus aspecting Mars, she was capable of great passion and the relationship between mother and daughter was close but not intimate.

With her Sun conjunct Venus and the 7th house cusp, it is necessary for Paloma to identify strongly with her husband and with Mars the ruler of both the Sun and the marriage house, in the 6th, they have a working relationship; he establishes her goals and encourages her in her work. As she states, "He saw that I should do this (jewelry design) on a grand scale, that I should not be shy..."

## Pisces on the 4th House - Virgo on the 10th House

Pisces ruling the 4th house is a prime indicator of a potential stepparent. Obviously, everyone who has this does not deal with pseudo parents; much depends on Neptune's placement. Often your family is religious...strongly so. Or there can be an air of mystery or glamor about your background and heredity ...the proverbial skeleton in the closet. You may have a parent who drinks to excess or is into drugs if Neptune

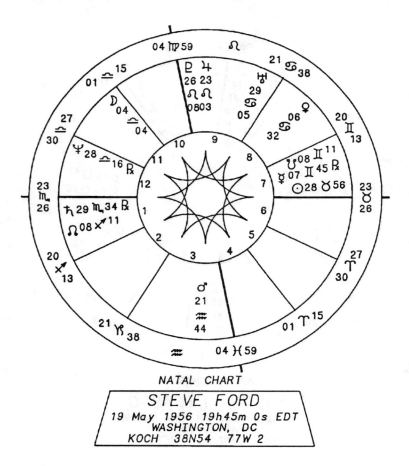

NATAL CHART

STEVE FORD
19 May 1956 19h45m 0s EDT
WASHINGTON, DC
KOCH   38N54   77W 2

has challenging aspects; or one who is musical if the aspects are harmonious. Your mother may not always be there for you, either because she works, or possibly because she has a health problem.

Virgo on the 10th describes a somewhat critical parent whom you try to live up to. Mercury's aspects show whether this is easy or impossible. You deal with authority by trying to analyze it out of existence, if you can. If you cannot cope, you may flee into the dreamy safety of your 4th house, seeking refuge with the parent represented there. We find many people who have the responsibility for an aged or infirm parent with this axis.

You look for both glamor and inspiration from your partner, as well as someone who can help you develop a strong family foundation. With mutable signs on the meridian, you will often have mutable signs on the horizon as well, and the placement of Jupiter, your 7th-house ruler plays a vital part in the traits of the partner you seek.

Steve Ford, son of the 38th President of the United States has this axis in his chart. Neptune rules his 4th house and is in the 12th, square Uranus, quincunx the Sun, trine Mars and sextile Pluto. His mother had quite a battle with the bottle and prescription drugs and Steve, his father and siblings were all very helpful in getting her to a clinic. Steve's Moon is in Libra in the 11th indicating that he views his mother as a friend, someone who seeks balance and harmony. His Moon has some very positive aspects and a square to Venus. Even though he was on good terms with his mother, there may have been disputes about his public behavior (Venus rules his 7th).

After some success as a rodeo rider, Steve has a career as an actor, appearing in a daily TV soap. With Virgo on the MC and the ruler in Gemini in the 7th, he has developed his ego by appearing in the public eye. His father is also represented by Mercury and the Sun in Taurus, suggesting that he could be a public person. With the Sun opposing Saturn, we can be sure that Steve is trying to follow in his father's footsteps, not necessarily in politics, though that could come later in his life, but in the limelight in some capacity.

## LESSON 4
# OTHER HOUSES IN RELATIONSHIPS

### The 2nd House in Relationships

The 2nd house does not represent any immediate family member or intimate relation, thus it does not play a great role in assessing how a relationship may work out. Its greatest significance is in analyzing the values of each person involved in the comparison. If their values are similar, the situation between them may run quite smoothly, sometimes almost too smoothly, thus lacking challenge or spark. If their value systems augment each other, but also have some challenges, the affiliation has the best chance of working. When their outlooks on life are totally divergent, it may be very difficult to align their goals and needs and thus a happy marriage or partnership, unless other factors are extremely supportive, has much less of a chance.

In speaking of values, we do not particularly mean how the person earns or spends money; this is significant, of course, but we are mainly referring to what is important to each individual in terms of possessions, viewpoint and understanding of life. The 2nd house is the area of life where you come to terms with your own self-image...your self-worth. If you are an extreme egotist, feeling that you really have it all together as far as knowing who you are, where you're going and how you will get there, it is unlikely that you will feel comfortable with a partner who is still searching for her/his identity, career goals and partnership needs. The 2nd house can help in these areas when judging the suitability of the partnership.

A student once brought in the chart of a young man she was interested in. In examining the horoscopes of both, there were a few nice connections between them. But, in viewing the 2nd house, it seemed as though there was little similarity in their value systems. She had Aquarius there with Uranus in Gemini in the 7th, indicating that she was drawn to unusual people and enjoyed interacting with intellectual groups. He, on the other hand had Cancer on the 2nd house cusp, with the Moon in Capricorn in the 7th. His tastes ran more to conservative interaction with other people. Saturn was also in his 2nd, so his attitude toward money was security oriented, while hers was "easy come, easy go." Uranus conjuncted Mars and both squared Jupiter so her self-worth issues were somewhat outré.

Saturn opposed his Moon; he was a bit unsure of himself in the ego department, but quite doggedly certain of what he wanted in a partner.

They married; it lasted three years; her comment was, "He was a tightwad from the word go. Can you imagine, he wanted to invest my money for me? I couldn't go for that for one moment." He was much less willing to comment about the demise of the partnership, only saying, "We just didn't see eye-to-eye on anything. We only agreed on not having pets."

## The 3rd House in Relationships

As the house of side-by-side relationships, the 3rd represents your siblings and shows how you relate to them. With Saturn there, you may have responsibility for younger brothers and sisters; Mars in the 3rd often indicates a lack of siblings or arguments with sisters and brothers or neighbors. Positive use of Mars here implies energy directed toward family relationships. The Sun in the 3rd may involve you in close personal or even business relationships with siblings or neighbors, while Mercury here naturally suggests that issues of communication arise between you and others. The way this works out depends on Mercury aspects. Jupiter does not always indicate a large family but does typify a very cordial familial relationship. Venus, contingent upon aspects, denotes closeness and possible financial dealings with relatives, and you may spoil younger siblings. The Moon here is very emotional when it comes to family affairs and often tends to mother or father siblings. Neptune sometimes clouds the family picture with step- or half sisters and brothers, or it can reveal a creative family streak. Uranus often suggests a sister or brother who is out of step with the rest of the family and Pluto occasionally indicates the loss of a sibling or intense involvement with him or her.

Brothers and sisters provide on-site peer interaction. If a girl has no brothers, her only male role model is her father. If a boy has no sisters, he only can look to his mother for a feminine role model. An only child may find it difficult to relate to peers because of the lack of interaction with siblings in the home. This is neither good nor bad, but does provide a clue for the astrologer in assessing how the person interacts with others. The only child may have difficulty in knowing how to share; the girl with no brothers has to learn to adjust to male traits through trial and error. The reverse is true for the boy who grows up without sisters.

We remind you once again, that you cannot tell from the chart whether a person has brothers and sisters, and nowhere in astrological annals is it written that you should guess. If guessing is your game, you may occasionally be right, but we would rather that you be right all the time, so ask!

Jeff Bridges has Scorpio on the 3rd house cusp; Pluto is in the 12th; Mars is in the 1st. (See chart on page 55.) His Sun is also in the 3rd house. The Pluto placement shows that he may work behind the scenes with a sibling; Mars position shows strong identification with a brother or sister and the Sun in the 3rd attests to a substantial sibling bond. He has worked in films (12th) with his brother, Beau*, and often mentions his close identification with him. Pluto's aspects are easy and flowing, but Mars squares Mercury, so obviously there have been disagreements between them. Although cinematically he has surpassed his big brother, Beau seems free of jealousy. "Jeff's victories are mine," he relates in an interview. "We have always felt that we're on the same team rooting for each other."

Prince Charles of England has Virgo on the cusp of the 3rd house and Mercury in Scorpio in the 4th ruling it. Mercury sextiles Saturn and trines Uranus suggesting that he has rather passive relationships with his sister and two brothers, based on family respect (4th house), a sense of responsibility (Saturn) and friendliness (Uranus). (See chart on page 131.)

Lorna Luft (see chart on page 45), with Cancer on the 3rd, quite naturally tends to nurture her sister and brother and expects the same in return. The Moon in Capricorn reinforces this inclination. Uranus in the 3rd, ruling her 10th implies a competitiveness with a sibling in career areas. She and her sister Liza Minelli both sing and act, and with Aquarius intercepted in her 10th, Liza achieved more recognition earlier. (See chart on page 7.)

With the Sun that rules his 3rd house exactly conjunct the Midheaven, it is not surprising that Peter Fonda's sister, Jane, is a star in her own right. His Sun opposes his Moon and quincunxes Pluto, so theirs has not always been an easy relationship, but the sextile to Mars suggests that he will stand up for her whenever necessary.

Let's look at the charts of two famous siblings and see if we can tell how they interact with each other.

Princess Anne of England has Jupiter ruling her 3rd house with Capricorn intercepted. Saturn is in Virgo in the 11th conjunct her Moon and Mercury, while Jupiter is in Pisces in the 5th. Jupiter is in a Grand Trine with Mars in the 1st and Uranus in the 9th. Her brother, Prince

---

* See chart data in Appendix.

Andrew, has Virgo on the 3rd and the ruler Mercury is in Pisces in the 8th sextile Saturn.

She views their relationship as friendly (11th), though somewhat competitive (5th). She probably feels close to all her brothers and they likely agree on philosophy, sports and what constitutes having fun (the Grand Trine in the 1st, 5th and 9th).

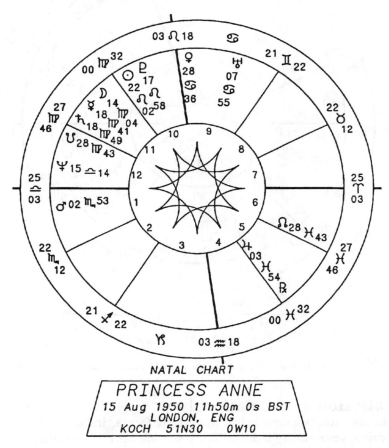

NATAL CHART

PRINCESS ANNE

15 Aug 1950 11h50m 0s BST
LONDON, ENG
KOCH 51N30 0W10

Andrew may be a bit critical toward his siblings (Virgo on the 3rd cusp) and with the sextile to Saturn in his 5th, he could take on some responsibility in organizing mutual sport and game activities. The quincunx to Uranus in his 1st, ruler of his 7th indicates an unusual method of communicating at times and a certain amount of unconventionality in his self-expression that his siblings may have difficulty understanding, but with his 2nd and 3rd houses tied together (Virgo on both cusps), it is likely that they share the same values. His Venus/Mars conjunction in his 6th house sextiles his Moon so he probably relates better to his sister, Anne, than to his brothers. The conjunction falls in her 3rd house intensifying the bond between them.

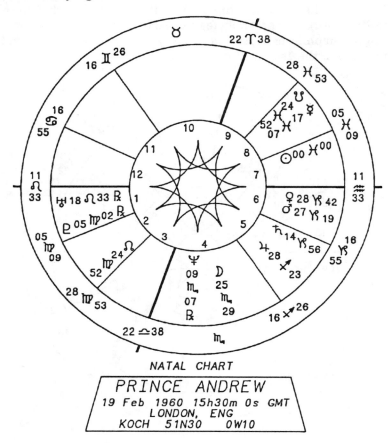

NATAL CHART

PRINCE ANDREW
19 Feb 1960 15h30m 0s GMT
LONDON, ENG
KOCH    51N30    0W10

## The 5th House in Relationships

This house encompasses many important facets, including your creative drive, your ability to have fun, your risk-taking disposition, speculations, pleasures, hobbies, sports, enterprise...but, when it comes to relating only two 5th house essentials are really significant; how you relate to your children and your attitude toward love and romance.

Even the most repressed Venus cannot stop Taurus on the 5th from enjoying sensual pleasures, while Aquarius there can be eccentric, even somewhat outré if Uranus has challenging aspects. On the other hand, Capricorn on the 5th does not have to project the inhibited lover; Ingrid Bergman had Capricorn here, but her Saturn conjuncts Mars. Her lover, then husband, Roberto Rossellini also has Capricorn on the 5th cusp, but he has Uranus in this house. You will agree that neither of them were particularly reticent when it came to love affairs.

Romantic movie idol of the 40s, Charles Boyer*, had supposedly unromantic Gemini of the cusp of the 5th, but Pluto and Neptune were in the 5th house and the ruler, Mercury, was in Leo in his 7th. Unlike his film image, his only real love was his wife of 44 years (ruler of the 5th in the 7th). Nearly obsessive in his love for former Playboy Bunny, Dorothy Stratton, film director Peter Bogdanovich* has Leo on the 5th with both Sun and Pluto conjunct in Leo in the house. Cher has Scorpio on the 5th and Pluto and Mars conjunct in Leo in that house. Need we say more?

Truly romantic was the allegedly platonic love affair between composer Johannes Brahms and Clara Schumann.

Clara (see chart on page 71) was an exquisite pianist, famous for her physical beauty and charm; she was 35, 14 years older than Brahms, at that time the mother of six children, and most importantly, the wife

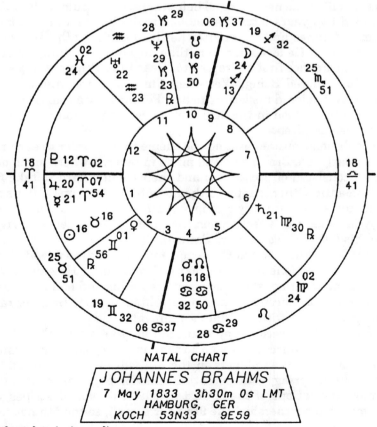

NATAL CHART

JOHANNES BRAHMS
7 May 1833   3h30m 0s LMT
HAMBURG,   GER
KOCH   53N33   9E59

* See chart data in Appendix.

of well-known composer Robert Schumann. Schumann was the man who opened musical doors for Brahms and made him his musical protege. His devotion to the couple was intense; gratefulness to Robert, adoration and a deep affection for Clara. Cancer on his 5th cusp, with the ruler, Moon in Sagittarius in the 9th of idealization, trine Mercury and Jupiter, suggests magnified feelings. Since it also sextiled Uranus, he enjoyed any unusual relationship; the square to Saturn suggests he might refrain from expressing love for fear of rejection. The Sun, ruler of the intercepted sign in the 5th, was in sensual Taurus in the 1st house; sextile Mars, ripe and ready for love; trine Saturn, disciplined in how he will express it; square Uranus, impetuous and stubborn in his pursuits.

A short five months after they met, Robert Schumann, long suffering from nervous troubles, tried to commit suicide by throwing himself into the river Rhine. Within days he was taken to an asylum and Clara, pregnant with her seventh child, was left to care for the family. Brahms immediately went to Dusseldorf and virtually sacrificed the next two years of his life to be near her and help wherever he could. Robert Schumann died two years later. Yet no one really knows what happened between Johannes and Clara after her husband's death. By Brahms' own testimony, "He loved her more than anyone or anything on earth" and correspondence first addressed to "Dear Frau Schumann" soon became "Most Adored Being." Yet when Clara was free, a new reserve seems to have colored his letters to her. Perhaps it was easier to idealize his feelings (Moon in the 9th) than to accept the domestic realization of seven children.

Speculation centered around the theme that in order to earn money, at an early age Brahms played piano in taverns where much of his audience consisted of prostitutes and their clients; hard to take for a young romantic. Others supposed that he suffered from an Oedipus complex, having an unnaturally strong attachment to his mother who supposedly lavished her affections on him and feeling a sense of rivalry toward his father (Moon square Saturn).

What we do know is that Clara and Johannes stayed friends for the rest of their lives (she died one year before he did). He gave her his passionate admiration, she recognized his genius and had the musical understanding to encourage and advise him. In fact, Brahms rarely published anything without Clara's approval.

What about the second important 5th house matter—the relationships with your children? The sign on the cusp, the position and aspects of the ruler, as well as planets in the 5th will explain your attitude toward your offspring, your potential behavior patterns toward them and your expectations of them. Just as the 7th house describes your first committed partnership, the 9th your second, so the 5th house depicts your first child, the 7th your second, the 9th your third and so on, but your feelings about your children are always seen in the 5th house. In judging your attitude to each succeeding child, remember to skip the house that represents a child that for some reason was lost (death, miscarriage, abortion).

Though the sign on the cusp and its ruler are usually the strongest indicators of how a house may perform, planets in the house give added meaning and shading. In reading the following, please remember our usual warning: We just cite possibilities. Any serious interpretation needs the consideration of the entire horoscope and the questioning of the individual whose chart is being delineated.

Saturn in **the 5th house** seems to generate many misconceptions, so we'll consider this planet first. Its placement here does not mean that you cannot conceive children. We have literally hundreds of charts of male and female clients, students and relatives who have this Saturn placement and have one or more children of their own. To mention a few famous people with this placement who are blessed with offspring: Shirley MacLaine (1), Debbie Reynolds (2), Tatum O'Neal McEnroe (2), Sir Winston Churchill (4), Billy Graham (5), Phyllis Schlafly and Happy Rockefeller (6 each). Saturn here, depending on its aspects and the position and aspects of the cusp ruler, can suggest difficulties in having children or in relating to them; it can also mean the loss of a child— such as President Kennedy who had two healthy children but lost the third. A bit too strict, or too protective, or too demanding of them, you may take the parenting role more seriously than necessary. In other words, you are very responsible when it comes to raising your progeny. It can also indicate literally working with your children, a family business or a shared profession.

If you have **Neptune in the 5th**, you may adopt a child, give one up for adoption, or idealize your offspring. With **Pluto** there your desire to have children can be intense, yet if Pluto has difficult aspects, you may have to overcome many hurdles to have them and then, as with any rare possession, dote on them excessively. With **Jupiter** in this house, you are liable to go overboard, either in having a large family, maybe more than you can afford, or in indulging them; but regardless of aspects, you are a generous parent.

**Uranus** in the 5th house can, of course, signify exceptional children, but more often than not it means that you are not really as fond of them as babies as you are when they are old enough to have minds of their own, so you can communicate with them and eventually become their friend.

When **Mercury** occupies or rules the 5th house, you feel the need to have some cerebral contact with your children. The verbalization of thoughts, both yours and theirs, becomes most significant; you probably also pay great attention to their education. **Venus** here augurs a warm relationship from parent to child, and even the hardest aspects will not make you a tough or uncaring person. Should the **Moon** fall in your 5th house, your maternal/paternal instincts are innately awakened and you yearn for children. Your relationship with them will depend on other factors in the chart including aspects to the ruler of the cusp as well as the Moon. The Moon, like the tides, has its ups and downs; thus your emotional temperament cannot be generalized.

Where the **Sun** resides in the chart is where you want to shine. If it is in your 5th house, you may want to show off your artistic talents or creative efforts. But often the horoscope indicates that you do not like to draw attention to yourself and may prefer to do your shining through another. With a 5th house Sun you can do this through your children, possibly as the proverbial stage mother (or father) where the heat of your Sun's rays will conquer many obstacles. With **Mars** in this house, energy, drive and enthusiasm are the keywords. As a result you want to be active with your youngsters, teaching them all kinds of sports, taking them skiing, to the beach or acting as Little League coach or Brownie leader. If physical activities are not your bailiwick, your participation may consist of encouragement and chauffeuring. With a very stressed Mars, your children may not get along very well together or you may be quite impatient with them.

Mia Farrow, mother of nine children, three with conductor/composer Andre Previn, one with producer/director Woody Allen, and five adopted, has Leo on the cusp; the ruler Sun is in Aquarius in the 10th (she enjoys acting in out-of-the-ordinary ways). Expansive Jupiter is in her 5th also. Martin Sheen's Aries 5th house is ruled by Mars in Leo in the 8th involved in a Grand Trine; Venus is in the 5th in another Grand Trine. No doubt that he ardently loves his children and that he gets along with them beautifully.

Brahms never married, yet according to biographers he had always wished for children in whom he hoped to see his own gifts developed (the Sun, ruling the 5th house interception is in Taurus in the 1st). Since this was denied him, he bestowed his affections on the children of others. With Cancer on the cusp of his 5th he enjoyed nurturing the young ones and with the ruler, Moon in Sagittarius in the 9th house, he must have delighted in teaching them and imbuing them with lofty concepts and visions. He apparently always had some sweets in his pockets to give to his "little friends." His beloved Clara, on the other hand, had seven children. When she resumed touring in order to support the family, Johannes supervised the children's schooling and music lessons and assisted the housekeeper with the care of the younger ones.

What about Clara's relationship to her brood? With Scorpio on her 5th house, she not only was intense in her approach to love, but also in her feelings toward her children. The ruler Pluto is in Pisces in the 10th, conjunct Saturn. We know that her creativity and artistic talents led to her career as a successful pianist (ruler of the 5th in the 10th); we can also surmise that she was a powerful (Pluto) influence on her children and diligently (Saturn) worked to see them succeed (10th). Co-ruler Mars is in Cancer in the 12th house, repeating the Pisces motif of Pluto and Saturn in that sign, which often manifests as musical talent; Cancer adds motherly caring and sensitivity toward her offspring. Her Moon is in Cancer in the 1st house, widely trine Pluto the 5th house ruler which helps to explain her fecundity. Because of her sensitivity she also gently explained, or maybe defended, her relationship to Brahms: "Like a true friend, he came to share all my grief," Clara wrote to her children after the death of her husband, "He strengthened the

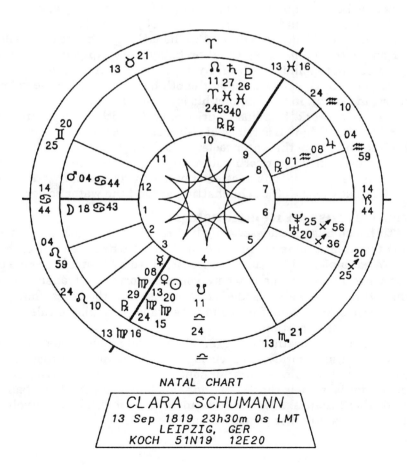

NATAL CHART

CLARA SCHUMANN
13 Sep 1819 23h30m 0s LMT
LEIPZIG, GER
KOCH   51N19   12E20

heart that threatened to break, he uplifted my spirit, brightened my soul any way he could. He was, in short, my friend in the fullest sense of the word."

## The 6th House in Relationships

Much like the 2nd house, the 6th has no profound significance when defining relationships. It reflects such varied areas as your health, including diet and hygiene; service you provide for others, either voluntary or paid; your habits and routine matters; your pets such as dogs and cats; your work and co-workers, your employees, as well as any servants you may have, and if you are a landlord, your tenants.

For our purpose of defining relationship needs, it may be of some consequence in how you get along with those working with or for you. It can even affect your spouse if you have Mars in your 6th house with tension aspects, and you keep yelling at the cleaning lady.

By the same token it is important to recognize your strengths and weaknesses before taking certain actions. If you have a peace-loving Libra Sun in the 6th and you want to be loved by one and all, or if Pisces is on the cusp and Neptune is in the 12th house, don't offer to collect the rent from your tenants; they could probably soft-soap you and you'll come home empty handed, or worse yet, you may loan them money.

A client with chatty Gemini on the 6th house cusp with the ruler, Mercury, in Gemini in the 7th, met his lady love around the proverbial water cooler at work. She has Capricorn on her 6th, with Saturn in Aquarius in her 7th; it also trines his Mercury. She knew immediately how to keep him from the water cooler...she brought him coffee into his office (down-to-earth Capricorn knows how to give service). They married and have children; she does computer and secretarial work from home; he's back in the office chitchatting around the water cooler.

## The 8th House in Relationships

The 8th house has an undeservedly bad reputation. Death and taxes are the two areas that immediately come to mind when speaking of this house. What a pity! This Scorpionic house, ruled by Pluto, has some of the Phoenix qualities; this is where you transform and transmute by letting certain characteristics "die" and then rise from the ashes, changed and ready to start again. Taxes and inheritance also play a role here, but not the most important one.

The 8th is your partner's (7th) 2nd house and as such can show the financial, spiritual, moral and psychological support you can expect from others. You will find few successful politicians who do not have strong 8th house focus in their charts. By the same token stockbrokers, bankers and other financial advisers seem to have much 8th house involvement—they deal in other people's money.

But for our purpose of relating, the most significant as well as the most fun facet of this house is sex. Ninety-five percent of all relationships start with that delightful chemical attraction that sizzles between two people. Call it flirtation, coming on, infatuation, falling for someone or by any other name you choose, it boils down to sexual attraction between two bodies, and nobody, except, of course, astrologers, knows why or when. Very few marriages or committed liaisons would take place if sex did not play a major role.

What you see advertised as "sexy" is not always necessarily so. Jim Morrison* of the musical group, the "Doors" was considered a sex symbol. He had Virgo on the cusp of the 8th and the ruler, Mercury, in Capricorn in the 11th house, not exactly sexually-oriented signs; but Neptune in Libra was in the 8th. Jim took the Neptunian escape route of drugs and alcohol, but he pulled off the illusion (Neptune) of a sexual being.

On the other hand Warren Beatty*, another male sex symbol, has ardent Aries on the 8th house cusp; Mars, ruler of Aries, is in freedom-loving Sagittarius in the 3rd, and both Venus and Uranus in Taurus are in the 8th. He obviously is sensual (Venus in Taurus) as well as sexually experimental (Uranus in the 8th).

Martyred president John F. Kennedy, (See his chart on page 17.) known for his sexual exploits, had Taurus on the 8th cusp and Venus, the planet of love in Gemini there conjunct the Sun. As if that weren't enough, Mercury and overdoer Jupiter, both in Taurus, are also in this house.

Former glamor and sex symbol Marlene Dietrich*, the lady with the gorgeous legs and husky voice, has Aries on the 8th and ruler Mars in Capricorn in the 5th conjunct Jupiter. Self-protective and supposedly inhibited Capricorn is not known as the most sexual or sensual sign, but when at ease, especially in the 5th house, it can become as lusty as the goat which it symbolizes.

Every sign of the zodiac has sexual properties and needs— otherwise the world would not be propagated with so many people.

**Scorpio** usually takes first prize for being the most sexual of all the signs. Actually that's an exaggeration. What they do have is extreme intensity and an animal magnetism that makes them come across as very sexy.

Our vote for sensuality goes to the two Venus-ruled signs, **Taurus** with its tactile enjoyments, and **Libra**, who's in love with love. These two signs truly enjoy sex, delight in being loved as well as being good lovers. **Aries**, with the fires of Mars burning from within, are eager and impetuous lovers, while sensitive and sometimes clinging **Cancer** enjoys switching roles by being nurturing parent or pampered, needy child.

* See chart data in Appendix.

Leo, the "star" of the zodiac, likes to be applauded for sexual expertise, and well should be, because romantic fervor, keynote of Leo's sexual behavior, is fun for all involved.

Pisces is also romantic and a utopian dreamer who wants to save humanity and will lay down her/his life, or body, to do so.

Sagittarius, though fiery by nature, is very interested in being free and usually dislikes any form of commitment, therefore the chase is as much, or more fun, than the conquest and sex itself is at its best when taken lightly. We've already talked about maligned Capricorn, so vulnerable and anxious to protect themselves, thus appearing uninterested and rigid until they are sure that their love is returned, then watch out.

Aquarius finds it easier to love humankind than to relate on a one-to-one basis and takes pride in seeing the large picture rather than focusing on an intimate level, preferring sex for the sake of sex, not love and this can lead to great experimental fun. Gemini is often consid-

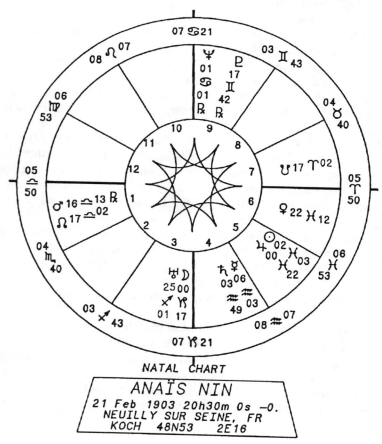

NATAL CHART

ANAÏS NIN
21 Feb 1903 20h30m 0s –0.
NEUILLY SUR SEINE, FR
KOCH   48N53    2E16

ered asexual or, at best, a cool lover. Not true, much of the time s/he just sounds cool and collected because s/he talks such an intellectual game and most people consider sex an instinctual function that should be acted out rather than discussed; if you ignore the verbiage, Gemini can be as sexy as any other sign.

The other Mercury ruled sign, **Virgo**, is often thought of as " All work and no play  can make Jack a dull boy." That's a bum rap. S/he may not be the sexiest sign of the zodiac, but with her/his love of work, service and learning, s/he "serves" sexual partners well, and quickly learns what the other likes or dislikes and enjoys doing it.

The above tongue-in-cheek discourse applies to archetypes, not Sun signs and should be taken with a smile and a few grains of salt.

Anyone who has read Anaïs Nin's diaries knows that she was an extremely sensual person to whom sex was as crucial, or maybe more critical than eating or sleeping.

Taurus was on her 8th house and Venus in Pisces in the 6th was in a T-square with Uranus and Pluto. Venus also rules her love-enamored Libra Ascendant and Mars is in the 1st house. It trines Pluto, indicating that she probably enjoyed many love affairs. She wrote (3rd house) about unusual matters (Uranus), especially about her passionate (Pluto), amorous escapades (Venus /8th house). Pluto in the 9th could indicate publishing, and with the Sun trine her Midheaven, it was easy for her to be successful in Venusian work (Venus in the 6th). Though we are mainly addressing the 8th house here, don't forget the 5th, which in Nin's case contains both the Sun and Jupiter in romantic Pisces, adding a very feminine touch to her sexual nature.

Author Henry Miller was one of her famous lovers, and no slouch himself when it came to writing about sex. His 8th house is Scorpio, ruled by Pluto in Gemini conjunct Neptune, and involved in an interplanetary yod; it was co-ruled by Mars in Scorpio in the 7th flanked by Uranus on one side and the Moon on the other. Here, as with Anaïs Nin, the 8th house ruler also ruled the Ascendant. To both, sex and their persona became as one, all encompassing. Miller's Pluto squared Jupiter, implying probable overindulgence in sexual matters. His Mars trine Jupiter sends a similar message, though in a more benign fashion, whereas Mars' conjunction to Uranus points to a great deal of experimentation and feelings of lust rather than love in his sexual expression. Since Mars in the 7th rules his Ascendant as well as his 8th house, it is easy to understand why Miller married so many of his lovers—though not Nin, who was not free at the time; neither, for that matter, was Henry Miller.

## The 9th House in Relationships
There are no intimate or one-to-one relationships in this, the 9th house. If defines your higher mind, religion, law, philosophy, distant travel,

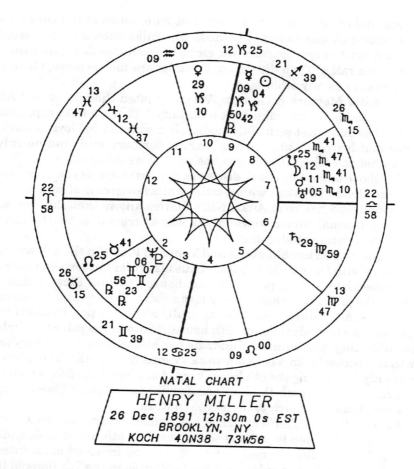

NATAL CHART

HENRY MILLER
26 Dec 1891  12h30m 0s EST
BROOKLYN,  NY
KOCH    40N38   73W56

foreigners, imports and exports, ethics, ideals, aspirations, vision, and on a more person-oriented basis, the clergy, teachers, and most important of all, that one special person who comes into your life when you are young—aunt, uncle, family friend, neighbor, teacher, minister, guru—and shows you a world you never knew before. That special someone who can make the difference and open your eyes to visions and ideals you might not accept from your parents. After all parents are there for you to love and obey, as well as to rebel against in order to prove that you are growing up, whereas the "special" one has no claim on you, so you listen, follow and agree on a voluntary basis.

A close friend has Virgo on the cusp of the 9th house. Mercury which rules it, is in Pisces conjunct a 3rd house Sun, sextile the Ascendant. She baby-sat for her neighbor (3rd house) who became her inspiration. Though the neighbor married young and had four children, she decided to go back to school to first finish her Master's degree, and then get her PhD, all the while raising her children.

They lived next door to each other for quite a few years; the girl watched her neighbor write the thesis and become a professor at the university. During this time she always found quality time for her children, exposed them to literature, art and music. Our friend followed in the neighbor's footsteps, married young, had children and is now finishing her PhD and she too always finds time for her children.

A client with Leo on the 9th house has the Sun in Aquarius in the 3rd, Virgo is intercepted in the 9th and Mercury is in Capricorn in the 2nd. Her beloved father was sickly and could not play with her or engage in some of the other activities fathers are supposed to do. A family friend who lived nearby had a fire in his apartment and during four months of repairs stayed with the client and her parents in their home.

He was different from anyone she had known before (Sun in Aquarius). A pianist, when he practiced Debussy's "Clair de Lune" she fell in love with classical music. He took her on walks through the forest and showed her where to find wild strawberries, told her why moss grows and how ants build a hill. He tossed her in the air and caught her. She was four, he was 34. He changed her values (Mercury in the 2nd), he showed her a new world (9th house) and she fell in love with it, and of course, with him!

## The 11th House in Relationships

Long known as the house of friendships, the 11th also encompasses any groups, organizations and clubs you may belong to and illustrates just how you will function in them. We find that if you have the Ascendant ruler there, you are much more likely to be a joiner than if your Sun is in the 11th. Very often the Sun here tends to be somewhat of a loner; of course much depends on aspects and other variants in the horoscope. On the other hand, many military people have active 11th houses.

But for this book, our main focus is the interaction between friends. The *Bible* states:

> *"Greater love hath no man than this, that a man lay down his*
> *life for a friend."* —John 15:13

and

> *"Forsake not an old friend; for the new is not comparable to him;*
> *a new friend is as new wine."* —Ecclesiastes 8:10.

Shakespeare has this to say about friends:

> *"Those friends thou hast, and their adoption tried, Grapple them*
> *to thy soul with hoops of steel."* —Hamlet, I, iii

It is often said that you have no choice in the selection of your family, but you choose your friends and are thus more tolerant of them. Goethe calls them *"Wahlverwandschaft"* or chosen relatives. Other things in the horoscope are indicative of friendship, but the 11th house shows your needs in this area. Look at the sign on the cusp to see what characteristics are important to you in attracting friends; if Aries, it may be that you are drawn to take-charge people, while Pisces there looks for empathy and understanding. It is not our intention to provide a compendium of astrological friendship traits, but we do want to point out how to assess this area of the chart.

As always, the ruler of the house, in this case, the 11th, will give information through its sign and house placement; so will any planets in this house, as well as aspects to them. With **Saturn** in or ruling the 11th, you have a tendency to be very particular about the friends you choose, often having only one very close friend, but several people in your life that you think of as acquaintances. With **Uranus** involved in this house, you may have several sets of friends, each group having nothing to do with the others. You may be creative with one set while you play with (sports or games) the other.

**Mercury** involved in the 11th finds you seeking articulate and communicative companions, or wishing to become involved in group activity, like the PTA or making friends with people you meet at the local gym or health club. **Venus** here suggests you look to have fun with your friends and possibly enjoy partying with them. If you have the **Moon** in or ruling this house, you tend to nurture those you cherish as companions, and if the Moon is in the 4th house, you may even choose to have them live with you.

With **Neptune** here, your friends may come and go, fade into and out of your life, but you always have myriads of acquaintances with whom you become entranced and with whom you spend much time. Another way Neptune can work here is that you are drawn to friends and acquaintances who share your interests in the arts, music and possibly involvement in religious groups. **Pluto** in the 11th is somewhat like Saturn in that you are quite discriminating in your choice of the people you like to spend time with. Occasionally you may have a tendency to become totally absorbed with one acquaintance, turning a deaf ear to others whom you have been friendly with in the past.

As remarked earlier, the **Sun** in the 11th can be quite outgoing and gregarious, but much depends on aspects. You may find that one or two close relationships are more than enough for you; but many 11th house Sun (in or ruling) people are the ones who define the word friendship, rarely meeting anyone that they don't take under their wing socially. **Jupiter** can act much the same way. You are open to many degrees of friendship with people from all walks of life. Your intellectual curiosity is piqued by their experiences and you nurture the friendship in an effort to learn. **Mars** in or ruling this house can attract energetic, outgoing companions with whom you vie athletically, socially or competitively on some level.

Since we (the authors) have been friends for many years, we felt that we could do no better than to use our charts as an example of what friendship is all about. We will look at it, not only from 11th house needs, but will also preview Part Two and chart comparison.

We are both Aquarians; Joan's Sun is in the 1st house, Marion's in the 3rd. Our Mercuries are conjunct and Joan's Venus conjoins them which is part of a Fixed T-Square in her horoscope. Marion's Fixed T-Square (Sun opposed Neptune square Jupiter) blends with Joan's (Sun opposed Neptune square Saturn). Joan's Mars trines Marion's Venus; her Jupiter sextiles Marion's Uranus. Marion's Jupiter conjuncts Joan's Saturn and activates her Grand Water Trine (Uranus, Pluto, Saturn), while both Suns trine Marion's Saturn.

The above are aspects formed between the two charts and they indicate a lot of accord as well as stimulation. But let's take a look at what each one looks for in terms of friendship. Joan has Jupiter ruling the 11th house. There are no planets in it, but it is linked to the 10th since Jupiter also rules that cusp. Jupiter is in Capricorn just into the 12th. We feel it should be read into the 11th also. This suggests that she is drawn to intellectual, philosophical businesslike friends, who can keep a confidence (Jupiter in 12th) and are serious, organized and trustworthy (Jupiter in Capricorn, sextile Saturn). She makes friends among her professional peers (10th and 11th linked), and is generous and outgoing toward them (Sagittarius on the cusp).

Marion has Scorpio on the cusp of the 11th with Pluto in Cancer in the 8th house and Mars in Aries in the 4th. Jupiter in Scorpio in the 11th rules her Ascendant. She is drawn to people with definite opinions, who view events and action in a similar way to hers; whose background is active (Mars in the 4th) and people to whom she can be supportive (Pluto in the 8th). She nurtures her friends (Pluto in Cancer), initiates their action (Mars in Aries), and is intensely interested in their goals and behavior (Scorpio on the 11th cusp). Since her Ascendant ruler is in this house, she really enjoys people and working with them in groups as well as individually. She values her friends for their intellect, philosophical views and openness to learning (Jupiter in the 11th).

The many similarities in our charts is what first drew us together, but it is the respect and love we have for each other which has contributed to the relationship's endurance. We met in 1968 in an astrology class, liked and admired each other, found that we could work together and have proceeded from there. Every friendship does not always evolve into a working relationship, but in our case, the Saturn factor and the

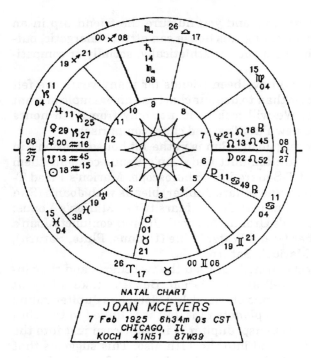

NATAL CHART
**JOAN MCEVERS**
7 Feb 1925   6h34m 0s CST
CHICAGO, IL
KOCH   41N51   87W39

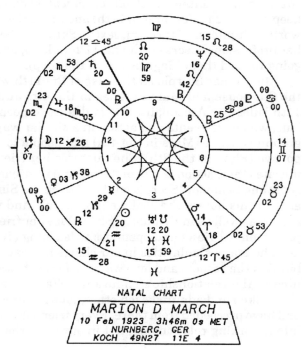

NATAL CHART
**MARION D MARCH**
10 Feb 1923   3h46m 0s MET
NURNBERG, GER
KOCH   49N27   11E 4

fact that our Midheaven rulers Venus and Jupiter are widely conjunct contribute. Some other apparent affinities include our Moon positions. Marion's is closely conjunct her Ascendant; Joan's closely opposes her Ascendant. This indicates that we both are nurturers. Marion's Moon sextiles her MC; Joan's trines her Midheaven. We approach our collaboration with emotion and commitment.

As Ralph Waldo Emerson said so eloquently: "A friend is a person with whom I may be sincere. Before him, I may think aloud." For us, that about sums it up.

## The 12th House in Relationships

The 12th, like the 2nd house does not represent any direct relationships, but it should not be ignored in judging a comparison of two charts. Just as the 2nd house shows values and issues of self-worth, the 12th is where you deal with hidden fears, development of your inner strengths and how you handle your limitations. What, you ask, does this have to do with interacting with others? From the sign on the cusp of this house, its ruler and any planets in it, you can find out a lot about your subconscious yearnings, as well as how you handle difficult and demanding situations you may have to face.

When you assess this house in connection with relationships, it is important to know how each person will relate to the other when dealing with feelings of inadequacy, how open either of you will be with issues of faith, loyalty and trust. Once you perceive where another person is coming from subconsciously, you have come a long way in understanding what to expect from her/him in moments of stress and tension. Also, when you can deduce what strengths are necessary for your partner to develop, you can help broaden her/his perspective in these areas.

With Leo on the 12th (or the Sun there), you may feel somewhat inadequate in expressing your ego. If your partner is aware of that from your horoscope, (it is unlikely you would be able to put it into words), s/he may be able to discover a way (through aspects from your Sun to her/his chart) to help you develop more self-confidence and good feelings about yourself.

If you are drawn to someone with Mercury in or ruling the 12th, you may find that you can encourage that person to share her/his knowledge with you, become a sounding board, thus helping her/him discover talents for speaking or writing that s/he didn't know were there. You can help each other, if you or your partner are aware that: with Moon in the 12th, feelings are much stronger and hurts go much deeper than you let on; with Venus in this house, the way you display your affectionate nature may be difficult except in intimate situations; with Mars here, your energies may be bottled up; with Jupiter, depending upon the Sun or Ascendant, you may feel embarrassed about revealing your religious and philosophical beliefs; with Saturn, you could experience problems in facing your fears and your partner could help you face anxieties or deal with repression.

With you partner's awareness and understanding, it will be easier to acknowledge your channel for individualistic expressions, with Uranus in the 12th. Your innate instincts and intuition can be productively directed with Neptune. Wherever Pluto is in the horoscope, power issues are paramount. If it is in the 12th, you may be drawn to a partner who can help you sort out your inner feelings about the way you wield or succumb to power.

Very often, if you have strong ties to another person's 12th house, you can be instrumental in helping her/him come to grips with her/his subconscious or unwillingness to deal with hidden feelings.

As you can see, all the houses are significant when you are comparing and analyzing charts of lovers, mates, friends, parents and children.

# DERIVATIVE HOUSES

There is another facet of interpreting houses that is illuminating in relationship analysis. It is the Derivative House System. In Volume I of *The Only Way to...Learn Astrology* on page 38, we briefly refer to this as "Houses Within Houses." As we explained at the time: Just as the 5th house shows your children, the 9th house (the 5th from the 5th) shows your children's children, i.e. your grandchildren. When counting houses in this manner, be sure to start with the house in question. For example, in the above explanation, the 5th house becomes house 1 as you begin your count, the 6th is house 2, the 7th house 3, the 8th is house 4 and the 9 becomes house 5. The 9th is five houses from the 5th.

In using this technique, each house has reference to various relationships. To cite another example: Your paternal grandmother (your father's mother) is represented by the 1st house. Father is the 10th, his mother would be four houses from the 10th. If the 10th is house 1, the 11th is house 2, the 12th is 3 and the Ascendant becomes the 4th house from the 10th and can describe one of your grandmothers. Your paternal grandfather is found in the 7th house, the 10th from the 10th.

Following is a list of the houses and the primary and secondary relationships they represent.

The 1st house represents:
  Your father's mother (4th from the 10th)
  Your mother's father (10th from the 4th)
  Your niece or nephew by marriage (7th from 7th)
  Your great grandchildren (5th from 9th)

The 2nd house represents:
  Your mother's friends (11th from 4th)
  Your children's boss (10th from 5th)
  Your friend's parents (4th from 11th)

The 3rd house represents:
 Your brothers and sisters
 Your children's friends (11th from 5th)
The 4th house represents:
 Your mother
 Cousins paternally related (5th from 12th of paternal aunts
  and uncles)
 In-law parent of opposite sex (10th from 7th)
 Stepmother
The 5th house represents:
 Children
 Second sibling (3rd from 3rd)
 Friend's spouse (7th from 11th)
The 6th house represents:
 Maternal aunts and uncles (3rd from 4th)
 Your employees
The 7th house represents:
 Your partner
 Third sibling (3rd from 5th)
 Nieces and nephews (5th from 3rd)
 Your mother's mother (4th from 4th)
 Your father's father (10th from 10th)
The 8th house represents:
 Employees of your siblings (6th from 3rd)
The 9th house represents:
 Your grandchildren (5th from 5th)
 Your in-law brothers and sisters (3rd from 7th)
 Your fourth sibling (3rd from 7th)
 Friends of your friends (11th from 11th)
The 10th house represents:
 Your father
 Your boss
 Cousins maternally related (5th from 6th of maternal aunts
  and uncles)
 In-law parent of same sex (4th from 7th)
 Stepfather
The 11th house represents:
 Friends
 Adopted children (5th from 7th)
 Foster children (5th from 7th)
 In-law children (7th from 5th)
 Your godchild
 Illegitimate children
The 12th house represents:
 Paternal aunts and uncles (3rd from 10th)

By counting around the houses, you can determine where any relationship can develop. Using this method can become very convoluted. We advise keeping it as simple as possible.

Sometimes astrologic works as well as real logic. There is no logical reason for skipping a house to describe the second child (7th house), the third child (9th house), the fourth child (11th house) and so on, but it works.

The same principle applies to marriage where the 9th house seems to outline the characteristics of the second partner, while the 11th portrays the third one and so on. Remember, however, that your attitude toward marriage is always described by your 7th house. The ensuing descriptions just provide more in-depth characterizations of each new partner.

# PART TWO: CHART COMPARISON
## INTRODUCTION

The art of comparing two charts, also called **synastry**, is probably the most frequent request astrologers receive. The comparison can, of course, be for future business partners, between parent and child, siblings, or—the most common questions: "Is Johnny the right man for me? Will Jane make me happy? Should we get married?" Most people, before they take the "big step" want to know if what they feel is a passing infatuation or the real thing.

Since intimate, one-to-one relationships are of most interest, we shall in this segment of the book mainly concentrate on them, but we will also talk about family and business affiliations.

The only way to assess charts for the purpose of comparison, is to **thoroughly** understand the natal horoscope first, which is, of course, the main reason we wrote Part One.

Only after understanding what each individual seeks and needs natally, can the interrelation of one chart to the other be appraised.

There are many factors to consider when correlating two charts, but first you must decide on an item that astrologers rarely agree on...namely **orbs**. We feel that five degrees (maybe six for the luminaries) is the the most that should be allowed when comparing two horoscopes. The tighter the orb, the stronger the contact. Please try it our way first, but if after a few months, this does not work for you, tighten or increase your orbs according to your experience. Astrology is a symbolic language and eventually each astrologer has to develop her/his own system which includes how large or small the orbs should be.

Following are some of the things we deem crucial in deciding how easy or difficult certain relationships may be, but again realize that even the easiest union between two people can end in disaster if the individuals do not communicate with each other or somehow endeavor to make the partnership last. By the same token, even the toughest obstacles can be overcome if both parties are willing to make adjustments and love each other enough to make allowances for their differences, as well as relish their similarities.

Examine what both people want from the relationship; in other words, what are their **7th house needs?**

Put the planets of one chart around the planets in the other and observe the **house positions** of the planets; realize what each person is bringing to the other; at the same time notice if one's planet(s) fill the other person's **empty house**(s). Note all aspects when merging two charts and search for new **configurations.**

See what each horoscope is missing—element, quality, kind of aspect—and check to see if the other chart can fill that **lack.**

Explore all **Saturn contacts,** since they have proven to be the most binding.

Probe for further **affinities,** such as one person's Taurus Sun feeling similar to, or fully understanding another's 2nd house Sun or Moon. Connections between the Ascendant of one to the Sun or Moon of the other, or between Sun/Ascendant rulers or 7th house rulers should be considered. So should the classic male/female draw of Moon or Venus to the Sun.

Explore the **sexual attractions** even though they may not always be lasting between Venus/Mars, Venus/Venus, Mars/Mars as well as the Sun, Moon, Venus or Mars to Uranus.

Inspect what connections other planets, such as Mercury (communication), Jupiter (ideals/religion), Neptune (charisma/fascination) or Pluto (intense/compulsive) have.

Compare **chart patterns.** Note harmony between **like elements,** regardless of aspect by orb. Keep in mind that **nodal contacts** can be very meaningful. See if one's **Ascendant sign** is the same as the other's **Midheaven** or vice versa. This often indicates an accord and innate understanding each of the other.

Last but not least, check the links between the **progressed charts.**

We will interpret each of these step by step, but do keep in mind that this list is not given in order of importance, just in the order we are accustomed to using.

## LESSON 6
# THE 7TH HOUSE PROMISE

As we pointed out in Lesson 2, the 7th house describes what you need from a partner. The sign on the cusp provides the first clue, the planet ruling that sign is very significant in terms of where you may seek your partner. For example, if that planet is in the 6th house, the work arena may be the place; if it is in the 9th, you could meet your intended on a trip; if the 7th house ruler is in the 11th, perhaps you both belong to the same athletic club. Since we explained your partnership wants and needs in Lessons 1 and 2, in this lesson we will teach additional refinements to describe the actual person. The physical appearance is next to impossible to outline, but characteristics and traits can be quite obvious according to sign, ruler, and planets in the 7th house.

With the **Sun** in or ruling the house of partnership, you will seek someone who is outgoing, friendly, a leader, who may be dramatic, possibly even egotistic. All of this depends, of course, on aspect and sign. If your Sun is in Pisces in the 7th, you obviously would not seek a partner who is as powerful as if your Sun was in Sagittarius or Aries. But you attract people who have definite ideas, a need to shine and sometimes to be competitive. With the Sun here, be careful not to pick a partner who eclipses you.

Prince Andrew of England (See chart on page 66) has the Sun in Pisces in the 7th house and Aquarius is on the cusp, ruled by Uranus in Leo in his 1st. He is looking for a unique individual, but one who will not steal his thunder; he has Leo rising. His wife, is lively, fun, entertaining; all Aquarian/Leo traits, but she is also compassionate, friendly and empathetic (the Pisces quality). Her Sun is in Libra right on the cusp of her 12th (Pisces) house and Mars, Neptune and Mercury are all in her12th. Her Moon is in assertive Aries in the Leo 5th house.

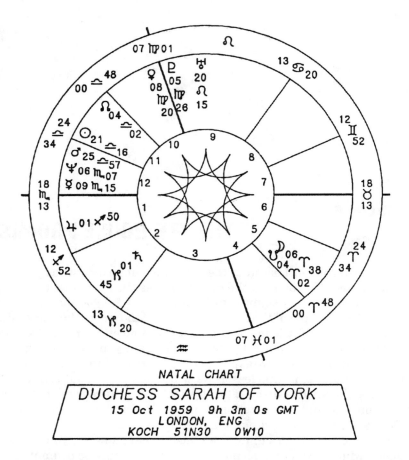

NATAL CHART

DUCHESS SARAH OF YORK
15 Oct 1959    9h 3m 0s GMT
LONDON, ENG
KOCH    51N30    0W10

If **Cancer** is on the cusp of the 7th, or if the **Moon** is in that house, you are looking for a nurturing, caring partner, one who is reminiscent of your favorite parent. If the Moon is in Gemini, communication will be significant in your relationship; if it is in Scorpio, intensity may well be the keynote. You definitely relate to people who are responsive, home and family oriented, sensitive and feeling. Of course, the sign the Moon is in will give added information. So will its house position.

Jane Fonda has the Moon ruling the 7th in the 7th in Leo. She attracts flamboyant, outgoing, limelight-loving partners; but they must have some home and family orientation as well as the ability to nurture. Since Pluto is also in that house, she desires intensity and drive in her partners and a struggle as to who is in control may arise. Her first husband was French film director Roger Vadim, (see chart on page 18.) who played a somewhat paternalistic role in their relationship. It was he who groomed her as an actress and controlled her career. Her second husband, Tom Hayden, one of the original "Chicago 7" is a California politician with a Sagittarian Sun and Moon. He is outgoing, dynamic and definitely seeks the limelight. Since her divorce from Hayden, Fonda married entrepreneur Ted Turner. (See chart on page 23.) Turner is a Scorpio, the intense, driving sort of partner her Pluto seeks. His Sagittarian Ascendant has the fire her Leo Moon as well as her Sun in Sagittarius responds to. Perhaps this is the match made in heaven.

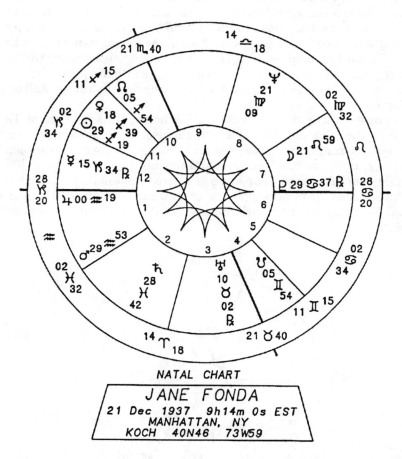

NATAL CHART

*JANE FONDA*
21 Dec 1937   9h14m 0s EST
MANHATTAN, NY
KOCH  40N46  73W59

With either **Gemini** or **Virgo** on the cusp of the 7th, or with **Mercury** in that house, you attract partners with whom you can converse, who share your views of life, and who enjoy the same type of fun and games that you do. Above all, Mercury needs a sounding board, a person who will listen and exchange ideas. Not for Virgo, Gemini or Mercury, a partner who is the strong, silent type; one who is not social, who withdraws and will not discuss problems or plans. No, indeed! You want someone you can confide in, one you can share ideas with, one who will listen while you rattle on. If it is Virgo you are dealing with, you may have to endure a bit of analysis or critique, but that is alright with you, as long as you have a sounding board.

A friend has Virgo on the 7th with Mercury there in Virgo, so she obviously attracts others who are verbal and communicative. Her husband also has Virgo on the cusp of the partnership house, however his Mercury is in Pisces conjunct his Ascendant. She is a homemaker and mother; he is a successful business man in a field where he deals with many employees. Both have Saturn in the 11th, so their friendship circle is small. She cannot wait until he arrives home from work to hear all about the daily happenings. They discuss everything about the business together and she gives him great insights into the people he has to deal with, while he enlivens her life by asking for her advice, and often taking it.

**Venus** is the natural ruler of the 7th house, thus if **Libra** or **Taurus** is on the cusp, or if Venus is in the house, you may expect all to go well with partnerships. As you realize by now, nothing is guaranteed in astrology. If Venus has favorable and flowing aspects, perhaps living happily ever after with your mate is a strong possibility. But what if Venus squares, conjuncts, opposes or quincunxes Saturn, Uranus or Pluto? You may have to work quite diligently to achieve a successful affiliation.

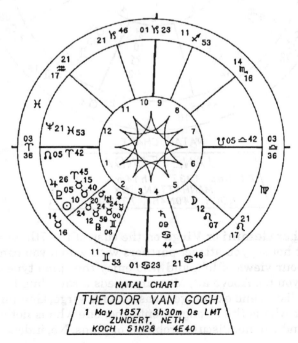

NATAL CHART

THEODOR VAN GOGH
1 May 1857   3h30m 0s LMT
ZUNDERT, NETH
KOCH   51N28     4E40

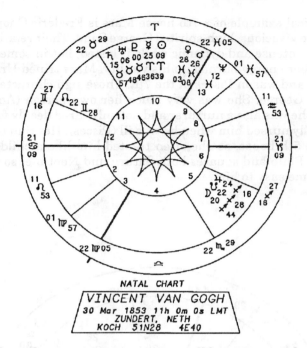

NATAL CHART
VINCENT VAN GOGH
30 Mar 1853 11h 0m 0s LMT
ZUNDERT, NETH
KOCH 51N28 4E40

With Venus here, your partner may well be quite social, charming, loving, cooperative and diplomatic (Libra) or artistic, sensual, affectionate, thorough and loyal (Taurus). To share the same value system with your mate becomes significant. With Libra here, discussion may be fun; perhaps you pursue artistic endeavors together. Taurus, on the other hand, suggests stability and strong sex drive; musical and financial matters may be predominant in the relationship. Whichever it is, you definitely have an ability to attract others to you.

Theodor van Gogh had Libra on this cusp with Venus in Taurus in his 2nd house. He and his brother Vincent had a working relationship, in which Theo supported Vincent while he painted.

An art dealer, he attracted artistic (Libra) people to him; he made a good income selling other's art works (Venus in Taurus in the 2nd). However, neither he nor Vincent lived long enough to profit from Vincent's prodigious talent.

As you can imagine with **Mars** in the 7th, or **Aries** on the cusp, you tend to attract others who are energetic, pioneering, inventive, sports oriented, dynamic and impulsive. How you handle all this energy, of course, depends on the sign and aspects of Mars. If you are somewhat passive, you may find it too challenging, and forever keep looking for Mr. or Miss Right. If you are relatively dynamic yourself, though there may be strife and arguments between you and your partner, the kiss-and-make-up part is worth all the hassle.

A typical example of a 7th house Mars is Frederic Chopin who attracted the vivacious, high-spirited George Sand. Their relationship was extremely intense and dynamic while it lasted, but in some respects it was as if her energy burned up his vitality. Mars trined Uranus, ruler of his 7th and was in Pisces in the 7th. Those sign characteristics well described George. She was very much her own person (Aquarius rising), but she was also a nurturer and not only cared deeply for Frederic, she literally nursed him when he was ill (Pisces). Her Sun was in Cancer in the 5th house, so she often treated him like a child. His Mars conjuncts Pluto and squares both Saturn and Neptune, so partnering did not come easy to him.

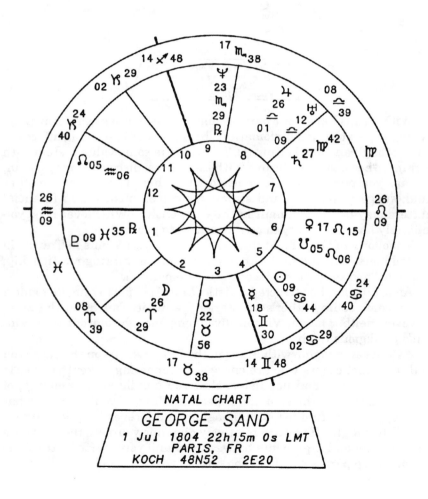

NATAL CHART

GEORGE SAND
1 Jul 1804 22h15m 0s LMT
PARIS, FR
KOCH    48N52    2E20

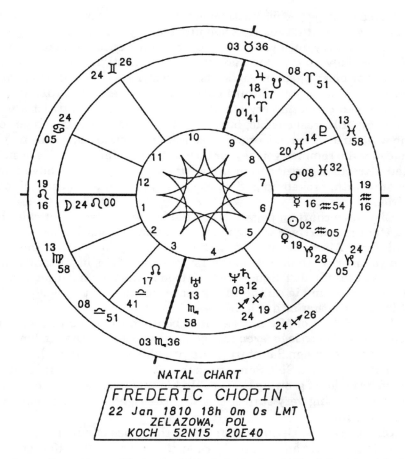

NATAL CHART

FREDERIC CHOPIN
22 Jan 1810 18h 0m 0s LMT
ZELAZOWA, POL
KOCH 52N15 20E40

Actor Burt Reynolds,* who long led the bachelor life, is typical of Sagittarius on the cusp of the 7th house. His Jupiter is also there. He had an early marriage to Judy Carne and then played the field for years before settling down, marrying Loni Anderson and adopting a child.

You 7th house **Sagittarians** value freedom and your behavior attracts footloose people to you. Commitment is just a word to you until the right person comes along. With **Jupiter** here you want your partner to grow with you. S/he must be an individualist, one who shares your philosophies, and possibly your religion, as well as an unbiased outlook on the world and its people. The aspects to Jupiter tell how easy or difficult it may be to finally find your ideal. Reynold's 7th house Jupiter T-Squares Mars and Neptune, so it is obvious that his motto for many years was, "Once burn't, twice wary."

The beautiful planet **Saturn** often gets a bum rap from astrologers, especially when it is in the partnership house. True, it can symbolize

* See chart data in Appendix.

delayed marriage; you may attract older (or younger) partners, you may feel that your partner restricts you in some way, but what's wrong with waiting to marry until you have a few romantic encounters under your belt? Certainly, in this day and age there is no stigma if you attract a younger or older partner. As far as the restriction goes, it depends on how you are using your Saturn energy. Saturn here, or **Capricorn** on the cusp can denote a very stabilizing factor. You can attract a mate who is capable, responsible, businesslike, a good money manager, one who will nurture you in a practical sense. In a female chart, this may be someone who reminds you of your father. We also find that this position often attracts a partner from the past; someone you may have had a romance with, broken up and not seen for years; or an old school mate or friend.

Cher (See chart on page 12.) has Saturn in the 1st and it rules her 7th. Her first marriage was to much older Sonny Bono; her second husband, Greg Allman, was close to her age; every lover since then has been younger. With Saturn in the 1st, partnership is important to her, but it is in a difficult T-Square to the Moon in the 7th and Jupiter in the 4th. She is looking in all the wrong places for the nurturing she didn't get from her father as a child.

Prince Albert of Monaco* seems to be in no rush to take on the responsibility of marriage, even though he has Saturn in the 7th house. It is in the bachelor sign Sagittarius and rules his 8th, and though it trines Pluto, it squares his Sun. Sometimes the latter aspect suggests that the person has a lot of growing up to do. In his case, with a 10th house Sun it relates to being very sure of choosing the right partner to help him rule in the future.

Obviously with **Uranus** in or ruling the house of partners, you are drawn to impulsive and unusual people; those of a totally different background, race, creed, color or habit. With Aquarius here, you have Leo rising and unless there are a lot of earth and water placements in your chart, you can be pretty dynamic and bombastic yourself, so you are hardly intimidated by outgoing, gregarious people. If, on the other hand, you are laid back and mellow, the attraction of opposites may well come into play.

Marilyn Monroe (see chart on page 13) had this placement and she certainly had a varied assortment of husbands. Her first was a welder, her second a ball player and her third a playwright. With Uranus in Pisces in the 8th house, the attraction was obviously sex and money. Unless you count a very wide conjunction to Mars and trine to Saturn, her Uranus is unaspected. As we mentioned before, it is not always easy to integrate an unaspected planet into the horoscope and in Marilyn's case, choosing a partner was never her forte.

* See chart data in Appendix.

Often with Uranus in the 7th house, your partnerships are varied and eccentric, or your behavior in this area reflects rather odd concepts. Author Henry Miller (chart on page 76) married five times (never more than seven years to any wife) and had many sexual liaisons. His literary output reflects many of his "romantic" experiences and his graphic descriptions were long banned as obscenity. Uranus conjuncts the Moon and Mars and is caught up in a formidable yod. Perhaps this reflects his indecisiveness and capriciousness when it came to partnership. The Ascendant square Venus did not help.

With **Neptune** in the 7th or **Pisces** on the cusp, you tend to attract others who lean on you, whether consciously or unconsciously. You are generally more than kind hearted and always willing to listen to other people and their problems, thus people seek you out for your advice and sound counsel. Spouses love the partner with Neptune in the 7th, because s/he will idealize you, but you must take care not to be toppled from your pedestal. If Neptune has difficult aspects, or if you have not properly incorporated its themes into your life, you may attract a partner with drug or drinking problems, or one who needs your constant support. On another level, musical and religious folks seek you out, because you can relate well to them with your empathy and kindness. You are often a counselor on a professional level: psychologist, parole officer, astrologer, therapist, minister, priest.

A busy practicing psychotherapist who has Pisces on the 7th cusp is a client. Besides her professional practice she volunteers two evenings and one day a week to help out in a disabled children's clinic. She has never married; she claims she is married to her job, and many little children are grateful for her care and kindness.

Fred Astaire (chart on page 139) had Neptune in the 7th and his first dancing partner was his sister, Adele. He had Pisces intercepted in the 3rd house of siblings. Eva Braun (chart on page 106) had a 7th house Neptune and was probably the only person in the world who could personally adore a man like Adolf Hitler.

**Scorpio** on the 7th cusp or **Pluto** in this house can be quite challenging unless Pluto's aspects are agreeable. Many times you can attract someone who tries to take you over, or one who inveigles her/his way into your good graces, only to throw you over on a whim. Power issues arise wherever Pluto is in your chart; in the 7th, it can indicate a struggle for supremacy between you and the other person. Sometimes you can be the dominating factor in a relationship and drive away the person you really care for. The lesson to be learned with Pluto in the 7th is to temper your desire with patience and lovingkindness. This applies as well to Scorpio on the cusp and Pluto's and Mars' positions will help you to discover ways to handle this.

Dictator Benito Mussolini (chart on page 22) had Pluto in the 7th in Taurus; it ruled his Ascendant and had very benign aspects except for a square to the Midheaven. He was very demanding in his relationships, yet held his marriage sacrosanct in spite of a deeply committed affair with Claretta Petacci*.

She had Scorpio on the 7th cusp, with Pluto in her 2nd house weakly aspected. He dominated the relationship totally, but she was completely devoted to him which is often noted with Scorpio here. The attitude toward partnership is intense and abiding.

---

* See chart data in Appendix.

# LESSON 7

# OTHER INDICATORS OF WHAT YOU SEEK IN PARTNERSHIP

Because the Moon rules the feminine principle in a man's chart and the Sun represents the male in a woman's chart, another way to judge the kind of mate you look for is to check what needs your Sun (in a woman's chart) and your Moon (in a man's chart) project. We are not overlooking the fact that the Moon in any chart is where you look to nurture or be nurtured, or that the Sun is where you want to shine, be admired, loved or praised as well as many other lunar and solar attributes—but in this book we discuss your needs in relation to others. If your Sun is in the 9th house, as a woman, you most likely respond to a man who is intellectual, aspiring, possibly involved in the law in some way, one who is spiritual, religious or metaphysical. This would also apply to a Sun in Sagittarius. If a man has the Moon in Scorpio, or in the 8th house, sex drive would be a prime requirement in his partner. He would also be attracted to a woman with deeply felt emotions, one who is self-contained as well as intuitive.

Another concept to take into consideration is the first applying aspect your Sun (in a woman's chart) or Moon (in a man's chart) makes. The key word here is "applying." As an example: In Roberto Rossellini's (chart on page 122) chart his Moon's only applying aspect is an opposition to the Sun, which does not exactly indicate that marriage is a comfortable situation for him. It also describes a mate who is stable (Sun in Taurus), down to earth and someone who will love travel and philosophy (9th house).

George Sand's Sun applies to a square to Uranus (see her chart on page 94), suggesting that she might find relating in marriage quite challenging. Her partner should be considerably different in background and culture, perhaps enjoying different social activities or values than she did. This aspect, of course, may account for her divorce in an era when women could rarely avail themselves of that privilege. You may ask why we did not mention the Sun's trine to Pluto. It is ten minutes past the applying orb. The only way this ancient method works, is by using applying orbs only. We suggest it for additional information only.

If your Sun or Moon makes no applying aspects, it does not mean that you will never find a partner, just that you will have to rely on other factors to describe what you want from your future mate. This calls to mind a phone call from a student many years ago. An amateur astrologer had told her that she would never marry because she had no planets in the 7th house and she was very upset by this information, as she was engaged and planning a wedding. Obviously, with only ten planets and 12 houses, it would be impossible to have a planet in every house and by now, we are sure you realize that people get married with no planets in the 7th, have families with no planets in the 5th and travel when they have an empty 9th house. She married, divorced a few years later and happily married again.

## Second, Third and More Relationships

We have explained your 7th house wants and the type of partner you may attract by considering this house, its ruler and tenants in depth. But what if you are embarking on a second trip down the aisle or a second committed relationship. Do you always marry exactly the same type of person? Of course not; although occasionally that happens. To describe what you are looking for from a second partner, you must consider the sign on the cusp, the ruler of and planets in the 9th house. Your attitude toward partnership is still the same (7th), but now there are added factors. Whatever the reason your first marriage or committed relationship ended, you learned something about relating intimately to another person. So when you embark on a second union, your outlook as well as your expectations, may have altered because of how the first one worked out. Thus the 9th house gives additional information.

If you commit to a third serious affiliation, look to the 11th and each succeeding odd numbered house for each following relationship, if you are Henry Miller or Mickey Rooney. We have found that third marriages or commitments sometimes are the best because the couple start as friends (11th house).

Judy Garland had Capricorn on the 7th house; she was looking for security and the fathering that was so illusive in her childhood. Her father died when she was 13 and she was, in her words "devastated." Saturn is in the 4th house square the Moon, compounding the need for a father figure, someone she could depend upon, who would be responsible and responsive to her needs. Her first husband, David Rose was older and to a young, romantic girl that certainly seemed to fulfill her desire for an understanding partner. They had a very wide social (Saturn is in Libra) circle, entertained a lot in their home but had a difficult time establishing a solid, intimate base. He was attractive, creative and musical, almost her mirror image, but Saturn squares Mercury in her 12th house and she found it very hard to communicate her deep-seated feelings and desires.

Her next marriage was to charming, urbane, also much older Vincente Minelli who fathered her first daughter, Liza. To the needs and wants represented by the 7th house, we must also add those of the 9th (2nd partner). Uranus rules the 9th and is in Pisces in the 10th conjunct the Midheaven. She would attract someone unique, distinctive or different. Minelli filled the bill; he was cultured and introspective; he could help further her career (Uranus conjunct the MC). In fact they met while filming "Meet Me in St. Louis" which he directed and she starred in. Empathetic and nurturing (Uranus in Pisces), Minelli seemed

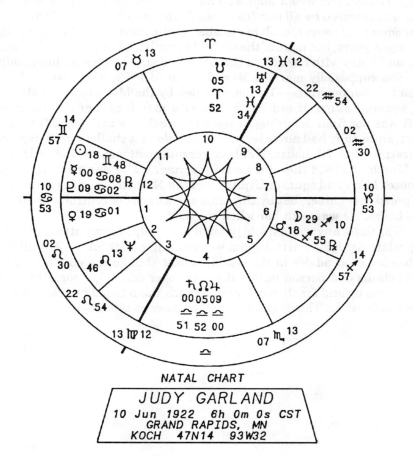

NATAL CHART

JUDY GARLAND
10 Jun 1922   6h 0m 0s CST
GRAND RAPIDS, MN
KOCH   47N14   93W32

to fulfill some of her *animus* desires. But Uranus has very troublesome aspects and Judy was still too young to have mastered the squares to the Sun and Mars and the quincunx to Neptune. She married him when she was 23; she had very little understanding of what was expected in a marriage and his sophisticated attitudes were anathema to her.

She married Sid Luft in 1952 when she was 30. With Saturn ruling the marriage house, it is easier to work in a partnership if you have passed your first Saturn return (age 28-30). Venus rules her 11th, the house representative of a third marriage, and is in her 1st house in Cancer with favorable trines to Uranus and the Midheaven. In this marriage, she could probably find it easier to express herself than in the first two.

Luft tried very hard to get her career on track, and this marriage had a good chance at surviving with the arrival of their daughter, Lorna and son, Joey, but the relationship was tumultuous from the beginning. Though she wed a man who may have fit her requirements, she still was tortured by all her 7th house doubts and Saturnian feelings of inadequacy. However, of all her husbands she stayed with him the longest, eight years, but none of them could bring back her childhood, where she could play with her dog on the lawn, and stay home with her daddy.

She supposedly married Mark Herron in 1963, which would have been her 4th marriage—1st house, ruled by the Moon opposed Mercury, square Saturn. If indeed there was a marriage (her divorce from Luft was not final according to some sources), it was doomed from the start, since Judy had never learned to handle that challenging T-Square concerning her 7th house. Her final commitment was to Mickey Deans on March 15, 1968 (her 3rd house marriage). The Sun rules her 3rd, opposes Mars and squares Uranus and the Midheaven. He also tried to help with her career, but by this time she was out of control with drugs and booze. He was with her when she died.

Was there any way astrology could have helped Judy attain a working relationship? As astrologers, we would like to think so, but all the unheeded good advice in the world, cannot change the circumstances and actions of a person unless the astrologer can help people to work things out by and for themselves and teach them to believe that everything is possible. This is the free will we always talk about.

# YOUR PLANETS IN THE OTHER PERSON'S WHEEL

Perhaps one of the easiest ways to check for compatibility between two people is to place the planets of one around the wheel of the other. From this you can realize what each is bringing to the other in terms of character, opportunity and accord.

## The Sun

Wherever your Sun falls in another's chart you will try to exert your own ego, sometimes to control that person, sometimes to further her/his ambition instead of your own. Of course, this works in reverse. Someone's Sun falling in an angular house in your chart is usually a major indication of attraction on one level or another. If it is your 1st or 7th house, the attraction can be physical, in the 1st there is also a sense of alikeness, especially if the Sun is in your rising sign. When the 7th house receives another's Sun the law of "opposites attract" comes into play. Since you are seeking the qualities inherent in your 7th house, when another's Sun is there, it seems in some way to fulfill your expectations.

If the Sun falls in the 4th or 10th, often the other person seems to reflect a parental feeling or attitude. In the 10th house your career may be impacted. When the Sun is in the 5th (romance and children) or the 8th (sex), it is obvious what the attraction and power play might be. If the other person's Sun is in your 6th, depending on aspects, you can work well together; in the 2nd, you may share similar values or s/he may show you the way to increase your earning capacity. If another's Sun occupies your 3rd or 9th house, conversation and philosophy may spur your relationship or you may learn from one another or explore distant horizons together.

Obviously, someone's Sun in your 11th house suggests amity and friendship between you. As always, the 12th house usually gets a bad shake—some astrologers warn that if another's Sun comes into your 12th house, this can be your worst enemy. We do not concur with this concept since we feel you have much to learn from this house and who better to teach you about your hidden strengths than one who is familiar with the sign you have there?

## The Moon

The Moon has much the same flavor in these cross positions, however it is more on the feeling, emotional level and you will find that other people's Moons falling in your various houses operate on an intuitive and perceptive plane. This works when it is someone else's Moon in your chart or yours in theirs. When another's Moon is in your 1st house, this person picks up on your feelings and attitudes, almost without words; in your 6th, it can be your physical feelings; in the 9th, it may be your yearnings and aspirations. With the Moon in the 2nd or 8th, issues of money, sex, or values are paramount; in the 3rd, communication can be by look or gesture; in the 4th, nurturing becomes significant; in the 5th, you intuitively know how to romance the other; in the 7th, taking care of one another may seem natural; in the 10th, dealing with public and career issues; in the 11th, social needs and in the 12th, unexpressed yearnings. You seem to be tied emotionally to the other person in the house where her/his Moon falls.

## Mercury

Wherever another's Mercury falls in your chart, the two of you will find it most easy to communicate—8th, about your sexual needs, 4th, about your deep-seated attitudes concerning home and family, childhood memories and your feelings of nostalgia. Aviator Charles Lindbergh's Mercury occupied Anne Morrow Lindbergh's 6th house. (See their charts on page 136.) They spent the early years of their marriage surveying the country by air to provide information for map makers. Any planetary interaction, using this method of comparison, is naturally dependent on sign and aspects in both charts. If the other person's Mercury changes a T-square in your chart into a grand cross, it will obviously have more impact on the relationship than if it makes few or easy aspects. See more about this in the lesson on configurations.

## Venus

Wherever another's Venus interacts in your horoscope, is almost always an area of accord and understanding. Even difficult aspects result in feelings of warmth and love toward the other, but may be tinged with a bit of jealousy or mutual excess. Venus, the great ameliorator indicates happiness and agreement on most issues pertaining to the house. Another with Venus in your 6th house with easy aspects may admire the way you dress and keep yourself. With hard aspects, you may tempt each other to indulge. If it is the 11th, you most likely have the same attitudes toward friends and social activity; in the 10th you agree on community involvement and the maintaining of status. Venus in either the 5th or 7th is one of the nicest placements between two people, because unless the aspects are most difficult, love flourishes and harmony prevails.

## Mars

Where another's Mars falls in either chart, it is easy to utilize that energy, and, as expected, physical attraction is enhanced, so obviously the 1st, 5th, 7th and 8th are very auspicious houses for this planet. But its action enables you to put new life into old values in the 2nd; to enliven communication in the 3rd; to warm the appreciation for home in the 4th; to motivate toward cooperative ventures in the 6th; to vitalize philosophical discussions in the 9th; invigorate public recognition or career in the 10th; give life to social activity in the 11th and awaken dormant concepts in the 12th. How easy or difficult it is for this interplay to work depends, as you have surely come to realize, on the aspects to Mars in each chart, the sign involved and last, but hardly least, how hard each person is willing to work on making the relationship blossom.

## Jupiter

Jupiter represents the principle of expansion, so the house where another's Jupiter is placed is where you can expect support, confirmation of your beliefs, reinforcement of your ideals and approval of your actions. For example, if another's Jupiter is in your 10th house, you may find that you receive backing in your career goals or if it is in your 5th, this person could be very supportive of your creative endeavors. Unless Jupiter is very challenged the area it occupies can experience growth and quite often good fortune.

Elizabeth Barrett Browning and Robert Browning (his chart is on page 24) have their Jupiters in opposition and they fell in each other's 1st and 7th houses adding mutual development and expansion to their personas as well as their relationship.

## Saturn

Saturn plays a very significant role in this sort of astrological synthesis. Saturn represents staying power, and while at times its presence in chart cross placement seems challenging and difficult, this planet typifies the glue that holds a partnership together. Another's Saturn will denote responsibility, tradition and endurance in terms of the house where it is posited. With someone else's Saturn in your 1st house, you

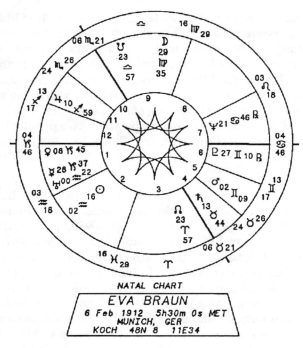

NATAL CHART

**EVA BRAUN**
6 Feb 1912   5h30m 0s MET
MUNICH, GER
KOCH   48N 8   11E34

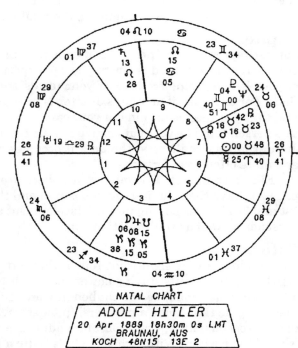

NATAL CHART

**ADOLF HITLER**
20 Apr 1889 18h30m 0s LMT
BRAUNAU, AUS
KOCH   48N15   13E 2

may find that you take yourself more seriously or the other person feels responsible for you; in your 9th, you could become interested in what the other's philosophy of life relates to, and if it is in your 2nd house, you may benefit from her/his budget and money handling expertise or just be willing to pay more attention to money matters.

Adolf Hitler and Eva Braun had Saturn square each other. Hers was in his 7th house conjunct his Venus/Mars. From what we read, he was enchanted and touched by this young woman's sincere feelings and supposedly she was the only one he was ever serious about. His Saturn was in Eva's 8th house. We do not know the inside story of their sex life, but it is known that Hitler had some strange quirks. It is obvious the relationship totally transformed Eva's life.

## Uranus

Since Uranus is the planet of "divine discontent," whichever house another person's Uranus lights up, is where you are motivated to self-examination and potential for change. In the angles, this becomes a very personal issue and depending on aspects, you may resist the tremors that you feel, before capitulating to the transpositions that are necessary to keep up with the partner. If the 2nd or 8th houses are implicated, this relationship may totally revise your value system or if Uranus is in the 3rd/9th axis, your communication and philosophical outlook may change dramatically.

Uranus is the planet of freedom and independence and where it touches another's chart it may not always bring the unexpected, but it does arouse feelings of "Don't push me or I'll push back." "I do my own thing." "I march to my own drummer."

## Neptune

The illusory quality mirrored by Neptune can confuse and obfuscate activity in the house where it falls. Unless your Neptune is well integrated in your own chart, you may find the action of the other person's Neptune nebulous and it is not until you know her/him well that you are able to discern the way it works in the relationship. Positive Neptunian action can bring inspiration and enlightenment to the house Neptune is in. Where you find it, you most likely idealize the person or affairs of the house. On the angles it can indicate allure and charm which create a charisma between the two of you or it can point to a veil over over exposure of the activities connected to the house. As always, sign and aspects determine the way it works.

## Pluto

Pluto's symbolism is much like that of Mars, only more intense and subtle. Martian action is overt; Plutonian action is covert. Where Pluto impacts your chart or vice versa, you may not always want to share and often prefer to keep the functions of that area to yourself. Just as it takes time to understand Neptune placements, so it does with Pluto. Another's Pluto position in your chart tends to show situations stirred up in an insidious way and the actions of that house may be intensified. Fortunately, most people's Pluto, as well as Neptune will fall in the area of your chart where you are already dealing with the planet's implications, unless you are attracted to someone of a different generation.

## Filling Another's Empty Houses

It is also informative to see if your partner's planets fill an empty house in your chart. For instance, if you have no planets in the 6th house and another's planets fall there, it provides a way for you to work out the energies in that house through the planet in their chart.

Prince Philip of England fills this need very nicely for Queen Elizabeth. (See their charts on pages 26.) She has no 8th house planets, but his Jupiter and Saturn fall there, bringing both expansion and support in sexual matters. She, on the other hand brings her Saturn to his empty 10th house, furnishing the royal status he enjoys. Dame Rebecca West* brings her Mercury and Sun to H.G. Wells* otherwise empty 10th house. His affair with her attracted attention and gained him notoriety as well as notice.

Charles Boyer had no planets in his 2nd house of shared values, but his wife's Venus fell there and theirs was a total love relationship. Shortly after her death from cancer, he committed suicide and left a note that said he could not live without her.

## The Importance of Lacks

Nearly as important as the 7th house needs are those caused by lacks in your natal chart. We have talked extensively about this phenomena in Volumes II and III, and have mentioned it as part of the Overview in this book. To briefly recapitulate: Any time something is missing in your horoscope, you tend to compensate for that absence in some way. If you lack an element or quality or even a specific aspect, you often seek to fulfill the lacking characteristic through your relationships with others.

A client has no planets in the earth element. He is strongly attracted to Virgo, Capricorn and Taurus women, because they reinforce his need for order, method and a sense of responsibility that he feels he lacks. You do not always actually lack the traits represented by the missing factor, but you at times feel inadequate in these areas. When you are with a person who fills the lack, you are intrigued.

Lacks can show up in diverse ways as mentioned above. All three of the houses of life, or those of substance, relationships or endings may be empty. Charles Lindbergh, for example, has no planets in his houses of endings (4th, 8th, 12th). Anne brings her Mars, Moon, Neptune, Mer-

* See chart data in Appendix.

cury and Venus to his 8th house, enabling him to look deeper into himself and his profound needs. (See their charts on pages 136.)

Both Joanne Woodward and Paul Newman have Moons which natally make no interplanetary aspects. By merging the two charts, she brings his Moon an opposition from Neptune and he does the same for her; his Mars also sextiles her Moon. By bringing oppositions into the relationship they help each other gain awareness of their emotional needs. (Their charts are on page 27.)

Most important is the fact that a natally unaspected Moon often lacks insight into her/his own feelings, in fact shies away from emotional expression. By bringing lunar aspects to each other, they are propelled into facing that responsive part of their being. Woodward and Newman seem to have done an excellent job in handling their lives as well as their marriage. Not all couples fare as well. To be impelled to look within is not everybody's cup of tea. Joanne and Paul may have been helped by their creative use of Neptune, acting in movies together or him directing her.

Quite often you are drawn to the person who embodies what you do not, only to try and change them to your ways rather than trying to adapt to theirs. Our files are full of such examples. A young man with no planets in fire signs fell in love with a delightful young lady with Leo rising and Sun in Sagittarius. After six months of wedded bliss, he began to complain bitterly about how his wife was upstaging him, how he was sick and tired of her eternal optimism and was there every going to be an event she was not enthusiastic about? That's human nature and must be evaluated when comparing charts.

## Hemisphere Emphasis

If you have seven planets or more above the horizon, you are generally quite outgoing and so could have a positive influence on someone with many planets below the horizon who may be somewhat reticent. Your social proclivities will make it easier for the other person to come out of her/his shell. This interaction also creates a balance between those with many planets east of the Meridian and those with more west. The eastern oriented person can enthuse the one with more western planets to take action, while the one with the western orientation often can provide wise counsel for one who may move too hastily.

## Affinities

There is another way that planetary cross placements work to contribute to the allure as well as the longevity of a relationship. In this instance we are only referring to Sun, Moon and Ascendant sign and house positions. After examining charts of hundreds of couples who had been together for 25 years or longer, one factor kept repeating. This is what we call "House/Sign Affinity." It is simple to find in the horoscopes.

Example: If one person has the Sun in Sagittarius and the other person has the Sun or Moon in the 9th house, or has Sagittarius rising, it is an affinity that almost guarantees longevity, if other factors indicate accord. What makes this work, is the concord between sign and house.

The alphabet system of astrology pioneered by Dr. Zipporah Dobyns is supported by this concept. She starts by relating Aries, Mars and the 1st house and progresses through the astrological alphabet to Pisces, Neptune and the 12th house, feeling that the sign, planet and house share certain common attitudes and outlooks.

Our investigation proves this in the area of astrological comparison or synastry. If your Moon is in Taurus, you are emotionally attuned to someone who has a 2nd house Sun or Moon or who has Taurus rising, because you innately sense where s/he is coming from. Examples abound. Sophia Loren's Aquarian Moon attracted Carlo Ponti's 11th house Moon. Cary Grant's* Moon in Aquarius enticed Dyan Cannon's 11th house Sun. Prince Andrew's Sun in the 7th house complements Fergie's Libran Sun.

Another affinity is interaction between planets in the same element, even if they are out of orb. For example: your Sun is at 12 degrees of Gemini and your lover's Mercury is at 27 Aquarius; the planets are **not** in orb to form a trine, but that certain feeling of innate understanding is there; not as strongly as when in aspect, but enough to count.

The charts of Civil Rights leader Martin Luther King and his wife Coretta, well illustrate how the needs and affinities of Lesson 8 work. She has a Taurus Sun, his rising sign is Taurus, so it was relatively easy for them to align their value systems, in spite of the fact that their 2nd house rulers make no aspect to each other. They both have their Moons in Pisces; hers is in the 6th, his in the 11th, suggesting that they handled feelings and emotions in similar ways.

In viewing the dispersion of each one's planets around the other's chart, we can make some informative observations. Her Moon, Jupiter and Uranus all fall in his 11th house indicating that she supported his political position. Her Mercury and Sun were in his 12th house, denoting that she provided behind-the-scenes support. Her Venus conjuncts his 2nd house cusp and trines his 10th house Mercury— she concurred in his public position and agreed with his value system. Her Mars and Midheaven conjuncted his 3rd cusp; perhaps they had arguments or discussions regarding her role in his public life (Mars co-rules her 7th). Their Uranus, Neptune and Pluto positions are conjunct, adding very little information, but her Saturn is in his 7th house and sextiles his 10th house Mercury. She reinforced and solidified his position.

When we place Martin's planets around Coretta's chart, we find that his Sun and Midheaven are in her 4th house indicating similar background and early home experience. This placement also suggests that she would carry on his work after his death. His Mercury is in her

* See chart data in Appendix.

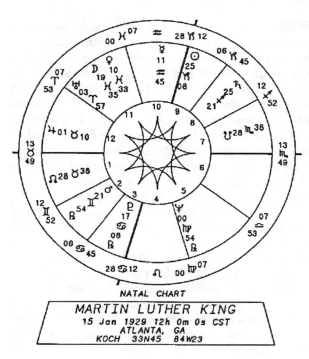

NATAL CHART

**MARTIN LUTHER KING**
15 Jan 1929 12h 0m 0s CST
ATLANTA, GA
KOCH   33N45   84W23

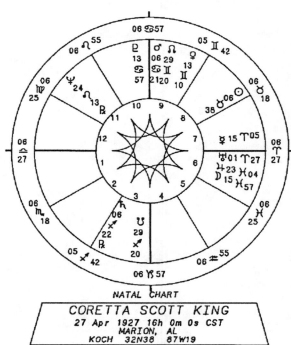

NATAL CHART

**CORETTA SCOTT KING**
27 Apr 1927 16h 0m 0s CST
MARION, AL
KOCH   32N38   87W19

5th and trines her Ascendant, surely a sign of positive communication as well as attraction between them. His Venus, Moon and Uranus fall into her 6th house, denoting that they could work well together since their Moons are both conjunct his Venus and her Jupiter and trine both Pluto positions, his in his 3rd, hers in her 10th. His Jupiter is in her 7th conjunct her 8th house Sun, a warm and convivial contact. His Ascendant falls into her 8th house—a strong sexual attraction. His Mars in Gemini falls in her 9th house, sextiles her Neptune and squares her Jupiter, which enhances their religious beliefs. His Saturn falls in her 3rd house conjunct her South Node which is also considered a karmic connection. More nodal information will be given in a later lesson.

There is another way affinities work. If one person has a Venus/Saturn aspect and the other has Venus in Capricorn or Saturn in Libra, this is also an affinity suggesting a similar outlook on love and loyalty. In the King charts, Martin has Jupiter trine Neptune, while Coretta has Jupiter in Pisces; they both have very strong religious beliefs.

In the King comparison charts, Martin's Sun and MC fall in Coretta's otherwise empty 4th house. He reinforces her psychological roots and sense of family. His Mercury is in her empty 5th house, providing a creative outlet for her. She brings her Neptune to his empty 4th house, reinforcing his family concepts and spirituality. Her Saturn in his 7th strengthens his public image by her show of support.

## LESSON 9

# INTERASPECTS

Observing the aspects formed between two horoscopes is one of the most effective ways of judging compatibility. Does your Moon conjunct his Sun? Could that classic male/female relationship destine the two of you to eternal bliss? Does your Mars trine her Venus and did you fall in love when first you met? It's not quite that simple, but there seem to be certain interplanetary actions that set off that certain *je ne sais quoi* upon first contact, whereas others can turn you off. Some of the strongest links are usually the hardest. You may call it "lessons to learn"– but once learned, these contacts become the most binding ones. Remember that conjunctions are the most potent aspects, then squares and oppositions; next are trines as well as quincunxes and least obvious in synastry are the sextiles.

As we keep reminding you, in astrology the principles of the planets and angles are always the same, whether referring to natal interpretation, progressions, electional, horary or chart comparison.

## The Sun

The Sun refers to your self-expression and inner personality, the only keyword you may wish to add in comparison is that all Sun contacts between two charts indicate growth potential. Conjunct Suns automatically understand each other's needs, but can bore each other to tears. Suns opposing each other can attract or repel, depending on the rest of the chart, whereas square Suns more often than not reveal conflicts, especially in the area they rule in each chart

Sun square Mars can manifest as hot temper flare-ups between you and your chosen other if the 3rd house is involved, as great sexual attraction if either planet is connected to the 8th, or it can denote lots of staying power between the two of you. The Sun in any interchart (interaction between charts) aspect to Neptune can prove seductive, while Sun/Uranus contacts can indicate startling and unforeseen consequences. Sun in aspect to Mercury indicates mental and verbal stimulation, whereas Sun in any relation to Jupiter projects a sense of ease with each other which can be misleading, because either of you may promise more than you can deliver. All Sun/Pluto aspects bring a sense of depth and intensity to the relationship, with the square, at times, connoting a power struggle between the Sun person's need to shine and the Pluto person's need to control.

## The Moon

The Moon shows your emotional responses, fluctuating moods and subconscious feelings. Easy lunar aspects between horoscopes disclose a sensitivity to each other's sensibilities and daily needs, whereas adverse Moon positions can symbolize domestic tension.

In synastry Sun/Moon contacts are considered among the most vital links, since the Sun in a woman's chart reflects the masculine or *animus* part of her nature, while the Moon in a man's horoscope shows his female or *anima* disposition. Any aspect is better than none. The conjunction is the most fulfilling; in fact, it is considered the classic bond in male/female unions and can help overcome otherwise difficult factors of the relationship. Trines and sextiles illustrate a feeling of harmony, but not necessarily longevity or that strong sense of needing each other inherent in the conjunction. Oppositions certainly imply attraction, though they may point to some emotional exchanges. Squares also characterize a draw, but they can suggest clashes as to who is the final authority, or similar power struggles.

The most amicable lunar interrelation is to Venus. Even the square can indicate an emotional high, since you feel you are picking up on your partner's sensibilities. The most difficult contacts are to Pluto where the Moon's emotionality can become too intense. This can be delightful for an air (Gemini, Libra, Aquarius) Moon, but hard to handle in an already susceptible horoscope. Moon/Mercury contacts combine the Moon's emotionality with Mercury's intellect. This can be stirring or irritating, depending on the type of aspect and your reaction to emotional stimulus. Connections from the Moon to Jupiter can reflect mutual admiration as well as emotional fervor for each other, while the joining of the Moon and Neptune can be idealistic or even spiritual; challenging aspects may hint that you could unintentionally fool each other.

## Mercury

Mercury connections are crucial since this planet represents your mental outlook and communicative ability. Even difficult aspects are better than none, because no relationship can survive if you and your better half cannot talk to each other. Without Mercury contacts there could also be a lack of mutual interests and nearly always an inability to understand each other. Mental and verbal exchanges are a must for a lasting union. Though squares and oppositions are considered challenging aspects, challenges can be stimulating and make a relationship worth cultivating .

Jimmy Carter's Mercury at 21 Virgo conjuncts Rosalynn's* Venus. Communicating with his wife was nearly always a pleasant and warm experience, hampered only by an occasional emotional outburst, since her Mercury squared his Moon. He could always get through to her; she might, at times, touch a raw nerve with him.

Aspects from Mercury to Jupiter can broaden your horizons; to Uranus, awaken each other's intellects and prevent boredom; to Pluto, deepen your understanding of each other or, with natally challenged Mercuries, require that you learn to tolerate your differences.

## Venus

Venus mirrors your true expression of love and affection and your Venus in harmonious contact to someone else's Sun is another classic male/female connection which can contribute to long-lasting relationships.

When both have Venus in the same element, you can express your love in a similar fashion; trines as well as sextiles can speak of enhanced, warm feelings between you, while the opposition shows you need time until you know each other well enough to understand each other's wants. The square may denote an inability to show your true feelings to each other or the potential of introducing one another to the finer things in life.

Venus connected to Pluto can be symptomatic of love (Venus) as a catalyst to transformation (Pluto), an intense love relationship, or the controlling need of one partner over the other, often manifesting as jealousy or possessiveness.

Venus/Jupiter aspects may represent mutual indulgence in the areas these planets are placed or rule. Connected to the 2nd house you may both spend more money than you should; to the 6th, neither one of you may feel like working as hard as you should. Except for such small peccadillos, all Venus contacts are basically helpful in intimate associations.

## Mars

Mars interaction will depict drive and energy including, of course, the sexual drive. Mars in easy aspect to Mars suggests that your sexual drives as well as your vitality agree; hard aspects still suggest sexual energy, but can connote bouts of jealousy or competitiveness.

Much more important than Venus/Venus or Mars/Mars are the Venus/Mars aspects. Since Mars represents your physical drive and

* See chart data in Appendix.

Venus your love nature, blending these can produce delightful and electric physical attraction. As always, the conjunction is the strongest aspect; the square and opposition are next in strength. All emphasize a super-charged magnetism. The quincunx, on the other hand, often typifies a one-sided sexual interest. The trine and sextile are pleasant, but less compelling and also less possessive when signs like Scorpio or Taurus are implicated.

Mars is always the go-getter and describes assertion in a comparison just as it does in the natal chart. Trines from another's Mars to any planet in your chart tend to show a feeling of strength and courage. Squares to Uranus, Neptune and Jupiter are not too hard to handle; they imply stimulation rather than aggravation. Squares to Mercury, the Moon and Pluto characterize irritation and can even provoke fights.

## The Ascendant

The Ascendant always describes your persona, your outer personality and body. Where and how it interrelates with another person can represent that first chemical reaction as well as peaceful or feisty behavior toward each other. Certain aspects to the Ascendant or Descendant give information about how a relationship gets started and also its endurance. For example, a strong connection between the Ascendant of one to the Sun of the other or contacts between the Sun/Ascendant rulers are very stimulating and helpful. Even links between 7th house rulers can be beneficial.

## The Midheaven

Your Midheaven (MC) denotes the status you bring to your mate, but any aspects involving it also have to be interpreted as an ego thrust which can strongly affect your counterpart.

## Jupiter

Jupiter contacts indicate areas of expansion as well as your ability to bring benefits to the other person; in fact, any time someone's Jupiter falls on your Ascendant, she/he'll probably try to spoil you rotten. Jupiter's optimistic side can lighten many heavy facets of an association. Its idealistic side can uplift or offer support in the houses it occupies or rules. Jupiter's down side may promise more than it can deliver in certain interplanetary connections, leading to disappointments; or you can induce one another into indulging when and where you shouldn't. Jupiter's missionary zeal can lead you into temptation as easily as into religious beliefs. This is particularly true of any Jupiter/Neptune aspects which can reveal mutual enlightenment, or you can convince each other to follow Jim Jones to Guyana. On the other hand Jupiter/Saturn aspects can combine the optimism and generous vision of Jupiter with the practicality and realism of Saturn, a wonderful fusion of talents, which is especially productive in a business relationship.

When combining Jupiter/Uranus energies, both partners are usually generous and give each other plenty of space, while Jupiter/Pluto aspects nearly always denote a need for growth and expansion, a great combination in business relationships.

## Saturn

Saturn shows limitations and lessons to be learned, but also the solidity of the relationship. In fact, without some strong Saturn contacts, any union rarely lasts. We consider the contacts to Saturn among the most binding in any serious commitment. Saturn symbolizes where you come face-to-face with the other person's reality. Whether you will use this positively or negatively is not only shown by the nature of the aspects, but also by the other person's attitude toward life in general. All Saturn contacts are noteworthy, but especially those to the personal planets. In synastry Saturn can overwhelm another person's planet and become a 'downer'—but it does not have to. Remember that improper use of a Jupiter aspect can express as overindulgence or license, while proper use of Saturn aspects can express as wise control.

Someone with Saturn contacts to your Sun can focus your goals or frustrate your ambitions; to the Moon the individual can stabilize your emotions or restrict your emotional expression. Someone with Saturn contacts to your Mercury can discipline your reasoning process or repress your ability to communicate. To Venus, the other person may cool your love nature and ability to experience pleasure or her/his love can hold like glue. A woman's Saturn conjunct a man's Mars can imply taming an overactive sex drive or causing psychological impotence, her demands sapping his energy; a man's Saturn in aspect to a woman's Mars usually connotes that her initiative is dampened or that he helps her to better organize her time.

Saturn/Neptune aspects typify the same in a comparison as they do natally, where we call them "the architect's aspects" since the combination of these two planets incorporates the dreams of Neptune and molds them into Saturn's reality.

Saturn/Pluto can indicate intense struggles for dominance even to the point of abuse, or it can point to incredible commitment, followthrough and tenacity in romantic relationships as well as organization skills for business associations.

## Uranus

With Uranus contacts, the other person is always stimulated, for good or bad. Uranus contacts are electric, fun and titillating, but not necessarily lasting. In close aspect to Venus, Mars, the Moon or Ascendant of another, it can indicate sudden attractions and what may seem like overpowering desires. If the aspect is a trine or sextile and there are other indications of affinity in the charts, this intense feeling can eventually turn into love. With discordant aspects, the infatuation may seem even more urgent, but rarely lasting. Uranus/Saturn connections between two charts are similar to Neptune/Saturn ones, since here too, Saturn motifs stabilize the often eccentric Uranus themes and can convert even oddball ideas into usable products. Trines, sextiles and oppositions are easier to integrate than squares and quincunxes. Uranus, planet of rebellion in aspect to Pluto often intensifies the Uranian needs for freedom or unique behavior patterns. Whether that is acceptable and stimulating or difficult because it demands the ability to adapt to new situations, depends on natal aspects and house placements of these planets.

## Neptune

Neptune may signify the height of ecstasy or great deception. Its aspects are illusory, magnetic, charismatic and always compelling. Since they are totally lacking in realism, they can be dangerous and rarely do the results live up to the expectations. Neptune/Mercury suggests the ability to make up great excuses to your partner or, with challenging aspects, even lie to each other. Venus/Neptune finds you cajoling your lover, or being lured into romantic situations you might later regret. On the other hand, you may inspire each other to produce some great artistic work.

Marlene Dietrich used to sing a song whose German lyrics read: "Men surround me like moths around the flame, and if they kick the bucket, I'm not to blame." That describes Neptune's powers, its allure and its perils.

In the 20th century, Neptune's largest separation from Pluto is a sextile. Such a generational aspect has little meaning when comparing two charts and all interpretations should concentrate on the houses and rulers involved, rather than on the sextile.

## Pluto

Where Pluto interacts, the other person may regenerate or gain new insights, but just as often Pluto may reveal intensification of some undesirable traits. Pluto is intense, sometimes compulsive and even obsessive in its passion. Pluto motifs can deepen the bond and intensify everything they touch; therefore Pluto contacts need to be carefully watched. The Plutonian commitment is nearly as lasting as the Saturnian one, but can be even harder to handle, since your feelings are instinctive and difficult for the conscious mind to conceive. If possible, a square from one person's Pluto to another's Mars should be avoided. In a volatile chart, this aspect could point to a certain amount of violence or sexual put-down (unless the people have constructive, highly competitive outlets).

All aspects between like planets seem to be less significant than other factors. They do allude to a certain feeling of harmony or innate understanding, which can be pleasant in an otherwise challenging relationship. The only time aspects between the same planets are consequential is when they rule the Sun, Moon or Ascendant.

It is also wise to remember the speed of the planets. Since the slower moving one stays longer in any zodiacal area it impacts, it ends up having the strongest significance. Your Mars to another's Jupiter—Jupiter is slower and will have more clout. Mars to Mercury, Mars is slower and is therefore more meaningful in the interrelationship.

The most essential point to keep in mind is that challenging or tension producing aspects are needed to make any intimate venture meaningful. Trines and sextiles are pleasant, but they rarely contribute to longevity or excitement in a relationship.

# LESSON 10

# CONFIGURATIONS

Now that you understand how important aspects between two charts can be, let's discuss the crucial forming of configurations and what happens when the simple square of one chart becomes a T-square by merging two charts; the T-square changes into a grand cross, the quincunx or sextile of one chart turns into a yod between the two horoscopes.

After working with thousands of charts, we have noted that when a configuration is formed between two horoscopes, especially the grand cross and yod, the relationship becomes a more binding or lasting one.... not easier, on the contrary, just longer in endurance, often until death dost them part.

The yod seems to indicate that the couple must make adjustments toward each other; reorganizing their habits or *modus operandi*, which in turn can lead to a give and take, a respecting of each other's values or attitudes. This, more often than not, leads to a long lasting union.

When a planet in one horoscope fills the missing opposition in another person's T-square, it seems as though a dark place has suddenly been lit; new awareness floods an area that wasn't really understood before, yet now becomes clear and workable. This can be a very binding combination, not only in charts of lovers, but also in those of friends, family or business associates.

The forming of other configurations is also significant, but not as crucial or predictable. The merging of two squares and/or an opposition into a T-square can show stimulation or irritation. In already difficult or tense charts it can depict more stress than the individuals are willing to handle. On the other hand, if the couple in question is easygoing, the push or challenge of the combined T-square may be exactly what is needed.

As strange as it may sound, the forming of a grand trine by combining two or three planets in both charts, is the least important configuration in one-to-one relationships. It represents harmony and flow which can be most inspirational, but not necessarily the willingness to work out mutual problems. The spark lit by a grand trine can motivate a sexual attraction, but it does not ensure a good or long lasting marriage unless there are other contributing factors.

Since learning is always easiest by example, let's look at some configurations in pairs of people you are familiar with.

## Forming a T-square

Ingrid Bergman's Mercury at 18 Virgo opposed Roberto Rossellini's Saturn at 13 Pisces and squared his Jupiter at 11 Gemini, as well as his Pluto at 21 Gemini. Ingrid liked to express herself precisely (Mercury, planet of communication, is dignified in Virgo, sextile Saturn), at times grandly (opposed Jupiter) and always a bit uniquely (quincunx Uranus). The opposition to Saturn and square to Jupiter formed by merging her chart with that of Roberto was not much of a problem for her since Ingrid knew how to integrate Mercury with Saturn and Jupiter. What must have been difficult was the intensity Pluto added to all conversations, discussions and arguments. Roberto was likely to have even more difficulties, stemming from this T-square, since his natal Mercury had only one aspect and Ingrid's mental and verbal approach may have overwhelmed him at times.

Their second configuration is even more intriguing, since it involves Roberto's Sun/Moon opposition at 17 Taurus and 16 Scorpio respectively in a T-square with Ingrid's Uranus at 13 Aquarius. Any Sun/Moon opposition is rarely easy to handle, and by the time Rossellini learned to live with it, Bergman came along to shake up the foundations of everything each of them stood for. In her case Uranus rules the 7th house of intimate liaisons and is involved in a yod with Saturn and Mercury, that same Mercury which forms the previously discussed T-square. The sparks must have flown in that household. But they also had some wonderful aspects that drew them together...her Sun and Venus conjunct his Ascendant, her Mars conjunct his Neptune, her Sun trine his Uranus.

Could they have made the marriage last? Of course; you can do anything you set your mind to. Did they care enough to really work on the union? Yes and no. Her 7th house needs (Aquarius, ruler Uranus in the 6th in Aquarius) were not really fulfilled by him. He has no Aquarian planets and only illusory Neptune is in the 11th, but his Virgo Ascendant partially fulfills her 6th house needs. She does not fulfill his main needs either. He has Pisces on the 7th house cusp with the ruler Neptune in Cancer in the 11th house. Ingrid was not at all Piscean. But she did reflect the Cancer feeling with three planets in Cancer.

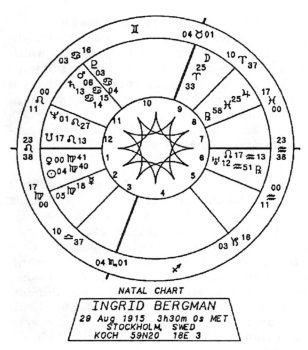

NATAL CHART

INGRID BERGMAN
29 Aug 1915   3h30m 0s MET
STOCKHOLM,  SWED
KOCH  59N20   18E 3

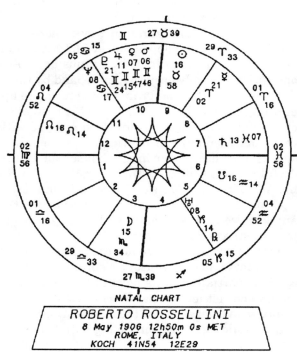

NATAL CHART

ROBERTO ROSSELLINI
8 May 1906 12h50m 0s MET
ROME,  ITALY
KOCH  41N54   12E29

Surely the love affair was more fun for Ingrid than the reality of marriage. Roberto's Uranus fell into her 5th house. Their first child, Robertino, was born out of wedlock—then they had twins—certainly not a run-of-the-mill family. His Saturn fell in her 7th house, and when the excitement of the 5th house romance turned into 7th house responsibilities, life probably became less fun and games for both of them.

Two strong T-squares are also formed by blending Ethel and Robert Kennedy's charts (page 124).

His Venus/MC/Jupiter conjunction at 15, 19, and 20 Capricorn, opposed his Pluto at 14 Cancer and all of these are squared by Ethel's Jupiter/Sun conjunction at 17 and 21 Aries. This can be a very stimulating configuration and the Pluto square intensifies it. Both Ethel and Bobby with their natal grand trines could stand the tension and challenges a T-square symbolizes.

A bit harder to handle is Ethel's Mars/Ascendant conjunction at 2 Pisces opposed to her Neptune at 27 Leo square Bobby's Sun at 28 Scorpio. Mars (fire) opposite Neptune (water) can display a lot of steam unless you find an escape valve; when you add his 7th house Sun to this seething kettle, things can get hot and heavy. It may be sexual attraction par excellence or can result in boiling over or blowing up situations. Having 11 children in a period of 17 years (July 1951 to December 1968) probably kept Ethel's Mars conjunct the Ascendant (physical body) too busy to worry about much else except giving birth and raising her brood.

Ethel's Mars/Ascendant falls into Bobby's 11th house. We can assume that they were always good friends. We might wonder if with his 5th house Neptune (hers is also there), he had twinges of bad conscience when he indulged in his dalliances while his "friend" was mothering, or if with Neptune's help he could spin beautiful fantasies and deny reality in that area. Since Robert Kennedy was assassinated in 1968, they were married only 18 years and we do not know if the union would have lasted, but viewing all the interconnections, especially between their Suns and Mercuries as well as Venus/Moon, Mars/Ascendant, Pluto/Saturn (and their religious convictions), we doubt there would ever be a separation or divorce.

## Forming a Yod

If forming a T-square between two charts can connote tension, the formation of a yod usually represents relief. Relief from the simple quincunx which you have so often ignored in favor of an opposition or square which leaves you with a feeling of guilt for not having taken action. If you are the person with the sextile, you may not relish having a quincunx added to your collection of aspects, but at least it will give both of you a chance to start working with the quincunx and making the required adjustments (favored keyword for this aspect).

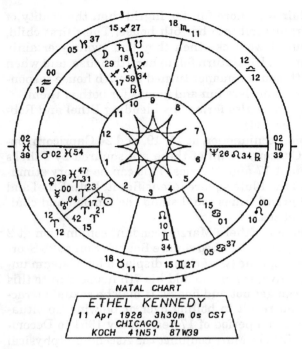

NATAL CHART

ETHEL KENNEDY
11 Apr 1928  3h30m 0s CST
CHICAGO, IL
KOCH  41N51  87W39

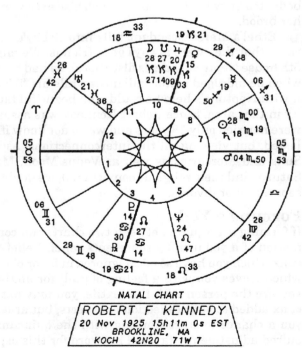

NATAL CHART

ROBERT F KENNEDY
20 Nov 1925  15h11m 0s EST
BROOKLINE, MA
KOCH  42N20  71W 7

Betty and Gerald Ford are a good illustration.When their charts merge, four yods are formed; two through Betty's sextiles, two through Gerry's placements. These are interesting in the sense that an area where you feel innately at ease can become complicated when you get involved with another person. Surely you have experienced this.

In Betty's case Mercury, ruler of both her Ascendant and Midheaven, sextiles Pluto, ruler of her 3rd house of communication. Though she always expressed in a fairly intense manner, she had no trouble saying what she wanted to say or being who she wanted to be. Gerald Ford, love of her life, has his Moon quincunx both her planets, forming a Yod. His Moon falls in her 4th house. All of a sudden she has to act like a congressman's wife; she cannot run her home as she did in Michigan. Bachelor Gerry has to make many adjustments also. His 7th house Moon has found the partner he always yearned for, yet was wary of (freedom-loving Sagittarius). Betty's Mercury falls into his 12th house of deep, inner feelings and her Pluto joins his Pluto in the 2nd of values and money. He obviously had to earn more money to support two instead of one, as well as adapt his values to blend with hers. For him it was now easier to work out his natal Moon/Pluto quincunx, because of the sextile from Betty's Mercury to his Pluto.

The second yod also involves the Moon/Pluto quincunx, but here Betty's Pluto becomes the "finger" of the Yod, while Gerry's Uranus sextiles his Moon and is quincunx Betty's Pluto. Jerry's own Pluto is out of orb for a quincunx to Uranus. We suggest using a tight five degree orb for this aspect. This yod as well as the other one is easier on Gerry than on Betty, who now adds another uncomfortable aspect to her natally very harmoniously aspected Pluto. His Uranus falls in her 5th house, and as she stated in her biography, due to the pressures of his job, Gerry was often an absent husband and father.

Their third yod is formed by Betty's Jupiter, ruler of her 4th in the 10th, sextile Saturn in her 11th, ruling her 5th. Both quincunx Gerry's Jupiter, falling in her 5th. That's a lot of Saturnian energy in the 5th house. Their first child was born about a year and a half after they married and we can assume that the original love affair turned into taking responsibility for children, a definite reorganizing of lifestyle, especially for the mother. In Gerry's chart Betty's Jupiter and Saturn fall into his 1st and 4th houses; obviously many personal (1st) and home (4th) adjustments were needed. Jupiter rules his 8th and it goes without saying that marriage brings sexual changes to a bachelor.

The fourth yod again involves Gerry's Jupiter quincunx his Mercury in the 4th house. Betty's Moon in Pisces sextiles Jupiter, giving Gerry not only the opportunity to work out his own quincunx, but since her Moon is in his 11th house of groups, she helped him to better understand his role in Congress, as well as helping him with the many polit-

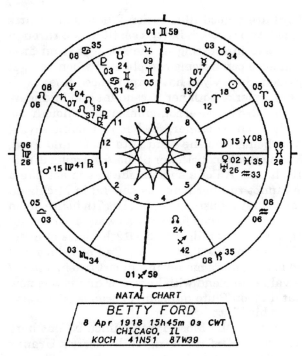

NATAL CHART

BETTY FORD
8 Apr 1918 15h45m 0s CWT
CHICAGO, IL
KOCH  41N51  87W39

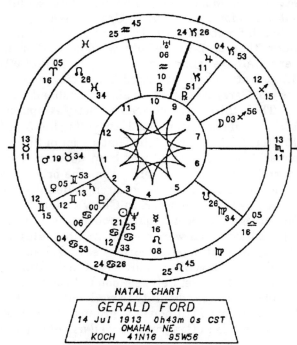

NATAL CHART

GERALD FORD
14 Jul 1913 0h43m 0s CST
OMAHA, NE
KOCH  41N16  95W56

ical groups that congressional wives become involved with. Betty's 7th house Moon rules her 11th, reinforcing what we see in Gerry's chart.

What does all of this mean? Are the four yods the reason the Fords have a long-lasting marriage, weathering many ups and down? Or is it the fact that he fills her T-square, which we will discuss later? Or maybe the grand earth trine they have together? The answer has to be very ambiguous... yes and no. No, because astrology does not "make you do something." Yes, because the tendencies brought out by their getting together may have forced them to take stock, talking out their problems or differences, and making the necessary adjustments.

## Forming a Grand Trine

As already stated, the grand trines formed when intermingling two charts are absolutely delightful, but they neither imply awareness of each other's needs, nor do they guarantee longevity of the relationship. They do reflect an innate feeling of harmony in the areas they rule or are posited.

Ingrid Bergman and Roberto Rossellini (charts on page 122) may have challenged each other with the T-squares their charts formed, but bliss must have reigned supreme in the areas of their two grand trines. The grand water trine was probably less important for Roberto than for Ingrid, since he has one natally. His Moon at 15 Scorpio trines his Saturn at 13 Pisces and both trine his Neptune at 8 Cancer. (Note: we stretch orbs a bit in defining natal configurations.) Ingrid tightens this grand trine considerably with her Saturn at 13 Cancer. Saturn rules her 5th house, Roberto's Moon falls into her 4th and his Saturn is in her 7th, just on the cusp of the 8th. That is a very nice flow for her, from love affairs (5th) to marriage (7th) and sex (8th).

Their emotions (illustrated by the grand water trine) may have brought them together, but the practicality of the grand earth trine aided them in their joint work. Ingrid's 1st house Sun at 4 Virgo rules her Ascendant and trines her 4 Taurus Midheaven; both trine Roberto's 5th house Uranus at 8 Capricorn, which rules his 6th house of work and falls into Ingrid's 5th. This time the 5th house involvement concerns both their creativity (5th), work (6th), career (MC) and her ability to personally (Ascendant) shine as an actress (Sun/Leo).

The Fords' grand earth trine encompasses his Ascendant at 13 Taurus, trine his 9th house Jupiter at 11 Capricorn, ruling his 8th. Both trine Betty's 1st house Mars at 15 Virgo, ruling her 8th and falling into his 5th. There is a lot of 5th and 8th house emphasis for him, which often reflects that magnetic something needed to get an affair started. Betty's 1st house Mars ruling her 8th trine his Jupiter in her 5th signals the same 5th/8th house scenario. With Gerry's Ascendant located in her 9th and his Jupiter occupying his 9th house, both of them likely pursued the same ideals, morals and religious principles, and these were important to both of them.

## Forming a Grand Cross

In the many charts we have studied and researched, the grand cross repeatedly appears as a difficult, but somehow very binding connection when combining two charts. As mentioned before, by filling the empty space, the opposition to the focal planet, a lack seems to become fulfilled; an area of confusion becomes imbued with awareness and new understanding. This is the positive part of this configuration. The tension producing and often difficult factor results from the two new squares formed.

Sophia Loren's biography is in Lesson 3. When combining her horoscope with that of her husband of many years, Carlo Ponti two grand crosses form. (See page 129.) Sophia's T-square includes Uranus, ruler of her 2nd house at 0 Taurus in the 3rd (conjunct the IC); it opposes her Midheaven at 0 Scorpio as well as her Jupiter at 25 Libra, ruling her 12th. This opposition is squared by Pluto in the 7th, ruling the MC and 11th at 25 Cancer. Career, marriage, income, her inner strength and communications are all involved. To this busy T-square, Ponti brings his Venus at 28 Capricorn conjunct Uranus at 1 Aquarius in her 1st house. He can, with love and tenderness, fulfill her and all her needs. He can in his own distinctive way (Uranus/Venus) help her become aware of what Pluto is all about and how to shape her career. That this grand cross takes place in his 1st, 5th, 7th and 11th houses is most helpful because it reflects his persona, his love given as well as his partnership needs and ability for friendship. Her focal planet, Pluto, conjunct his Neptune in his 5th, mirrors the intensity and endurance of their love for each other.

Carlo also has a T-square: the Ascendant at 27 Pisces square his MC/Jupiter conjunction, opposed to Pluto at 29 Gemini in the 4th (Pluto rules the 8th, Jupiter the 9th and 10th). He too, has many control (Pluto) issues as well as career (MC) and partner's money (8th) matters to work out. Sophia's Sun at 28 Virgo right on Carlo's Descendant turns this T-square into a grand cross. She brings her radiance and warmth to his house of partners. With her he becomes fulfilled and better able to understand himself. These two configurations are about as strong a bond as you would ever wish to find.

Let's review another pair of fascinating charts, fascinating because this couple too fills each other's T-square, but while we know the Pontis relationship has lasted since 1950, we do not know if Prince Charles and his lovely Diana will work out their differences. In the not too distant past, divorce would have been out of the question for a royal couple.

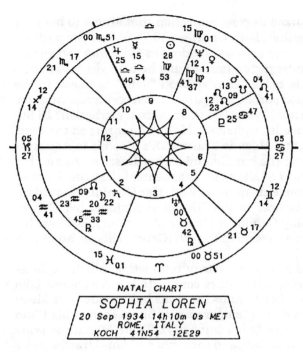

NATAL CHART

SOPHIA LOREN
20 Sep 1934 14h10m 0s MET
ROME, ITALY
KOCH 41N54 12E29

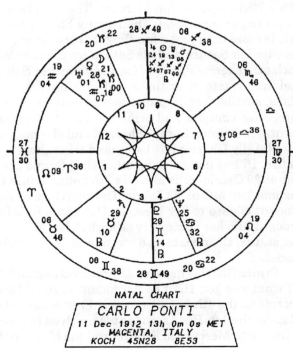

NATAL CHART

CARLO PONTI
11 Dec 1912 13h 0m 0s MET
MAGENTA, ITALY
KOCH 45N28 8E53

There is a dynamic fixed degree connection that seems to hold the English royal family together. Both Charles and Di fit into the pattern. Surely you remember their grandiose wedding in 1981 when she was a charmingly innocent kindergarten teacher and he a 33 year old bachelor looking for a suitable bride. They've been "done" to death in the tabloids...unfaithful... good parent, bad parent...divorce...reconciliation.

What astrological factors symbolize their mutual attraction? Di fulfills Charles' 7th house needs exquisitely. He has Aquarius on the cusp, ruler Uranus in Gemini and Moon in Taurus. Di's Moon is in Aquarius in the 3rd (Gemini) house; she has Gemini on her Descendant and her signature (predominance of qualities and elements) is Taurus. Charles does not meet her requirements quite as well. Her Gemini Descendant is ruled by Mercury in Cancer in the 7th house conjunct her Cancer Sun. Charles has no strong Gemini or Cancer placements, however his Sun and three other planets are all in the 4th (Cancer) house, an important interconnection.

Both have an abundance of planetary interaction which explains their romance and marriage. His Mars conjuncts her Ascendant (she finds him sexy) and trines her Uranus (he finds her unique); his Moon trines her Mars (their emotional temperaments blend easily); his Pluto trines her Ascendant (she feels his intensity). Their Mercuries trine highlighting their ability to understand each other and his Uranus (ruler of his 7th) conjuncts her Mercury. They can talk to each other, but best on an impersonal level. Their many Saturn connections indicate that this is more than just a fun fling. Saturn aspects are enduring. His Sun sextiles her Saturn and his Saturn sextiles her Sun/Mercury (they take each other seriously); his Moon squares her Saturn (she can make him feel inadequate or at times, old), his Saturn conjuncts her Pluto and Mars, sextiles her Neptune and quincunxes her Jupiter. He can help direct her energies and bring her dreams to reality; he can be instrumental in helping her face herself and she may not always like it.

Natally Charles has two grand trines, one mostly in earth and one in fire. Di has none, but together they form a grand air trine. His Uranus at 29 Gemini falls into Di's 7th house, trines her Moon at 25 Aquarius and her MC at 23 Libra. The marriage obviously added a certain amount of ease to her lifestyle. Her Moon falls into his 7th house (she brought him her femininity as a wife); her MC is in his 4th (she brought her status, clean slate as a virgin and good family background into his home).

Prince Charles has a most provocative chart. What you see is not at all what you get. His Leo Ascendant is ruled by a very private Sun in Scorpio in the 4th house in mutual reception with "I'm in charge here" Pluto in the 1st. His Ascendant is involved in a stubborn, set in his way T-square to Mercury in Scorpio and the Moon in the 10th in Taurus. To

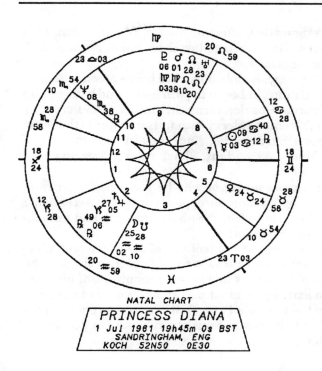

NATAL CHART

PRINCESS DIANA
1 Jul 1961 19h45m 0s BST
SANDRINGHAM, ENG
KOCH   52N50   0E30

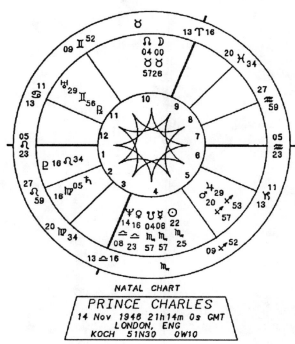

NATAL CHART

PRINCE CHARLES
14 Nov 1948 21h14m 0s GMT
LONDON, ENG
KOCH   51N30   0W10

this very convoluted configuration, affecting his 1st, 3rd, 4th, 10th, 11th and 12th houses, Princess Diana brings her chart ruler, Jupiter, at 5 Aquarius to form a grand cross.

Di also has a fixed T-square. It embodies a 3rd house Moon in Aquarius, opposed by its ruler Uranus in Leo in the 9th house and both square Venus in the 5th in Taurus. Charles turns this into a grand cross by adding his Scorpio Sun (his chart ruler) which falls into her 11th house. These two grand crosses are truly vital, since they include the core of both partners— Sun, Moon, Ascendant, chart rulers, Mercury and Venus.

Will Charles become more aware of who he really is (apart from being the Crown Prince) by gaining an opposition to his Ascendant? Does he want to? Does he wish to feel the abundance, joy and uniqueness that Di's Jupiter can bring him?

Is Diana willing to give rein to the feelings of deep love and affection that her 5th house Venus in Taurus is capable of once she lets the rays of Charles' Sun awaken Venus and become cognizant of her true feelings? This is where astrology cannot and should not try to provide answers. This is where the person's **Free Will** reigns supreme. All astrology can do is point out the positive outlets available to people, including Charles and Diana.

# LESSON 11

# OTHER KEY FACTORS

## The Nodes in Synastry

How you interpret the Nodes, more than anything else in astrology, depends on your beliefs. Since we sincerely feel that moral, religious, spiritual and even political convictions are very private privileges, we have, in this teaching series, been careful not to overstep the thin line of educating versus proselytizing.

In Volume II of *The Only Way...* we explained that in our approach the South Node is where you egest knowledge, ideas, attitudes and morals that are already part of you, based upon your memories, your childhood, or if you use the esoteric technique, in your past lives. The North Node on the other hand is where you ingest new knowledge, ideas and ideals; as you gain in learning, you gain in confidence. As you gain confidence, you gain inner security and eventually reach the highest point of inner fulfillment that your horoscope promises.

Depending on your beliefs, you may see the Nodes as one of the most important indicators of whence you came and where you should go; you may see them as keys to your social attitudes; as an area of monetary gain (North Node) or you may find them relatively unimportant.

In *The Only Way to...Learn About Tomorrow* we barely mentioned the Nodes, because in our experience they play a lesser role by progression, direction, transit or in solar and lunar returns. The one exception seems to be death, an event that rarely passes without prominent nodal interconnections. You can however, have a chart with many aspects to and from the Nodes without death occurring.

In synastry the Nodes seem highly significant. For some people they represent the cement that keeps them together, to others they denote the secret ingredient that brought them together in the first place, and for those who believe in reincarnation and karma, they are keys to that special something that helps you work our past, present and future *raisons d'être.*

Whichever your favorite interpretation, there is one thing that seems to apply to all nodal chart comparisons; someone's North Node contacting one of your planets or angles seems to be experienced positively, as though s/he is giving you her/his strength and good vibrations. The South Node in the same position is where you often find it easy to give to the other person or, depending on attitude and aspects, you may feel as though they are a sponge soaking you dry.

Johannes Brahms' South Node was exactly conjunct Clara Schumann's Moon and within four degrees of her Ascendant, confirming the fact that she was his inspiration and possibly the reason he never married.

Joanne Woodward and Paul Newman have strong nodal contacts. His South Node conjuncts her Mercury and Mars, indicating that she may have been the one who set the tone in the relationship. Her South Node conjoins his Midheaven; through him she had a chance to show her talents and further her own career.

The reverse of this is Ernest Hemingway's North Node on Mary Welsh Hemingway's Midheaven; he brings her the chance to become better known through his glitz and glamor. The Hemingways have another, more interesting nodal connection; her North Node (and Neptune) conjunct his Venus, making him feel wanted and loved, while Mary's South Node on Ernest's Moon could have drained him emotionally.

Even the most tragic or evil personalities feel attraction for each other and especially for staying together. Such was the case with Adolf Hitler and Eva Braun whose North Node was not only conjunct his Sun and Mercury, but also his Descendant, probably helping him feel better about himself and his thinking when she was present.

The Rossellinis, Ingrid and Roberto, have reversed nodal connections; her North Node at 17 Aquarius is conjunct his South Node at 16 Aquarius. We have found this to be a mutual attraction, but not necessarily something to make a relationship last.

## Patterns in Chart Comparison

Less important, but still revealing is to note the chart patterns between you and the other person and observe if a new pattern evolves when merging the two charts by putting one around the other. Of the nine existing patterns (Bowl, Bucket, Bundle, Fan, Locomotive, Seesaw, Splash, Tripod and Wheelbarrow) the ones to watch are the narrow, contained ones, such as the Bundle where all the planets are placed within a trine, or the Bowl where they occupy no more than six houses.

In either of those patterns it is important to see where the new outlet lies, or if a different pattern unfolds, which planets are involved.

Charles Lindbergh natally has a Fan Pattern; eight of his planets are in the 1st, 2nd and 3rd houses, Pluto and Neptune, widely conjunct, form the handle to the Fan from the 7th house. Anne Morrow Lindbergh has a Seesaw Pattern natally, with two planets from the 4th and 6th houses opposing the other eight planets in the 10th and 11th.

When the two horoscopes are superimposed, they still form a Seesaw, perhaps a bit wider; in Anne's case adding some action in her 5th and 9th houses. The major change occurred in Charles' chart where the Fan, which filtered all action through Neptune and Pluto, had to learn to adapt to the ups and downs, backs and forths of a Seesaw. The loner that we knew "Lindy" to be, probably had a hard time adjusting to married life.

When a Bundle or Bowl becomes a Locomotive, a new emphasis is added. A client and his wife have this. Her Uranus is the engine of the Locomotive in the combined chart. It was fascinating to observe how this rather conservative gentleman became more relaxed as time went on. With Uranus leading the way, his gray flannel suits soon gave way to sport jackets, the bland plain color ties progressed into stripes and diamonds; it took one year to go from clean shaven to a beard. Vacations in Hawaii and Vail have metamorphosed into an excursion to Bora Bora, explorations of the Himalayas and Sri Lanka.

Quite often you may find that a pair of horoscopes form a Bucket. In that case the "handle" or singleton becomes the critical planet. Its sign and house position can be the key to the relationship. More often than not the combining of charts results in some sort of Splash Pattern. We have found that to be of little importance.

## Homosexuality in Synastry
In Volume IV of *The Only Way to. . .Learn About Tomorrow* on page 43 we talk about homosexuality and the many so-called signatures that do not work dependably and should be viewed with skepticism. We briefly cite how some psychological problems could lead to the preference of ones own sex, but that none of them confirm homosexuality. They can just as easily contribute to to other difficulties such as sexual hang-ups, amatory excesses, abusive relationships with children, fear of being a parent, withdrawal from any relationship—to mention just a few.

Now it seems that we can even go a step further. According to recent scientific studies, mainly by biologist Simon LeVay of the Salk Institute, homosexuality may be rooted in biology. (*Newsweek* September 9, 1991) It seems that one tiny section of the brain of homosexual men is less than half the size of that in heterosexual men. Though this study is still considered preliminary, (LeVay only analyzed tissue from 41 cadavers) he found that one bundle of neurons in the hypothalamus

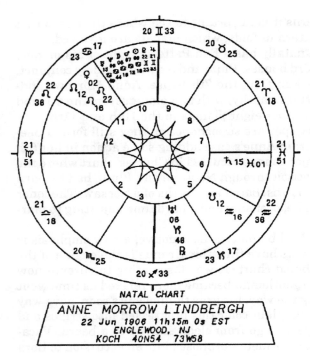

NATAL CHART
ANNE MORROW LINDBERGH
22 Jun 1906  11h15m 0s EST
ENGLEWOOD, NJ
KOCH  40N54  73W58

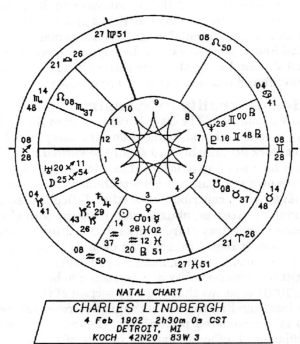

NATAL CHART
CHARLES LINDBERGH
4 Feb 1902  2h30m 0s CST
DETROIT, MI
KOCH  42N20  83W 3

was nearly three times as large in heterosexual men than in homosexual men or heterosexual women.

This study fits emerging theories that sexual orientation is determined as much by nature as nurture. In 1978 experiments made on male primates found that lesions in the hypothalamus left the monkeys' sex drive vigorous, but made them lose interest in females. At the University of California, Los Angeles, neuro-endocrinologist Roger Gorski is learning that male rats need plenty of testosterone early in life; if they do not receive it, they will exhibit behavior typical of the female rat. By injecting these males with testosterone, they can be returned to maleness, but only if done during the first five days of life.

Most experts at this point seem to feel that sexual preference has biological as well as psychological causes. They also explain that biological changes occur throughout life, as a consequence of experience.

What does all this have to do with astrology? We're right back to what we said a few years ago; you cannot know about sexual preference. Don't guess; ask your client!

One thing is sure; astrologically, sexual attraction shows up exactly the same way whether it is woman to man, man to woman, woman to woman or man to man. We have a fairly large homosexual clientele, and have found that all the different modes described previously, work in those charts, including passing fancies versus long-lasting commitments.

## LESSON 12

# DIFFERENT KINDS
# OF RELATIONSHIPS

Thus far, we have mostly given examples of partnership and parental relationships in describing needs and attractions and have used pair charts to illustrate configurations, aspects and lacks to mention a few. Now we would like to explore some other kinds of relationships to show you how to blend charts of friends or business partners; how relationships work between grandparent and grandchild, mother/son, father/daughter and vice versa.

## Working Partners

When comparing charts of people who work together, it is wise to look at the 6th house in each chart, to see if their habit patterns and work ethics are compatible. The movie dance duo, Ginger Rogers and Fred Astaire took the world by storm with their intricate steps and fascinating flair, performing everything from the Carioca to the Piccolino. Theirs was an enduring work relationship where according to the press and biographical material, no romance ever blossomed.

Neither Fred or Ginger foresaw that they would score such a hit with their first film "Flying Down to Rio" that would turn a run-of-the-mill ingenue comedienne and a thirtyish, none-too-handsome stage performer into the most popular and stylish dance team ever to grace the screen.

Astaire had Taurus on the 6th house cusp with the ruler, Venus in Aries in the 4th, suggesting dedication to perfection (Taurus on the 6th) and a need to be adventurous and pioneering in his approach to work (Venus in Aries). With both the Sun and Moon in the 6th, work

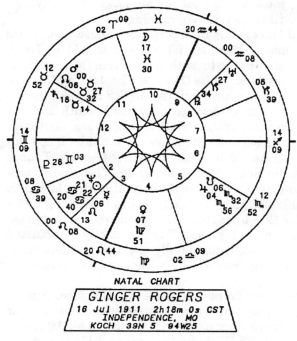

NATAL CHART

GINGER ROGERS
16 Jul 1911   2h18m 0s CST
INDEPENDENCE, MO
KOCH   39N 5   94W25

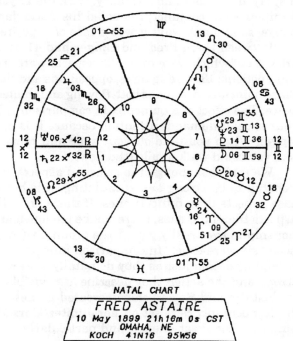

NATAL CHART

FRED ASTAIRE
10 May 1899 21h18m 0s CST
OMAHA, NE
KOCH   41N16   95W56

that satisfied him was a must and he put his all into it, not only performing, but much of the time also choreographing.

Rogers has Pluto and Mars ruling her Scorpio 6th house cusp. Pluto is in Gemini in her 1st house; Mars is in Taurus in the 11th. These placements indicate great dedication to method and order (Mars in Taurus), a personal interest in work habits (Pluto in the 1st), agility and flexibility in motion (Pluto in Gemini) and the ability to make money (Mars in the 11th— money from career) from her good health and mobility. You can see the similarity of their work approach and attitudes.

Comparing other factors between them, we note that he has a 6th house Sun in Taurus sextile her 10th house Moon in Pisces. His Taurus Sun also sextiles her Cancer Sun, which is in her 2nd (Taurus) house— a sign/house affinity. One of the reasons their relationship lasted so long, (ten movies from 1933 to 1950) is partly due to the strong interchart Saturn aspects. Her 12th house (dancing) Saturn (form and discipline) conjuncted his Sun, while his rising Saturn exactly quincunxed her Sun and opposed her Pluto. Undoubtedly she had to make some adjustments in the relationship, possibly by becoming even more disciplined in her work.

Pluto rising suggests a need for power, while the trine from Jupiter in Scorpio in the 5th not only indicates her creative ability, but also her sexy appearance. Astaire on the other hand, with Saturn in his 1st house displayed elegance and formality. With the 12 year age difference, their Jupiters were conjunct; his ruled his Ascendant; hers ruled her 7th house, so in many ways it was a case of opposites attracting.

Between them Fred and Ginger had 41 aspects (using a 5 degree orb), six of which were exact. 23 aspects were trines, sextiles and easy conjunctions; 18 were squares, oppositions and challenging conjunctions. Since quincunxes count as both flowing and challenging, they are counted twice. The effect of a quincunx in comparison is like having a pebble in your shoe; it demands attention because it is uncomfortable (the challenge). When you take off your shoe and remove the pebble, you feel like you could walk a mile (the flow).

We find that though the stressful aspects are necessary for a relationship to be strong and stimulating, it is better to have a few more easy aspects than difficult ones. If there are a third more challenging aspects than mild ones, there can be too much antagonism for the relationship to ever really get off the ground. Of Astaire's and Rogers' aspects, six were exact. In comparison interpretation exact aspects need careful attention just as they do natally, because the significance is so strong and the action they describe is so visible.

Astaire and Rogers charts created no new configurations, but his Jupiter conjunct hers set off her Jupiter/Mars/Mercury T-square, tapping into her great energy, and particularly important, provided him with the squares he lacked natally. He spurred her to great efforts in her work (his Pluto exactly conjunct her Ascendant) and she returned the favor (her Midheaven exactly square his Sun). Since dancing brought them into the limelight, it can be symbolized by the strong 12th house/ Neptune/Pisces factor. He has Neptune angular; hers conjuncts her Sun; Pluto, his 12th house ruler conjuncts his Descendant. Her Venus is angular and rules her 12th, she also has Saturn there and her Moon is in the 10th house in Pisces.

When Rogers and Astaire parted company and went on to separate, (and successful) individual careers, Ginger told an English magazine writer, "I love Fred so, and I mean that in the nicest, warmest way. I have such an affection for him artistically. I think that experience with Fred was a divine blessing. It blessed me, I know. And I don't think blessings are one-sided. We had our differences—what good artistic marriage doesn't?—but they were unimportant."

Several writers of the era commented that Ginger was fiercely competitive, while Fred was deemed to be a perfectionist. He recognized the perfectionist streak in her (Pluto ruling the 6th, Saturn sextile the Sun) and described her as "the hardest-working gal I ever knew." Together, they had it all. As Katharine Hepburn once said, "She gave him sex and he gave her class."

## Mother/Son Relationship

French painter Suzanne Valadon enjoyed a successful career as an acrobat and artist's model. Encouraged by some of the artists she posed for, including Toulouse-Lautrec, Renoir and Degas, she started to draw and paint. Her style was strongly linear and objective and her subject matter mostly nudes. Valadon became pregnant at age 18. Her son Maurice Utrillo was later adopted by his father, a writer also named Maurice Utrillo, but his parents never married. As Utrillo grew up, he developed a severe drinking problem and his mother thought to divert him by teaching him to paint. Pursuing this therapeutic distraction between sanitarium confinements, he achieved even more success in this field than Suzanne and is best known for his paintings of cathedrals, villages and Parisian street scenes. His paintings of Montmarte contributed to its eventual recognition and fame. Other than his drinking bouts, his life was outwardly uneventful—long periods of residence in Paris interrupted by short trips to the provinces in search of material.

In comparing the charts of mother and child, you must look to the 5th house in the mother's chart to describe her feelings for, and attitude to her offspring and how she will deal with him. When looking for the mother in a child's chart, start with the 4th house and the Moon. Consider all of the other comparison devices we suggested earlier...affinities, aspects between the charts, any configurations that are formed and where each one's planets fall in the other's chart.

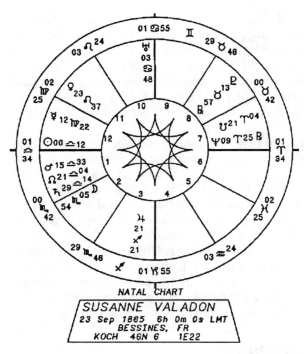

NATAL CHART

SUSANNE VALADON
23 Sep 1865   6h 0m 0s LMT
BESSINES, FR
KOCH  46N 6    1E22

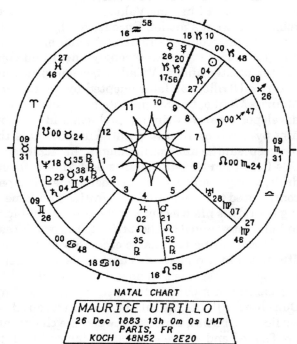

NATAL CHART

MAURICE UTRILLO
26 Dec 1883  13h 0m 0s LMT
PARIS, FR
KOCH  48N52    2E20

Valadon is a double Libra with the Moon in Scorpio in the 2nd house. Her 5th house is ruled by Uranus in the 10th conjunct the MC, indicating that her child would be unique and possibly well known. Uranus ruling the 5th can denote a child born out of wedlock, but further suggests one who is unusual or different in some way. Uranus squares her Sun and Ascendant; obviously he stirred up her life and forced her to grow up quickly, but with Saturn trine Uranus, she took her responsibility seriously and did her best for him.

Her nurturing abilities were intense. The Moon in Scorpio trines Uranus and conjuncts Saturn which rules her 4th house of caring and encouragement. This aspect also reflects her sense of responsibility toward her child.

Utrillo is a Capricorn with Taurus rising and the Moon in Sagittarius. The Moon rules his 4th (mother) as well as his 3rd (learning). It is not surprising that there was a very close bond between mother and child and that she was able to teach him her craft, with such astounding results. His 7th house Moon opposes Saturn and Pluto in the 1st, sextiles his 10th house Venus and Uranus in the 6th and trines Jupiter in the 4th. His love and admiration for his mother knew no bounds, and her involvement in his career is confirmed by these aspects. He viewed his mother as philosophical and independent (Jupiter in the 4th and Moon in Sagittarius), someone he could learn from and rely upon. The fact that Utrillo led an outwardly placid life is indicated by the emphasis of earth planets in his horoscope. This strong earth domination also reflected his tangible and concrete subject matter. Capricorn is on his MC; Mercury the ruler of both his 2nd and 6th houses is in Capricorn in the 10th. He has a grand earth trine from his 6th house of how he performs his work (Uranus) to his 10th of recognition and fame (Venus) to his 1st of self-projection (Pluto).

Both mother and son have Saturn in the 1st house; she has a Libra Sun and Ascendant, he has a 7th house Moon; they both have Moon/Pluto oppositions, though hers is a bit wide. These affinities mirror mutual accords, likes and dislikes and an innate understanding of each other. His Sun, Mercury and Venus in Capricorn all fall in her 4th house. His Capricorn Sun in her 4th house fills her Sun/Ascendant/Neptune/Uranus T-square and makes it a grand cross, fulfilling her 4th house needs. Is it any wonder that he lived most of his life with her? Her Sun and Ascendant in his 6th reinforces the similar talent and area of work that they shared.

## Father/Daughter Relationship

Fans of blues rocker Bonnie Raitt may not be aware that her father John Raitt is a famous veteran Broadway star who has appeared in many musicals including "Oklahoma" and who originated the charac-

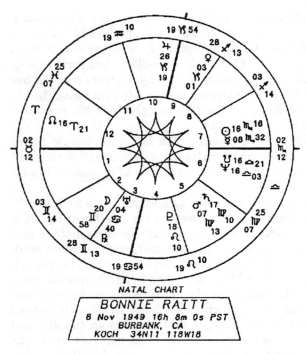

NATAL CHART

BONNIE RAITT
8 Nov 1949 16h 8m 0s PST
BURBANK, CA
KOCH   34N11 118W18

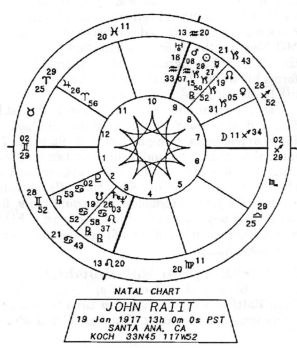

NATAL CHART

JOHN RAITT
19 Jan 1917 13h 0m 0s PST
SANTA ANA, CA
KOCH   33N45 117W52

ter of Billy Bigelow in "Carousel." Though he was on the road a great deal while Bonnie was growing up, they have a solid father/daughter relationship.

Affinities abound in a comparison of their charts. He has the Moon in the 7th; her Sun is there; her Ascendant ruler is in the 9th house as is his. She has an earth grand trine from Venus in the 9th to her Taurus Ascendant and Mars in the 5th. John's Venus conjuncts hers and reinforces this configuration which suggests amity and accord. He has a T-square from Sun/Mercury in the 9th opposing Saturn in the 3rd, all squaring Jupiter in the 11th. Bonnie's Jupiter conjuncts his planets in the 9th, reinforcing this configuration.

Her 10th house representing father is ruled by Saturn in her 5th; her Sun is in Scorpio in the 7th sextile Saturn and the MC. Pluto square her Sun leads to a T-square when we add John's 10th house Uranus falling into her 10th. Saturn squares the Moon and trines the MC. It is obvious that her father is very visible, not only in her view, but also publicly. The relationship between her parents may have seemed shaky to her as she was growing up (Moon square Saturn) and her parents did divorce and though he married someone else, they eventually remarried. The sextile between the Sun and Saturn suggests respect and admiration for her father. She stated that she and her two brothers felt that their father was "flexible, always understood his children and what they wanted to do." With Saturn in the 5th ruling her MC, it is not surprising that she followed in his talented footsteps.

How does John Raitt relate to his daughter? Mercury rules his 5th house of offspring and is caught up in his T-square, however it also trines his Ascendant; on some level he most likely sees her as an extension of himself. Mercury conjuncts his Sun, so though they may have had differences as well as disagreements, he feels close to her on a personal level. The opposition to Saturn mirrors the responsibility he feels for his daughter, as well as lack of understanding of her kind of music when she first started her career, but since her tremendous success, his pride in her accomplishments has replaced those feelings. Mercury square Jupiter reflects that his Quaker ways (nonsmoking, nondrinking) may have been strained to the limit by her drinking problems, but since she has been sober, their relationship has become even stronger than it was before.

## Grandparents/Grandchildren Relationship

In describing the relationship between grandparent and grandchild, be sure to check which house represents which grandparent in the child's chart. Refer to the Derivative House System presented on page 83. As an illustration we will use both a maternal and paternal grandfather. In the grandparent's chart, the child is portrayed by the 9th house (the 5th from the 5th of children).

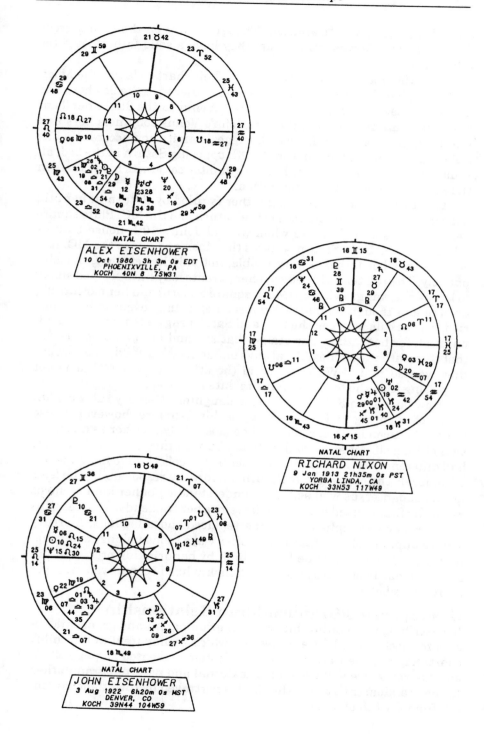

NATAL CHART
ALEX EISENHOWER
10 Oct 1980   3h 3m 0s EDT
PHOENIXVILLE, PA
KOCH 40N 8  75W31

NATAL CHART
RICHARD NIXON
9 Jan 1913 21h35m 0s PST
YORBA LINDA, CA
KOCH 33N53 117W49

NATAL CHART
JOHN EISENHOWER
3 Aug 1922  6h20m 0s MST
DENVER, CO
KOCH 39N44 104W59

Alex Richard Eisenhower is the son of Julie Nixon and David Eisenhower. His maternal grandfather is  ex-President Richard Nixon. His paternal grandfather is John Eisenhower, son of President Dwight Eisenhower. In viewing Alex's chart his maternal grandfather is signified by his 1st house (10th from the 4th), and his paternal grandfather by his 7th (10th from the 10th).

With Venus rising, it is obvious that his grandfather Nixon indulges him somewhat, but also expects him to be disciplined (Venus in Virgo). Alex has Leo rising, with the Sun in Libra square Nixon's Capricorn Sun, so while they may get along while he is a child, as he matures and develops opinions of his own, he may not always see eye to eye with his grandfather, yet Nixon's Sun falls in Alex's 5th house, so there is a lot of love between them. Alex's Sun is in the 2nd house, so his grandfather Nixon may be instrumental in influencing his values and image of self-worth. The potential for an inheritance is significant.

Alex's Sun trines his grandfather's Moon; his Uranus/MC is T-squared by Nixon's Moon while his Pluto is trined by Alex's Moon. Venus rules Nixon's 9th house, significator of grandchildren and is in Pisces in his 6th, square Saturn, so it is unlikely that he finds it important to instill discipline in the boy. Venus sextiles Mercury, Mars and Jupiter and trines Pluto, so his feelings toward his grandchildren are deep and compassionate, and in the privacy of his home (4th) he may find ways to communicate with them. Alex has no interplanetary oppositions, but grandpa brings his Saturn to oppose Alex's Mars/Uranus conjunction which though not easy to work with, will eventually help him to become aware of his goals and needs.

Alex's Sun in Libra rules his 1st house (maternal grandfather) and like a true Libran,  he will make an effort to get along with almost everyone, unless they try to control him (Sun conjunct Pluto). Venus in the 1st is charming and that charm, of course, will be evident in his relationship with his elders. With Venus widely square Mars, he will certainly stand up for his beliefs, but with Mars in the 4th sextile Jupiter and Saturn, he has respect for all family members, especially his elders. He has a Bundle chart occupying only four houses and Grandpa Nixon's planets fill five of his empty houses, suggesting Grandpa Nixon has the ability to broaden Alex's perspective. Together their planets form a grand earth trine from Nixon's Ascendant, to his Sun, to Alex's Midheaven, suggesting ease of relating and that his grandfather could influence his career plans.

What about Alex's relationship with his paternal grandfather, John Eisenhower? Having the same wheel immediately implies an affinity and comfort with each other; they tend to experience events in a like manner and Alex can profit from John's knowledge if they talk about viewpoints and expectations. You must look to his 7th house to see how he views this grandparent and what his expectations are of him. He has Aquarius on the cusp and Uranus in the 4th conjunct Mars, sextile Jupiter, opposed the Midheaven and square the Ascendant.

Obviously John Eisenhower is not the indulgent grandparent the 1st house describes. Alex more than likely relates to him on a friendly (Aquarius), but cautious level (Uranus in Scorpio with tension releasing aspects). However, he feels at home with him (4th house), but not always sure just what he can get away with.

Grandpa Eisenhower has Leo rising with his Sun in the 12th house, so he may be a bit reluctant to show his feelings, but his Sun trines Mars, ruler of his 9th house of grandchildren and Mars is in Sagittarius in the 4th. Obviously, this first grandson is the apple of his eye. Mars trines Neptune so he is willing to overlook any faults. Alex and his grandfather have a grand water trine from Alex's Mercury to John's Uranus and Pluto depicting their great mutual sensitivity. Grand water trines between charts often can intuit each other's moods and reactions.

The ties between their charts are many and varied. Both have Leo Ascendants, 4th house Mars's; Taurus Midheavens and 2nd house Saturns and Jupiters. Alex's Sun conjuncts John's Jupiter (he can learn from him); his Jupiter conjuncts John's Venus and his Neptune conjuncts his grandfather's Moon. Alex may choose to follow in John's footsteps as far as career is concerned since both have the MC ruler in Virgo in the 1st house. Their Mercuries square each other which can reveal stimulating conversation and discussion.

## Synastry by Progression

Have you ever met someone and immediately experienced a mutual attraction? This can happen with a lover, friend or business acquaintance. As time passes, the relationship intensifies, only to cool off and within a year or so, you find that you each are going your own way. What you both thought might be long-term love, friendship or whatever has faded away.

Often this phenomenon is the result of progressions, directions or it can be related to the transits of the outer planets. This may be a wonderful way to start a relationship if there are some natal contacts, but sometimes there is nothing truly compatible between two charts, yet you are drawn to another person and can find very little in the comparison to explain the intensity of your feelings for each other. Check to see if by progression or solar arc direction your Sun, Mars, Venus or Uranus is contacting the Ascendant, Sun, Moon, Venus or Mars of the other person. If there are one or more strong connections (conjunction, opposition or square), they are more than likely what is setting off the fireworks.

The progressed Moon may also be the trigger, but it only contacts another planet for a month to six weeks, just long enough for a hot and heavy romance, especially if it connects with the other person's Uranus, Mars or Venus.

The progressed or directed planet's significance can endure for a year to 18 months, and if at that time your progressed Moon is also hitting off the other person's chart, you can experience a very intriguing, but seldom long-lasting interlude.

A student once brought her and her husband's comparison chart to class because they were contemplating a divorce. It soon became apparent that there was very little compatibility between the charts and someone asked what had attracted them in the first place. She responded, "It was love at first sight; he intrigued me like no other man I had ever met. We became engaged on our second date and were married within six weeks of meeting." When questioned further by the class, she revealed that the marriage was pure bliss for about a year-and-a-half and then the roof caved in. He met someone else; so did she. They couldn't communicate with each other and both felt it was over. For financial reasons they held on for three more years which was why she brought the charts in. Could we see what happened?

Natally they had very few connections between their horoscopes...no Saturn aspects either way; no Sun/Moon/Ascendant affinity; no Venus/Mars. Their 2nd house rulers trined each other. After much discussion, one student suggested we look at the progressions for the marriage year. Her Sun and Moon natally were conjunct at 5 and 6 degrees of Scorpio. His Sun was a 0 degrees Sagittarius. The November they met, she was 24 years old and her Moon (by solar arc) had just conjuncted his Sun, to be followed a year later by her Sun. His natal Mars was in Libra and the year they met, it had progressed to conjunct her Scorpio Sun. Is there any question that the attraction was mainly physical? There were no strong Mercury contacts, either natally or by progression, but each had the progressed Moon moving through the other's 8th house.

Both had strong 2nd/8th house placements natally and they had tried to make a go of the partnership for financial as well as sexual reasons. After she viewed the charts and realized from the class discussion, just how challenging their relationship was, she persuaded him to go with her for counseling. They hung on to the marriage for two more years, finally divorced after wrangling over the financial settlement and each remarried. They had never had children.

This illustration is not intended to discourage marriage when and if there are challenging and stressful connections between the charts. Our intention is to point out that you should not mistake any and all attractions shown by passing aspects for the real thing. If the rules we have presented for long-lasting commitment are not present, caution is suggested.

A note about friendships that come and go. The same principles apply. If progressions and transits are all you have going in any relationship, be prepared to "seize the moment" and when the attraction has gone, try not to cling to the relationship.

## Finding Other People in Your Chart

Just a reminder that you can find out how you relate to anyone, by following the Derivative House System on page 83. For instance, your aunts and uncles on your father's side of the family are discovered in your 12th house (3rd from the 10th), so their children, your cousins are found in the 5th from the 12th or the 4th house. After you use this system a few times, you will find it gets easier to calculate. Be sure to start your count in the house where you begin, i.e., to find your cousins in the above example count the 12th house as number 1 and proceed from there.

Happy people hunting!

# PART THREE: THE COMPOSITE CHART
## LESSON 13

# THE MATH

The idea of **composite charts** is a rather recent one; it originated in Germany right after World War I and was first successfully used by Dr. Walter Koch of *Table of Houses* fame. By the 60s, like any idea whose time has come, the application of it spread like wildfire and composite charts are now widely used and taught all over the world.

These charts are based on the astrological concept of midpoints. Many astrologers consider midpoints an important factor in interpreting natal charts. For those not familiar with midpoints, Reinhold Ebertin's excellent book The *Combination of Stellar Influences* explains the subject in great detail, as does Michael Munkasey's *Midpoints* book.

## Math Instructions for Composite Chart

To mathematically figure midpoints, use the simple principle of adding and then dividing in half. For example:

Your Sun is at 8 Libra 04; another's Sun is at 13 Scorpio 48.

|      |      |      |                                            |
|------|------|------|--------------------------------------------|
| 6s   | 08°  | 04'  |                                            |
| +7s  | 13°  | 48'  |                                            |
| 13s  | 21°  | 52'  | + 2 = 6s carry 1 sign or 30 degrees        |
|      | 51°  | 52'  | + 2 = 25° carry 1 degree or 60 minutes     |
|      |      | 112' | + 2 = 56' or 25 Libra 56'                   |

When calculating midpoints for composite charts, always use the closest midpoint between the two zodiacal signs in question. Obviously late Libra is the closest point between early Libra and Scorpio, but here is another example:

Your Moon at 4 Pisces 16' and another's Moon at 20 Taurus 24'. By simply doing the math as just shown, the resulting sign will be Libra, yet the closest midpoint is Aries.

```
 11s   04°  16'
+01s   20°  24'
─────────────────
 12s   24°  40'  ÷  2  =  6s 12° 20' or 12 Libra 20'
```

When you look at an actual horoscope, you will note that the closest and real midpoint between Pisces and Taurus is the other side of the pole...Aries.

In the composite chart two horoscopes are combined and become one. The safest way to calculate the combined cusps is to start with the Midheaven. Be sure to be logical and continue the sequence you have started. If the closest midpoint between the Midheavens of two charts is Gemini, your 11th house should be Cancer, or Leo if there is an interception; it should not be Capricorn or Aquarius, even if that is the closer midpoint. In other words, use the MC as a guideline for the rest of the house cusps.

After you have calculated the house cusps, figure the planets, beginning with the Sun, then Mercury and Venus. Remember that Mercury cannot be more than 28 degrees distant from the Sun, and Venus no more than 46 degrees away in the natal chart. Here again you must use logic rather than the closest midpoint and be guided by the zodiac sign of the Sun. Then calculate the seven remaining planets and the Nodes.

There is an alternate way to figure the house cusps. Rob Hand calculates the combined Midheavens, and then, using the latitude where the people reside, takes the rest of the cusps from the Table of Houses, just as you would in any natal chart calculation. We do not think this method is viable, since it only works if the people in question live in the same place. Business partners could operate from different locations; which latitude do you then choose? But we do recommend Hand's excellent book *Planets in Composite* for additional learning.

After placing the combined planets in the wheel, the composite chart mirrors the picture of the relationship, whether commitment, marriage, partnership or family. It is an excellent method to determine the compatibility of two or three or ten people united as one.

Strange as it may seem, composite charts also work well for groups of people...an entire family, a business partnership of several members or any other combination of individuals. Be sure to remember that however many charts you add together, you must divide by that same amount. Five partners, add all five charts and then divide the total by five.

Some students ask if the artificial result of midpoints between two or more charts really helps to explain how people relate when brought together. The answer is a resounding **yes**! We would not dream of advising a client on any type of relationship, especially commitment or marriage without erecting a composite chart. We have found that when people are in specific situations with other people, they behave differently than when functioning on their own as individuals.

Surely you have observed a husband and wife at a party when they sit together at a table, as opposed to being seated at different tables. In the first instance, they play off each other; one might shine, the other sit quietly by; one tells the jokes, the other winces at hearing the same joke week after week, or laughs loudest to show support. When sitting at separate tables, each can be her/his individualistic self. That is what composite charts are all about . . . the new personality that you develop when involved with another.

The same, of course, applies to a family. Where in family situations, each member plays a role as parent, mother, father, child, son or daughter; on their own, each can be who they really are. Interpretation of the composite chart is similar to any natal horoscope, except that this is a union of two (or more) people. Therefore you need to use a bit of common sense in your analysis. The 6th house of health, for example, does not indicate one or the other's physical health, but rather the health of the relationship, as well as duties, habit patterns and other 6th house matters.

Before you can interpret a composite chart, it is important to know how to construct it. If you have a computer that calculates composites, that's fine, but be sure that it uses the system that calculates the chart starting with the closest midpoint of the combined Midheavens and does midpoints for each of the other cusps, rather than taking them from the *Table of Houses*. Also be sure that if the Sun is in Taurus, Mercury and Venus should be within 28 and 46 degrees respectively. Some computer programs reverse the positions of these planets.

For ease of learning, we show you the mathematics of combining the charts of Ernest and Mary Welsh Hemingway.

## Math Example

Here is an example of how to set up a composite chart, using the charts of Ernest and Mary Welsh Hemingway:

| | | |
|---|---|---|
| 1. Add the two MCs: | 8s 24° 16' | Mary |
| | + 2s 03° 22' | Ernest |
| Divide by 2: | 10s 27° 38' | |
| | 5s 13° 49' | = 13 Virgo 49 |

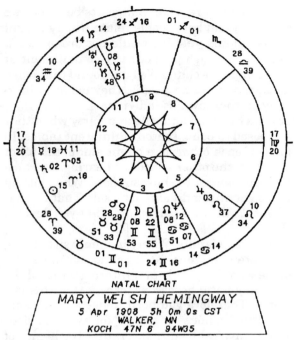

NATAL CHART

MARY WELSH HEMINGWAY
5 Apr 1908   5h 0m 0s CST
WALKER, MN
KOCH   47N 6   94W35

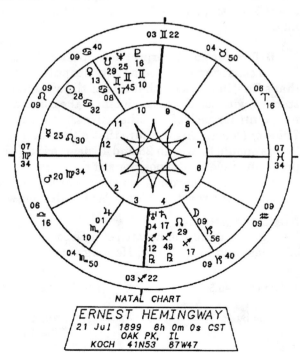

NATAL CHART

ERNEST HEMINGWAY
21 Jul 1899   8h 0m 0s CST
OAK PK, IL
KOCH   41N53   87W47

but the closest midpoint between 24 Sagittarius and 3 Gemini is not Virgo but Pisces; therefore the composite MC is 13 Pisces 49.

2. Add the two 11th house cusps:

|  | | 9s 14° 14' | Mary |
|---|---|---|---|
|  | + | 3s 09° 40' | Ernest |
| Divide by 2: |  | 12s 23° 54' |  |
|  |  | 6s 11° 57' | = 11 Libra 57 |

If the MC is Pisces, obviously the 11th house cusp has to be Aries, not Libra. The 11th cusp is 11 Aries 57.

3. Continue the same method for the next 4 houses until you have the entire wheel.

5. Now combine the 2 Suns:

|  | | 0s 15° 16' | Mary |
|---|---|---|---|
|  | + | 3s 28° 32' | Ernest |
| Divide by 2: |  | 3s 43° 48' |  |
|  |  | 1s 36° 54' | or 2s 06 54' |

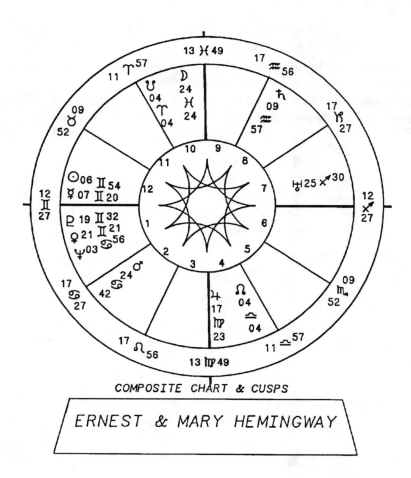

COMPOSITE CHART & CUSPS

ERNEST & MARY HEMINGWAY

6 Gemini 54 which is also the closest midpoint between their Aries and Cancer Suns. Do not worry about dividing uneven minutes; you can round those up or down, whichever you prefer.

5. Combine the 2 Mercuries:

|  | | | |
|---|---|---|---|
|  | 11s | 19° | 11' | Mary |
| + | 4s | 25° | 30' | Ernest |
| Divide | 15s | 44° | 41' | |
|  | 7s | 37° | 20' | |
| or | 8s | 07° | 20' | = 7 Sagittarius 20. |

The closest midpoint between Pisces and Leo is Gemini, therefore composite Mercury is 7 Gemini 20. But even if the closest midpoint were Sagittarius, with the Sun in Gemini, Mercury cannot oppose it, thus it has to be in Gemini.

6. Continue with Venus and use the same logic as you did with Mercury.

7. Now add the two Moons together:

|  | | | |
|---|---|---|---|
|  | 2s | 08° | 53' | Mary |
| + | 9s | 09° | 56' | Ernest |
| Divide by 2: | 11s | 17° | 109' | |
| or | 5s | 24° | 24' | |

The closest midpoint between Capricorn and Gemini is Pisces, therefore the composite Moon is 24 Pisces 24.

8. Continue with the remaining planets and nodes and check your math with the Hemingway composite chart on page 155.

9. For additional information, after you have interpreted this composite chart, you may wish to place both Ernest's and Mary's natal planets around it. This will show you how each one is interacting with the composite.

# HOUSES IN THE COMPOSITE CHART

In the composite chart when you describe the new entity formed by combining two charts, you must analyze by looking for keywords that can apply to two, not just one, persons. When examining the Sun, for example, you should not talk about the heart, upper back or spleen, all anatomical depictions of the Sun astrologically speaking. You should use such illustrations as sense of identity, the wish to shine, masculine principle, authority or title. Once you understand the theory, you won't have any problems. To help you, here are some useful interpretations of the composite houses and planets.

## The 1st House

The 1st house of the composite chart shows the inner state of your partnership, as well as the persona you, as a couple, want to show the world. Of course, any planets in this house amplify the description of how the couple sees and feels the relationship as a unit. You must remember that this chart unites the individual charts and creates a new entity, that of the two (or three, or more) people acting as one.

Most significant is the sign on the Ascendant and the position of its ruler. Where this planet is located and how it is aspected can provide additional clues as to what drew you together. If the sign is Capricorn, for example, the couple more than likely view the relationship as a serious one, perhaps devoted to business or social activity, definitely with a need to achieve some sort of success or recognition. Since Capricorn is the natural sign of the 10th house, all 10th house as well as Capricorn keywords apply. If Saturn is in the 4th house, home, family, real estate and building a firm foundation would be significant in the way they view their affiliation.

In the composite chart of Benito Mussolini and his wife Rachele Sagittarius rises with Jupiter in the 5th house.

Obviously religion, a similar philosophy of life, love, and children were the main focus of their union. Technically Jupiter is unaspected, which suggests that they handled their lives according to their own rules. Despite many difficulties their marriage lasted a lifetime and with the 5th house placement of Jupiter in Aries, the romantic element appears to have been fiery, to say the least.

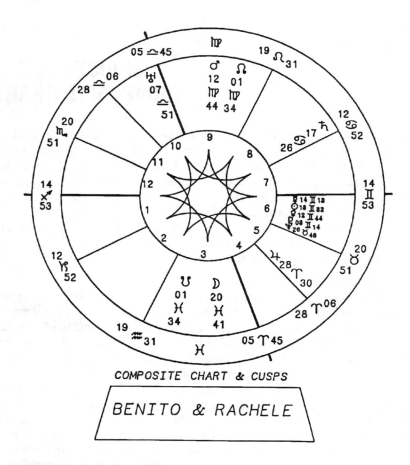

COMPOSITE CHART & CUSPS

BENITO & RACHELE

## The 2nd House

The 2nd house shows your shared values, your assets, as well as your financial outlook and how you will mutually handle your money. It also (with the 4th house) describes your security needs. If Mars rules this area of the composite chart and is in the 8th house with tension producing aspects, you might wish to carefully discuss which one of you is going to handle the budget or if you might benefit from outside help in this area and how you will reach major decisions on purchasing and saving. Even if Mars has only trines and sextiles, you both may be quite indulgent of each other and your spending could get out of hand. Of course, much depends upon other factors in the composite chart.

Martin Luther and Coretta King have Leo on the 2nd house cusp in their composite chart with the Sun in Pisces in the 8th and Neptune in Leo in the 2nd.

Their strong religious values are sharply mirrored by these placements. Neptune trines Venus in the 10th, while the Sun which con-

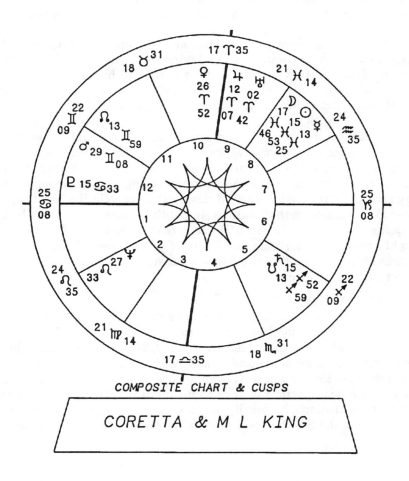

COMPOSITE CHART & CUSPS

CORETTA & M L KING

juncts the Moon and Mercury squares Saturn in the 5th. Sincere and dedicated, they attracted a large following because the values they stood for appealed to the public and their patriotic (new Moon) stance was admired as pioneering and acceptable to many. Neptune in the 2nd natally, or in the composite, is often referred to as "leaky pockets" because of too much idealism and an unrealistic outlook toward finances, so money just trickles away.

## The 3rd House

This house has to do with communication and the immediate environment and as such is a barometer of how you will interrelate on an everyday as well as conversational level. It can describe your day-to-day relationship, whether you and your partner see eye-to-eye on mundane situations and if you have a good understanding of each other. It also denotes your mutual family relationships and how you both feel about them. If Mars is there it is reasonable to expect that you will put a lot of energy into neighborhood activity as well as communicating your ideas to each other.

The van Gogh brothers, Vincent and Theodor had Cancer on the cusp of the 3rd house and we can imagine that much of their conversation involved creativity with the Moon in the 5th house.

Whether they always understood each other is questionable with the Moon quincunx Mercury, Uranus and Neptune and opposed to their Mars.

In their composite chart Ted Turner and Jane Fonda have Pisces on the 3rd house cusp with Neptune, the ruler in the 9th conjunct the Moon and square Mars. Saturn is in the 3rd house. Obviously their conversations can range far and wide embracing subjects from philosophy and travel to religion and politics. With Saturn in the 3rd, they are most likely serious in their outlook, but with Neptune ruling this house, they can also be quite fanciful. The square of Neptune to Mars suggests mighty arguments and the possibility of pitched verbal battles. Their communication capabilities are awesome and we doubt they ever run out of subjects to discuss.

## The 4th House

Obviously the 4th house refers to your home and surroundings, the establishment of your joint estate, but more importantly it indicates the roots of the relationship and how it will end. With Leo here you will, no doubt, want a large home and family, with much light, laughter and fun. Libra on this house in the composite chart suggests that social activity will be important in your home and it may be the scene of parties and celebrations. Naturally, much will depend upon the placement of the rulers, the Sun in the first instance and Venus in the latter.

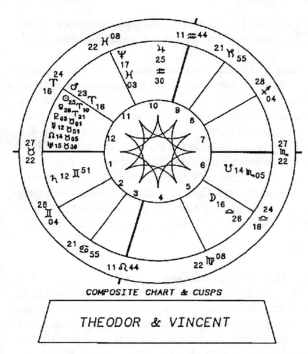

COMPOSITE CHART & CUSPS

THEODOR & VINCENT

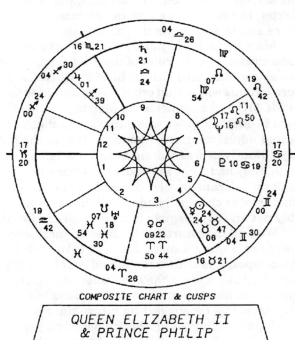

COMPOSITE CHART & CUSPS

QUEEN ELIZABETH II
& PRINCE PHILIP

Queen Elizabeth and Prince Philip have Taurus on the 4th house cusp with the Sun and Mercury there in Taurus suggesting a sumptuous home.

Venus is in Aries in their 3rd house, so conversation and discussion play an important role as does an occasional disagreement over daily affairs (Venus squares Pluto in the 6th) or perhaps travel or philosophical issues (Venus also rules the 9th). Venus's trine to Neptune in the 7th presents a beautiful picture to others and with the Sun in the 4th house, you know that their home is the heart of their relationship. Their philosophical differences are reinforced by the Sun's opposition to Jupiter and its as well as Mercury's quincunx to Saturn in the 9th house. There is a solidity to Taurus on the 4th that promises a secure and long lasting relationship; so does their ability to understand each other and present a united front with Mercury in Taurus in the 4th trine the Ascendant.

## The 5th House

Besides indicating the children of your relationship, the 5th house also depicts the fun things you do together as well as shared creativity. It shows your mutual enjoyment and your romantic feelings for each other. If the composite chart is one of a married couple, aspects (by solar arc direction) to the ruler of, or planets in the 5th can give timing for the arrival of children. In the composite chart of Jimmy and Rosalynn Carter, the 5th house leaps into prominence. Jupiter and the Moon are there and Uranus rules this house.

Married in 1946, Rosalynn gave birth to Jack in 1947 when Neptune quincunxed the ruler of the 5th house. Composite Jupiter, by solar arc also quincunxed Venus. In 1950 when their second son, Chip, was born Uranus was within orb of an opposition to the Ascendant, the square to the MC and a quincunx to Mercury. When their third son, Jeff was born in 1952, Jupiter was quincunx to Pluto. Obviously each birth required adjustment and reorganization of the partnership. After three boys, Rosalynn was willing to call it a family, but 13 years after Jeff's birth, they had Amy, the daughter Jimmy had yearned for. At that time composite Uranus, ruler of the 5th house squared Pluto in the 10th (their status changed) and the 5th house Moon opposed Mercury, probably not an easy pregnancy for 40 year-old Rosalynn.

We find that starting the directed measurements at the date of the marriage is quite a successful way to move this type of chart ahead. If the composite is not for a married couple, begin any measurements to significant events for the time when the relationship first started. We would also like to point out that transits to the composite chart can be very revealing for suggesting future timing.

Jupiter ruling (or in) the 5th house suggests that you may choose to have a large family, while Capricorn on the cusp often shoulders the responsibility for other's children. We have a client and her husband who have Capricorn on the 5th house in their composite with Saturn in the 5th house opposing a Cancer Moon in the 11th and they own and operate a very successful preschool.

Often with the emphasis in this house, you may both be creative or involved in sports or risk taking of some sort such as investing in a race track.

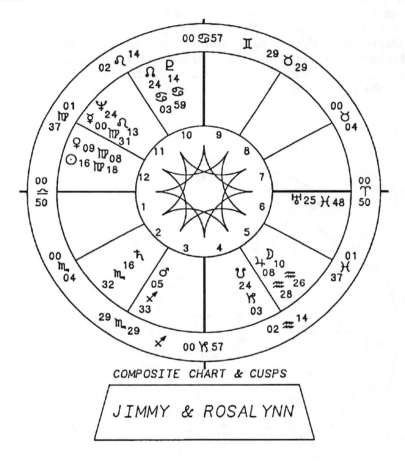

COMPOSITE CHART & CUSPS

JIMMY & ROSALYNN

## The 6th House
Sixth house placements are ideal for the couple who work together, but this area of the composite chart also reveals your habit patterns and how you can expect to relate to each other when it comes to things like who will lock up and turn off the lights, who puts the cap back on the toothpaste, and who will cook or who will clean up. The sign on the cusp

will give a clue. If it is a dual sign (Gemini, Sagittarius or Pisces), often you will share and share alike with everyday chores. Taurus or Scorpio here implies a deliberateness or intensity toward everyday living which may lead to locking horns occasionally, but you most likely agree that organization is paramount. Virgo denotes a certain amount of criticism in day-to-day affairs or an ability to work out the necessary details. Air signs (Gemini, Libra, Aquarius) often spend a great deal of time discussing daily routines and whose turn it is to take care of correspondence (Gemini), social activity (Libra), or group involvement (Aquarius). Capricorn on the 6th may point out an area where control issues need to be resolved, especially those pertaining to business affairs, while Cancer can mirror similar issues concerning the home. With Aries or Leo on the cusp or Mars in the 6th, you may argue about things like

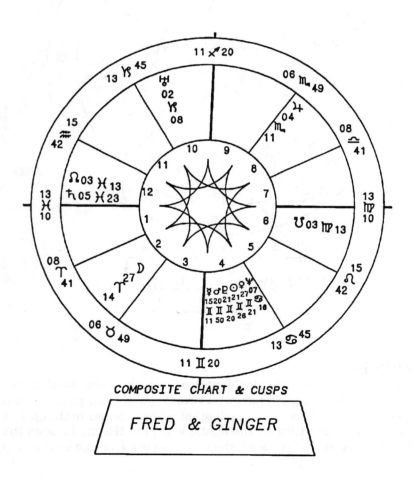

COMPOSITE CHART & CUSPS

FRED & GINGER

this. With Sagittarius there you may put tasks off until you both have to pitch in and help each other. Some astrologers refer to this area as the health of the relationship, but we feel this defies definition.

Ginger Rogers and Fred Astaire have the Sun in the 4th house ruling the 6th of their composite chart.

They enjoyed showing each other off with their dazzling choreography and most likely felt quite at home with each other. Their Sun is in a huge stellium with Mercury, Mars, Pluto and Venus, all in Gemini. No wonder they moved so gracefully together. The South Node is also in the 6th, so working together was something they just naturally found easy.

Jeff and Beau Bridges, who performed so well together in *The Fabulous Baker Boys*, have Jupiter in the 6th house and the ruler, Neptune in the 12th of movies and performing, while the Brownings have the Sun, Mercury and Mars in the 6th house.

## The 7th House

This area of the composite chart reflects how friends, relations and others view you. Here is the picture you present to, or how you function as a unit toward, the world (along with the 10th house) and the sign on the cusp is the indicator of your outer behavior. The common purpose of your relationship is also explained in this house. If it is **Aries** others may view you as an assertive couple, ready to take on the challenges of the world. **Taurus**, on the other hand, comes across as a very stable, productive duo who gives attention to detail and may appear prosperous. If you have **Gemini** on the 7th cusp, others see you as very distinct individuals, each sometimes moving in different directions within the relationship.

With **Cancer** here, the world may view your relationship as devoted and family oriented; often very publicly visible, possibly because you, as a couple, are involved in politics. Joanne Woodward and Paul Newman have Cancer here and they are both very visible, not only in their performing careers, but also through the causes she supports and he with his vending businesses. Pluto, the planet that describes their unconscious need for each other is in the 7th house...a very intense bond. Ted Turner and Jane Fonda also have Cancer on the 7th cusp in their composite and they also are very visible, cheering at ballgames, traveling all over the world together, and getting their pictures in the tabloids.

The composite chart of Claretta Petacci and Benito Mussolini has Leo on the 7th house cusp and their relationship was undoubtedly lively, exciting and carried off with a lot of flair. At least this is how others perceived them.

With **Leo** here, you tend to exude warmth and leadership and others often follow your social or business lead, depending of course upon where your Sun is. (All of the foregoing descriptions are dependent on the placement of the sign ruler.) With **Virgo** here the public may view you as an organized, studious, even analytical, couple. Together you give great attention to detail and are somewhat contained, modest and staid, unless the ruler, Mercury is in Aquarius, Leo or Sagittarius.

**Libra** on the 7th house can indicate that as a couple you are social, seek balanced behavior in others and like to maintain the status quo. On the other hand you may appear quite combative, always on the alert for a slight or excuse for a discussion or argument, or in extreme cases a war. The composite chart of World War II antagonists, General George Patton and Field Marshal Erwin Rommel*, has tactical Libra here with Venus ruling it in the 9th conjunct Jupiter, square Mars in the 6th and the Moon in the 12th. This well illustrates their relationship as it ap-

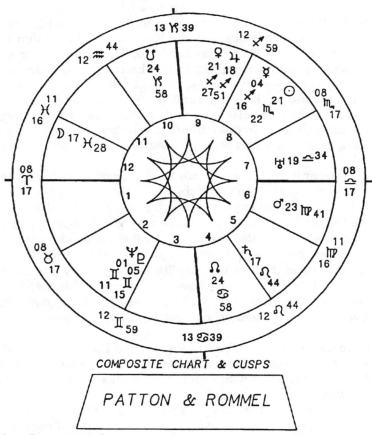

COMPOSITE CHART & CUSPS

PATTON & ROMMEL

* See chart data in Appendix.

peared to the public...bellicose, detailed (Mars in Virgo), far-reaching (Venus in Sagittarius), idealistic (Jupiter in Sagittarius) and manipulative (Moon in the 12th). Both Generals viewed war as a strategic game (Uranus in the 7th), rather than thinking of it as a bloody battle. These wartime adversaries, though they respected each other, were locked in an untenable, antagonistic relationship.

With **Scorpio** on the 7th house others view you as reserved, private and at times exuding great sexuality. There is an intensity to your relationship that may overwhelm people, but when they get to know you they may find that you are not so much overwhelming as you are strongly opinionated and very sure of yourselves. We have as clients two businessmen who are extremely successful in the real estate field. They are brokers who work as a team developing and selling large commercial ventures. Their rise in the field has been meteoric and we attribute that in part to their composite chart which has Taurus rising, Scorpio on the 7th cusp and Venus, Mars and Jupiter conjunct in the 10th in Aquarius. Though they can be intimidating at first meeting, they are also quite charming and such innovators and so sure of themselves that their buyers and sellers are more than willing to trust their judgment.

With **Sagittarius** on the 7th cusp in your composite chart other people view both of you as broad-minded, philosophical and open to new ideas. Friendly, optimistic and fun to be with in social situations, you are usually accepted by others at face value. **Capricorn** here may be viewed as responsible, dependable and businesslike. People are attracted to you because of the sense of security and success you project. If you have **Aquarius** on the 7th house cusp, others are drawn to you because of your willingness to try new things, to embrace unusual concepts, to organize groups and your innate friendliness to all the people with whom you come into contact. With **Pisces** here you may seem sympathetic, gentle and easily swayed to some, confused, empathetic and indefinite to others. Everything depends on Neptune's placement in the composite.

## The 8th House

Besides representing your sexual interaction, needs and habits, the 8th house also shows the mutual support you provide for each other. Situations and events that you do not find easy to discuss with each other are hidden here. This is another of the financial houses and your joint holdings and financial matters outside the relationship show up in this house as well as the 2nd. The 8th house also denotes possible transformation through each other, but be careful not to overemphasize that facet. Real transformation takes a long time and will not affect short-term unions.

Clara Schumann and Johannes Brahms had Capricorn on the 8th house cusp with both Neptune and Uranus in Capricorn in the 8th.

The ruler, Saturn, was in intellectual **Gemini** in the 1st house quincunx their 8th house Uranus. Theirs was truly a romantic, ethereal (Neptune), unusual (Uranus), yet practical and businesslike (Capricorn) alliance; very personal (ruler in the 1st) and imbued with problems to overcome (Saturn quincunx Uranus).

Cher and Sonny Bono had a very active 8th house in their composite chart with the Sun, Mercury and North Node in Aries there. Obviously, their mutual talent earned them money as well as recognition and their humor was often tinged with 8th house/Scorpio nuances.

With **Taurus** here you both enjoy comfort, touching, patting and hugging and this is a very significant part of your lovemaking. **Virgo** and **Capricorn** both display a surprisingly earthy attitude toward sex, but the touch sense is not quite as pronounced as with Taurus; **Virgo**

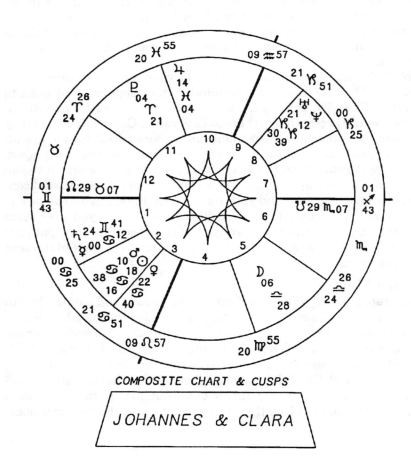

COMPOSITE CHART & CUSPS

JOHANNES & CLARA

often being more detail and cleanliness oriented while **Capricorn** tends to be lusty, with definite ideas of when and where to indulge. Venturesome, **Aquarius** is willing to experiment with what others would consider unique and outré, while **Pisces** takes a romantic, often dreamy approach to sex. **Libra** also opts for romance, but likes to create a beautiful atmosphere. **Cancer** suggests that you both nurture each other, while with **Leo** here, your sexual interaction may verge on the dramatic. **Aries** or **Sagittarius** suggests that each partner needs room to be independent, while **Scorpio** intensifies the sexual drive.

## The 9th House

The 9th house, besides illustrating your religious and cultural attitudes, your travel potential and interest in ethics, it also depicts in-laws on both sides and how you mutually relate to them. Shared education concerns often play a large role. Receptive (water and earth) signs here

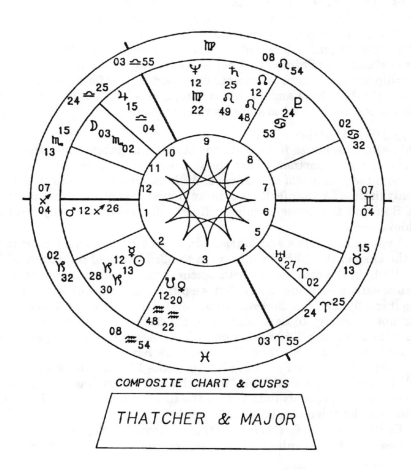

COMPOSITE CHART & CUSPS

THATCHER & MAJOR

suggest harmonious action; fire signs may imply some strife in this area; air signs certainly indicate much intercommunication in all 9th house areas. All of this, of course, is modified by the placements of the ruler of the sign on the cusp, as well as any planets in this house.

Britain's ex-Prime Minister Margaret Thatcher* and current Prime Minister John Major*, her former protege, share a most interesting composite chart. (See page 169.)

Creative Neptune, solid Saturn and the North Node all occupy the 9th house and the Sun which rules it is in the 2nd. Saturn and the Sun are in mutual reception suggesting that they share similar views and outlook on values (2nd) and political ethics (9th). Neptune is intercepted in the 9th and rules the interception in the 3rd; it squares Mars in the 1st and trines the 2nd house Sun and Mercury, so though they may not always agree, they do see eye-to-eye on important issues and can easily express their opinions. (Note: John Major's time is not exact, so though the planets are correct in the composite chart, the cusps are somewhat iffy. The Moon may move as much as a degree.)

If Mars rules your composite 9th house, there may be much verbal interaction on philosophy and outlook and though you may not always agree about the affairs of this house, yours can be a stimulating relationship because you never run out of subject matter for a good confrontation. On the other hand if Libra is here, it may be peace at any cost, so discussions are limited to subjects you agree upon.

## The 10th House

While the 10th house represents any status and public honor that you share with your partner, it also shows your potential achievement and the possible prestige of the alliance. With the Sun here, your potential is only limited by your feelings of mutual inadequacy and the aspects to the Sun and the house it rules will provide avenues for any kind of achievement.

In Joan McEvers's and Marion March's composite chart Scorpio is on the cusp of the 10th, with Mars in the 3rd house of communication and Pluto in the 6th. We are both teachers as well as authors; we both lecture extensively and to say that we put our all into our work is putting it mildly. The fact that we are successful in what we do proves that it is not necessary to have planets in the 10th house to succeed. But Pluto involved in a T-Square (opposed the Ascendant and square the Moon) helps to reflect our challenge to work hard.

Gerald and Betty Ford have Venus in the 10th and they were very well thought of by the public even though Venus has challenging aspects. Betty probably didn't enjoy the limelight as much as her husband, but she stood by him and did her best.

Recognition was fairly easy for them to come by. Neptune trines the Midheaven which it rules and Jupiter; Neptune sextiles the Sun.

* See chart data in Appendix.

With Saturn ruling this house, you are more than likely quite ambitious, with a strong need to make the partnership succeed. Jupiter in or ruling the composite 10th, suggests success in business undertakings, depending of course, on other factors in the chart.

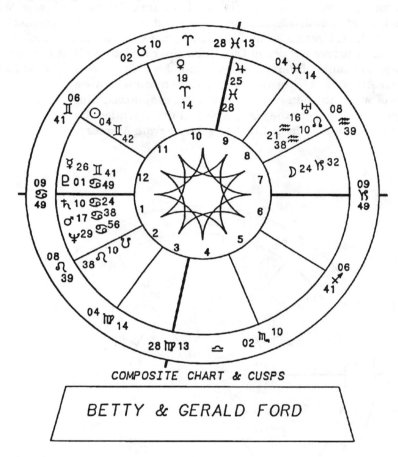

COMPOSITE CHART & CUSPS

BETTY & GERALD FORD

## The 11th House
This house portrays the friendship the two (or more) of you feel toward each other as well as the friends you share. It also outlines your goals, hopes and wishes for the future of the relationship. It can describe your involvement with groups and your social life in general. To a certain extent it also depicts circumstances beyond your control. This must be understood in the right context. This is the Uranian house and as such can reflect the unexpected through outside circumstances, rather than by your mutual actions.

Since it is the house of alliances as well as friendships, we will use it to illustrate an "unholy alliance," that of Adolf Hitler and Benito Mussolini.

Their composite 11th house is ruled by Mercury in the 8th in Gemini conjunct Venus and the Sun and square a 5th house Pisces Moon. That their so-called friendship would end in death and destruction is self-evident. Uranus in the 11th house, rules the end of the relationship 4th and squares Saturn in the 9th, a clear indication that they did not share the same philosophies and that the alliance was doomed to fail. Their Ascendant (Scorpio) rulers, Mars and Pluto were conjunct in the 7th of war and open enemies and both conjuncted illusive Neptune as well. Not only were they bellicose and unprincipled, but they were unconscionable and deceitful. The sextiles from Mercury, Venus and the

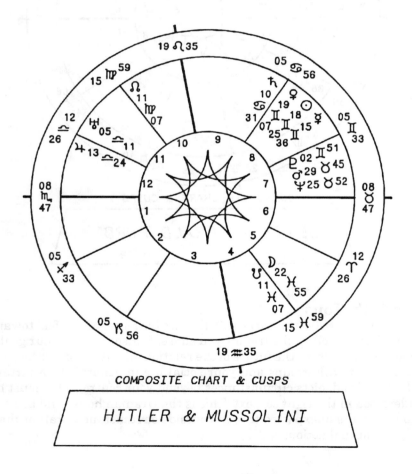

COMPOSITE CHART & CUSPS

HITLER & MUSSOLINI

Sun to the Midheaven, as well as their trines to Jupiter, may have led them to believe that they could conquer the world, but in viewing their composite, it is easy to see how they deluded themselves (Neptune square the MC).

If you have **Gemini** on your composite 11th, you undoubtedly have a very communicative, sociable circle of friends. With **Cancer** here, your mutual hopes and wishes may be involved with home and family issues, while **Scorpio** here suggests that you are intense in your relationships with others. **Leo**, **Aries** or **Sagittarius** on this cusp or the Sun, Mars or Jupiter in this house may find you sharing interest in sporting events. **Sagittarius** also suggests travel with friends or as a long-term goal. **Taurus** here, as well as **Virgo**, can be quite discriminating in your choice of friends, while Saturn in the 11th or **Capricorn** on the cusp often indicates a small social circle, by choice. On the other hand, with **Libra** on the 11th, both partners can be quite devoted to public service and involvement in group organizations. With **Pisces**, you may be active with charitable functions and/or foster children. With **Aquarius** on this cusp, you may associate with individualists or unusual people.

## The 12th House

Probably the most difficult of all houses to interpret, the 12th covers a lot of territory. It governs all sorts of limitations, sorrow and subconscious longings, but it also represents the repository of your greatest strength when used positively. In the composite chart, it can represent a clandestine relationship, if it is heavily emphasized, but just as often it can portray a solid, respectable, well-supported alliance in which both of you understand and back each other. It can also indicate what you do in the privacy of your home.

Ernest Hemingway wrote many popular and well-received novels, but he could not have done this without the advice, coaching and sometimes financial help of editor Max Perkins*.

Ernest, on the other hand had the adventures and shared them with Max who rarely left his offices in New York. With the Sun in and ruling the 12th and with Mercury and Saturn both there, we can see the many facets to this most supportive relationship. That each was always there for the other is most evident. Mercury ruled the 10th...they both became famous because of their affiliation; Saturn rules the 5th...the basis of their partnership was creativity, practical and pragmatic, but creative nonetheless. The Moon ruling their 11th house is in the 3rd exactly sextile the Ascendant...they never ran out of conversation. It also sextiles Saturn in Virgo strengthening the critique Max applied to Ernest's work; the trine to Venus in the 11th reinforced the bonds of friendship.

* See chart data in Appendix.

In a lecture presented to students in an extension course on book publishing conducted by New York University, professor Kenneth Mc-Cormick asked Perkins about Hemingway. Perkins said Hemingway needed backing in the beginning of his career, and even more later, "because he wrote as daringly as he lived." He believed Hemingway's writing displayed that virtue of his heroes, "grace under pressure." Hemingway, he said, was susceptible to overcorrect himself. "He once told me he had written parts of *A Farewell to Arms* 50 times," Perkins said. "Before an author destroys the natural qualities of his writings, that's where an editor has to step in. But not a bit sooner."

With the Sun and Venus in the 12th and Mercury, their ruler conjunct the 12th house cusp, but in the 11th, the Carters display much hidden strength...together they can move mountains and best of all, with the Sun sextile Pluto and Saturn, they love doing it. Mercury square Mars displays their extra energy to overcome many challenges.

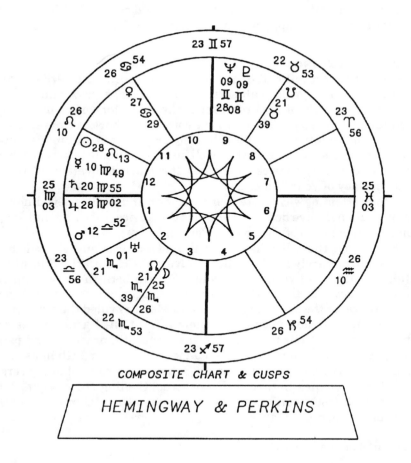

COMPOSITE CHART & CUSPS

HEMINGWAY & PERKINS

**LESSON 15**

# PLANETS IN THE COMPOSITE CHART

## The Sun

The Sun portrays the basics of the relationship as well as the usual astrological meanings, particularly their sense of identity, as well as how and where they wish to shine. In a minor way, in a male/female composite the Sun also describes the man's basic personality or field of endeavor. (To a lesser degree, Mars works in a similar fashion.) Some astrologers feel that for a marriage a 1st, 5th, 7th, 8th or 11th house Sun is best. That is true if the rest of the chart supports it, but we have noted that 2nd house (sharing values) or 6th house (sharing work) Suns are just as rewarding.

In the Joanne Woodward/Paul Newman composite chart, the Sun is conjunct the Moon in the 2nd house in Aquarius and Venus is in the same sign and house. This tells us that their marriage is a real partnership of shared values, shared income and shared love. With the Sun, Moon and Venus all in the same house in Aquarius, there seems to be an innate understanding between Joanne and Paul, of the male and female expressions in the relationship. Both luminaries oppose Neptune, disclosing the possibility that both idealize their union and maybe do not always see it clearly.

Prince Charles and Princess Diana have a 5th house Sun in their composite chart.

As mentioned earlier, we will have to wait and see if the marriage survives, but a 5th house Sun would indicate a union based on love and eventually a need to shine through their children. It appears that in order to keep their love alive, many adjustments are needed with the

Yod that is formed in the composite chart from Saturn and the Sun to the Ascendant. A Bucket Pattern where the emotional Moon in Pisces in the 12th is the handle, suggests additional modification. They will also have to focus on their exact (within 5 minutes) Mars/Neptune conjunction in Libra in the 7th house. This aspect characterizes lots of steam (Mars's fire and Neptune's water) which will eventually explode unless some outlet is found, or it can reflect all sorts of nebulous (Neptune) action (Mars).

Since the Sun, in a secondary way, also depicts the male's behavior pattern or field of endeavor, a 5th house Sun in Virgo, trine Jupiter and the MC, sextile Saturn, describes a meticulous, analytical, discriminating, thoughtful, disciplined and creative man, anxious to do everything well. The quincunx to the Ascendant implies that Charles and Diana do not really care what others think of them, but by being who they are, they have to change the way they come across in order to be accepted by the public.

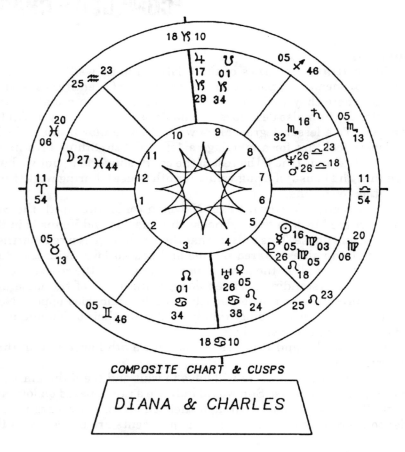

COMPOSITE CHART & CUSPS

DIANA & CHARLES

In entertainers Cher and Sonny Bono's composite, the Sun is exalted in Aries and Mars is angular. Both positions suggest that he was the dominant figure in the relationship. Cher readily admits the Sonny "ran the show" and it wasn't until after their divorce that she developed her own strengths.

## The Moon

The Moon symbolizes your emotional expression, your daily habits, subconscious motivations and subjective sensibilities. In the composite chart, its position by sign, house and aspect best imparts how you feel about each other and it depicts the instincts, moods, fluctuations and reflex actions of the union. In a male/female composite it also represents the woman, her character, personality and interests. So does Venus to a minor degree. George Sand's and Frederic Chopin's composite Moon is in Gemini in the 1st house. A Gemini Moon well portrays the fact that Sand was a writer, independent (1st house), different (trine to Uranus)

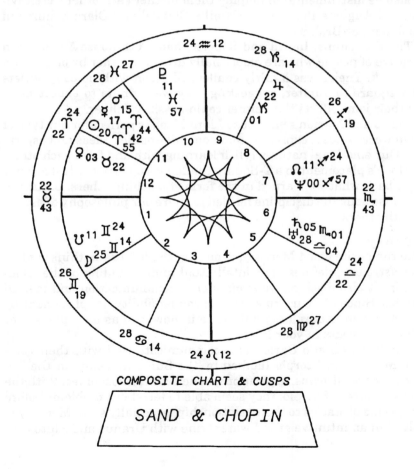

COMPOSITE CHART & CUSPS

SAND & CHOPIN

and successful (trine the MC). A 1st house Moon usually suggests an emotional relationship where the feelings are close to the surface and visible to the world. When the Moon is here, very often the woman controls the relationship and in this case Sand did exactly that. She was older, wiser and better able to make decisions and manage their affairs. With the Moon involved in a grand air trine, both Sand and Chopin seemed to treasure their love and their freedom. The sextile between the Moon and Sun often reveals a delightful compatibility and friendship between the couple. The quincunx to the 8th house Jupiter infers an exquisite love affair that raised eyebrows and necessitated changes in their public behavior if they expected support from others.

A 5th house Moon is very advantageous for any intimate or love relationship, since the duo are able to express their emotions through enjoying each other's company or having fun together, as did Benito Mussolini and Claretta Petacci. The deep emotions of a 5th house Moon can also be instrumental in helping them further each other's creativity, as did Auguste Rodin with Camille Claudel and Clara Schumann with Johannes Brahms.

The Rossellinis, Ingrid and Roberto, had a 6th house Moon, often indicative of people who are emotionally drawn together by or through their work. Theirs was a fairly challenged Moon with no easy outlets and a square to Jupiter, suggesting they were prone to expect more from their joint efforts than either could possibly deliver.

Joan's and Marion's 9th house Libra Moon is perfect for our type of shared work, since it expresses common philosophies, ideas and aspirations. Our emotional natures relish learning with and from each other. The Moon's placement in a T-Square challenges us to not only learn but to give back what we learned in the form of teaching others. Saturn in that house adds the discipline needed to share our philosophy of astrology with others.

## Mercury

In the composite chart Mercury, symbol of the left brain, thinking factor in astrology, defines your intellectual understanding of the  relationship. It also discloses your manner of communication and mental attitudes. Since Mercury rules the reasoning ability, its placement by house and sign makes a big difference in how, you as a couple, see or analyze the events in your lives.

Sophia Loren and Carlo Ponti communicate well with their composite Mercury in Scorpio flanked by the Sun and Venus in the 9th house of shared dreams, aspirations, beliefs and philosophies. With the probing nature of Scorpio, they seem able to ferret out problems before they become obstacles to their relationship, especially since Mercury is involved in an intuitive grand water trine with Uranus and Pluto.

Jimmy and Rosalynn Carter's composite Mercury is in down-to-earth Virgo in the 11th house of friendship, setting a realistic tone for this excellent marriage. Their union seems to gain much of its strength from the support both exhibit as well as the respect they have for each other.

Composite Mercury in Taurus in the 4th house indubitably illustrates the stability of Queen Elizabeth's and Prince Philip's marriage, helped by the conjunction to the 4th house Taurus Sun and the trine to the Ascendant. Their ability to patiently talk to each other, to depend on each other's good common sense, practical and conservative approach to life would be beneficial factors in any liaison.

## Venus

Whether you interpret a natal or composite chart, a progression or transit, Venus is always the planet of love. It alludes to your affectionate nature, your romantic make-up and in a lesser way, your sexual feel-

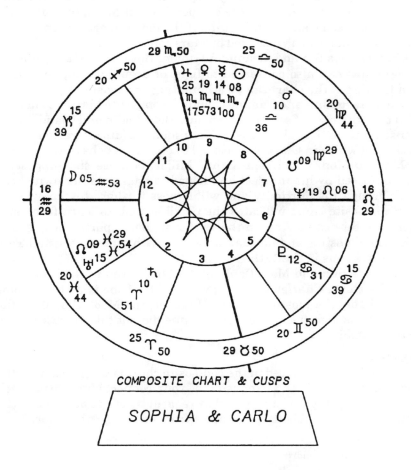

COMPOSITE CHART & CUSPS

SOPHIA & CARLO

ings, especially if you are female. It also helps to describe the woman in the composite chart by expanding on what you have already discovered when you examined the Moon.

Ingrid Bergman and Roberto Rossellini had their composite Venus in Cancer exactly conjunct Neptune.

This certainly helps us understand the magnetic attraction and blind love they felt for each other, so strong that Ingrid left her daughter, husband and thriving American film career and moved to Italy to be with him.

## Mars

Mars always deals with energy and initiative. It expresses your sexual drive. In the case of a difficult Mars, it can disclose areas where you intimidate each other or where you exert a lot of physical activity. (In our client files we have a composite chart where Mars in Virgo in the 3rd house squares a Sun/Mercury conjunction in Sagittarius and they both run marathon races.) In the composite chart Mars, to a lesser degree, conveys some additional details of the man's character and traits. The fiery enthusiasm symbolized by Mars can carry a relationship from nothingness to a fun and meaningful union. But the Martian principle of aggression can also cause you to fight or argue, which, depending upon the rest of the chart can be stimulating or devastating.

Auguste Rodin's and Camille Claudel's composite Mars was in Cancer in the 8th house of sexual enjoyment. Both Rodin and Claudel were intense individuals and composite Mars square Pluto suggested a power struggle which in Claudel's case led to obsessive behavior.

Marilyn Monroe married Arthur Miller* because she supposedly was impressed by his intellect and hoped to stimulate her own sharp mind through his proximity and willingness to share his knowledge. Their composite chart indicates the possible wish to learn from each other with Saturn in Virgo in the 1st house, but it particularly shows their sexual desires and mutual attraction with Mars in sensual Taurus sextile Venus in the 11th.

With the Sun and Mars flanking the Midheaven in the Lindbergh composite chart, Charles was the most visible of the two and in some ways probably the most dominant. However, the Moon though in the 12th house, is dignified in Cancer, so Anne did not take a back seat in the relationship.

## Jupiter

Wherever Jupiter is placed in the composite chart is where you find the potential for growth and expansion of your connectedness with each other. A strong Jupiter indicates that regardless of the outcome of the relationship, you will both have gained from knowing each other. Jupi-

---

* See chart data in Appendix.

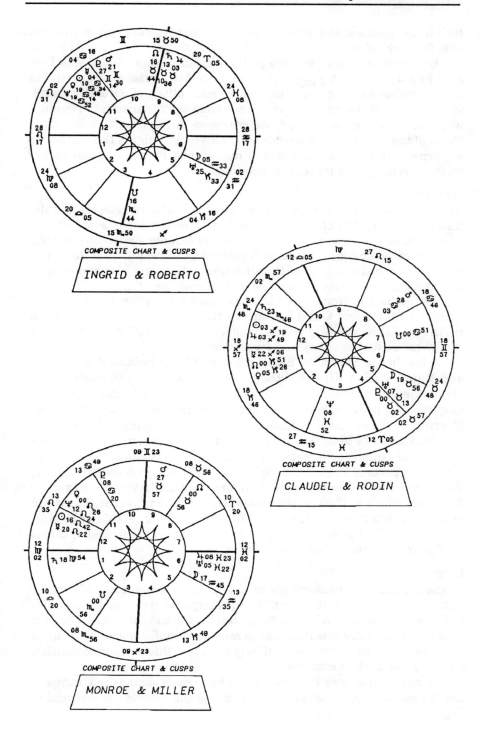

COMPOSITE CHART & CUSPS

INGRID & ROBERTO

COMPOSITE CHART & CUSPS

CLAUDEL & RODIN

COMPOSITE CHART & CUSPS

MONROE & MILLER

ter's house position and aspects also reflect the type of support you provide for each other.

Ernest Hemingway and his publisher, editor and friend, Max Perkins had Jupiter in Virgo in the composite 1st house, well describing their relationship of critical analysis of each other, of carefully detailing what should be added to or deleted from the manuscripts Hemingway wrote and Perkins edited and critiqued. Jupiter sextiles the Moon (ruler of the 11th house of friendship) and Venus, ruler of the 2nd house of earned income. Both benefitted immensely, personally and monetarily, through their mutual association.

## Saturn

In the composite chart Saturn plays a very significant role, since it determines the solidity of your relationship. Of course it can also indicate areas where you experience feelings of inadequacy or insecurity with each other or toward outsiders. Wherever you encounter Saturn you are faced with the reality of the situation, which is a blessing easy to accept for some, nearly impossible to deal with for others.

Saturn in the composite 1st house may have represented for Johannes Brahms and Clara Schumann the fact that living with seven children and the memory of a beloved husband who died could destroy the romantic feelings they had for each other.

A 5th house Saturn in Sagittarius may have indicated to Coretta and Martin Luther King that their love (5th), mutual philosophies and ideals (Sagittarius) were enough to conquer the world (trine the MC) despite some possible sexual differences (square to the Sun, Moon and Mercury in the 8th house), leading to rumors of dalliances by him.

Jane Fonda's and Ted Turner's 3rd house Saturn in Aries gives evidence of ardent conversations; communication is one of the most significant aspects of their relationship, particularly with Saturn trining Venus and Pluto. The square to Mercury does not have to be negative; it often symbolizes the need to constantly talk to each other. But it can also indicate that one partner is not always telling the total truth (Mercury in the 12th) or that the other does not totally understand; therefore clear communication is imperative.

## Uranus

Uranus, planet of awakenings or the unexpected, speaks of similar themes in the composite chart. The principle of freedom it embodies and the need to do one's own thing can create unrest in the house it occupies, since activities in this area may need conformation and one or the other, or both parties are unlikely to expect this of the relationship and may not wish to conform.

Prince Charles and Princess Diana have their composite Uranus in the 4th house. Their home life, according to the tabloids, is unusual to say the least, with each going their own way much of the time. But maybe that is exactly what is needed in order to keep the relationship alive; freedom to explore their own strengths and weaknesses. The trine to their 12th house Moon could indicate that privately they have agreed on this lifestyle, whereas the square to the 7th house Mars/Neptune conjunction may signify that neither they, nor the public, see the situation as it really is.

The Rossellinis with Uranus in the 5th in Capricorn may not have given each other enough space, neither in their creative efforts where he always directed her, nor in their love life. Uranus's opposition to Neptune can characterize a lack of clear vision. The opposition of Uranus to Venus may have manifested as a most exciting affair, but if that is all a relationship has going for it, it usually ends as abruptly as it started. In their composite chart the yod formed by Uranus quincunx Mars, Pluto and the Ascendant must have plagued them much more than they let on. Both seemed to easily accept what some others considered their scandalous behavior...her abandonment of her family and Robertino's birth out of wedlock. The yod leads us to believe differently.

## Neptune
This illusive planet may lead you in two totally diverse directions in the composite chart. At its most ideal it can represent your spiritual potential and creativity. It can also disclose the where and how of your mutual dreams. More often though it seems to manifest as disappointment or even deceit.

Ethel and Robert Kennedy's composite Neptune is in Leo in the 5th opposed Venus in the 11th. Does this indicate that he deceived her? Or is this where they dreamed of continuing the Kennedy clan by having 11 children?

Cher and Sonny Bono earned a good income through their creative use of a 2nd house Neptune trine Uranus. (See page 184.)

The public responded to their brand of music and banter and considered them unique and entertaining, but not everyone accepted them right away (Uranus squares the Ascendant). They had to work hard for their success (Neptune conjunct Mars).

If you have a 7th or 10th house composite Neptune, it often reflects the fact that the public is attracted to you and that together you come across with charisma.

## Pluto
Astrologically speaking Pluto is characterized by the word power. In the composite chart, it usually indicates an area of power conflicts. Pluto also shows your unconscious needs for each other and, esoterically speaking, it can indicate your karmic connections. It reveals the areas where change and transformation are most likely to take place. Wheth-

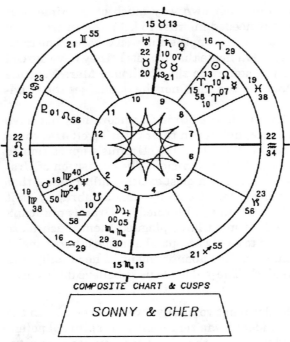

COMPOSITE CHART & CUSPS

SONNY & CHER

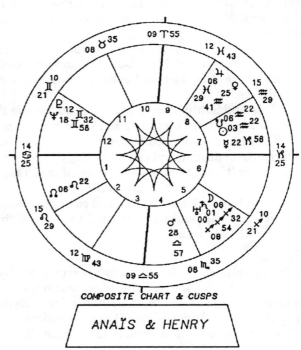

COMPOSITE CHART & CUSPS

ANAÏS & HENRY

er positive or negative depends not only on aspects, but also upon your attitudes toward life in general. Anaïs Nin and Henry Miller had a 5th house Moon opposing Pluto and squaring an 8th house Jupiter, forming a T-square. Each definitely changed through their love affair. The emotional challenges (opposition Moon) and sexual indulgences (square Jupiter; Venus also in the 8th trine Mars and Neptune) were probably seen through rose-colored glasses (Pluto conjunct Neptune; Venus trine Neptune), but in the long run both profited from the experience, not only by broadening their horizons (Jupiter/Pluto) but by writing about their liaison and making good money from it (Moon in the creative 5th trine MC).

Ernest Hemingway and Max Perkins used their 9th house composite Pluto for the purpose of publishing; the Rossellinis applied their 10th house Pluto for career purposes, to garner publicity and to grapple for professional dominance; as did Marilyn Monroe and Arthur Miller with Pluto in the same position.

In most composite charts the generational planets Uranus, Neptune and Pluto are in the same signs as they are natally in each chart, so their position by house, rather than sign, is most meaningful.

## The Nodes

Though there seem to be some very definite meanings for nodal contacts when comparing two horoscopes, in the composite as in the natal chart, there are many disparate characterizations of the real meaning of the Nodes, alternating from the karmic to the social and group oriented.

We have no absolute wisdom here and would advise you to interpret them as you do natally. We pay more attention to the house position than sign and aspects and find that the North Node can be helpful in determining where the relationship is headed. The South Node indicates an area of comfort with the old and familiar; the North Node, one of challenge of the new and unexplored. Wherever the Nodes fall in the composite chart, there is a need to balance polarities and avoid extremes.

A 2nd house North Node could indicate the ability to make money together or the need to share values. If the South Node is there, this is taken for granted and rarely thought about. A 4th house North Node may suggest that much rapport can be found by establishing a home together and the challenge to achieve this. A 10th house North Node can describe a common career, whereas the North Node in the 12th often signals a hidden strength in the union, not apparent to outsiders. The South Node in the 5th house may describe a very familiar, loving relationship, but remember to maintain balance because the North Node in the 11th house can indicate much social involvement at the cost of your loved ones.

## Aspects in the Composite Charts

In the composite chart aspects show the energy pattern, thus configurations including stellia, become even more important here than in natal charts. Therefore, do not hesitate to widen orbs when you feel it necessary.

## Composite Charts for More Than Two People

As we have remarked previously, it is possible to construct composite charts for any number of people. The important thing to remember is to add and divide the total of each cusp and each planet by the correct number. If you are doing a composite chart for a family and there are 11 members, you must first add all 11 and then divide the total by 11. As an example, here are the charts of well-known singing trio, Peter*, Paul* and Mary*.

Mathematics for finding their composite Sun:

| | | |
|---|---|---|
| Peter's Sun | 2s 9° 08' | 9 Gemini 08 |
| Paul's Sun | 9s 8° 51' | 8 Capricorn 51 |
| Mary's Sun | + 7s 17° 01' | 17 Scorpio 01 |
| Divide total by 3: | 18s 34° 60' | = 6s 11° 40' or 11 Libra 40 |

To find the nearest midpoint, place all three Suns in one chart (it doesn't matter which one). For our example place them all in Peter's natal chart, His Sun is in the 6th house; Paul's Sun falls in Peter's 10th; Mary's is in his 8th. It stands to reason that the composite Sun will fall on the side of the chart where the most Sun positions are...the eastern hemisphere; thus, the composite Sun's shortest midpoint is in Libra and is in the 11th house of the composite chart. We know this sounds a bit complicated, but after you do a few charts, it will become clearer. Unfortunately no computer program does this currently, so you're on your own. Good luck!

## Interpreting the Compound Composite Chart

You delineate this compound composite chart just as you do any other. The rising sign describes how these people relate to each other. Here it is Scorpio, with the rulers Pluto in Cancer just barely into the 9th house and Mars in Aries in the 5th. These placements suggest that this is a mutually supportive trio (Pluto in Cancer), who travel together (Pluto in the 9th), and who are actively creative (Mars in Aries in the 5th). Pluto is caught up in a T-Square with Jupiter and Venus and the empty leg of this configuration activates their all important 5th house of entertainment where co-ruler Mars is located.

At times, the constant travel they engage in must seem challenging (Jupiter opposed to Pluto), but Pluto's trine to Saturn indicates that

---

* See chart data in Appendix.

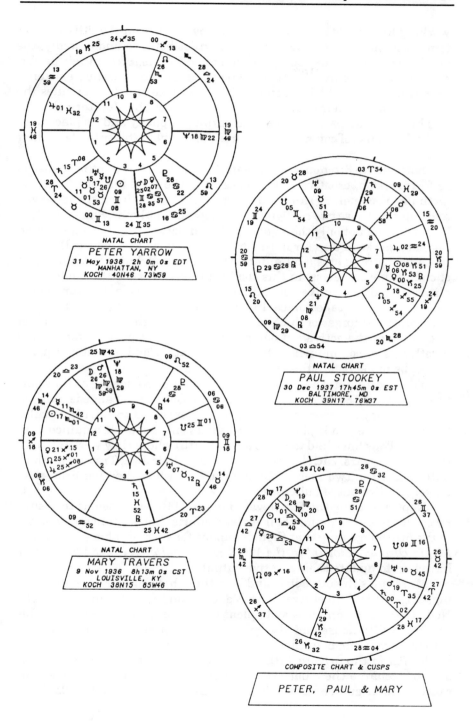

NATAL CHART

PETER YARROW
31 May 1938   2h 0m 0s EDT
MANHATTAN, NY
KOCH   40N46   73W59

NATAL CHART

PAUL STOOKEY
30 Dec 1937  17h45m 0s EST
BALTIMORE, MD
KOCH   39N17   76W37

NATAL CHART

MARY TRAVERS
9 Nov 1936   8h13m 0s CST
LOUISVILLE, KY
KOCH   38N15   85W46

COMPOSITE CHART & CUSPS

PETER, PAUL & MARY

working hard together is what they enjoy (Saturn in the 5th). Jupiter trines the Moon and Mercury; Pluto sextiles both, so undoubtedly, the accolades (Moon in the 10th) and the money earned from their performances (Mercury in the 11th) compensate for the unsettled existence they lead. Venus which is squared by both Pluto and Jupiter rules the 7th, confirming their drawing power with the public. Jupiter rules the 2nd house of values, self-worth and earning capacity and its placement in the 3rd house of communicating, reinforces their ability to blend their voices.

Saturn, the 3rd house ruler is in the 5th, which is another house of self-expression, creative in this case. It is the focal planet of one yod (actually a boomerang) and figures in another involving the Midheaven and Jupiter. These two configurations suggest that Peter, Paul and Mary have changed not only their goals (MC and Saturn), but also their singing patterns with Jupiter in the 3rd (more folksy, less political).

A boomerang acts a bit differently than a yod, but it is a harbinger of change nevertheless. In this configuration Saturn is the point of application and quincunxes the Midheaven and Venus, but Saturn is not where the action takes place. In a boomerang, it takes place at the opposition to the finger of the Yod; here Mercury is the opposition planet and becomes the activation point. Obviously, their purpose for coming together is to communicate, but reorganization and and adjustments had to be made before they hit the big time.

Their peripatetic lifestyle is reflected by the boomerang as they perform in 10 or 12 cities in a two week period. Constant change is a way of life when they are performing. It is not unexpected that Uranus rules their 4th house and is placed in the 6th; its only aspect is a quincunx to the Sun. They have had to make a home (4th) where they work (6th). In the last few years, each has made a home of their own, Travers in Manhattan and the two men in California. But when they perform, they travel and live out of suitcases.

Neptune ruling the 5th elevated in the 10th house seems to assure recognition and fame for their artistic efforts, but it quincunxes Mars in the 5th, suggesting that though famous for such numbers as *Puff the Magic Dragon, Blowin' in the Wind* and *Leavin' on a Jet Plane*, they have had to update their creative output.

Mars rules the 6th house and is in the 5th; their work is entertaining, original and inventive. With Venus ruling the 7th and the South Node there, they find it easy to please their audiences. Venus is in Libra in the 12th house and also rules it, which probably explains why so little information about their private lives is available. The ruler of the public 7th in the private 12th reflects their need for occasional seclusion to recharge their batteries. Venus in Libra mirrors their acceptance by their audiences. Their music has endured since the 60s. Mercury, ruling the 8th house, is in the 11th with flowing aspects as well as the challenging opposition to Saturn...a nicely balanced Mercury which also conjuncts the Moon in the 10th, more indication that the public loves the way they communicate and gives them lots of support. The Mercury/Saturn aspect, no doubt, contributes to the longevity of their relationship.

The ruler of the 9th, the Moon in the 10th, is a classic aspect of travel connected to career and achievement, but here it also reflects their philosophy in their musical output. Mercury in and ruling the 11th suggests that Peter, Paul and Mary, not only work together, but are friends as well. Jupiter in the 3rd house sends the same message of mutual support and understanding, especially with its trine to Mercury/Moon and its sextile to the Ascendant.

# PART FOUR: PUTTING IT ALL TOGETHER
## LESSON 16
# ANALYSIS OF NATAL CHARTS AND SYNASTRY

## Gwen Verdon and Bob Fosse

We've given you a lot of information in the first three parts of this book; now it's time to put it all together. In this final section of the book we will compare the charts of Gwen Verdon and Bob Fosse and we will also interpret their composite chart by going step by step as we have explained in Lessons 14 and 15.

First and foremost, before we can judge how these two people will get along with each other, we have to see what their individual natal needs, wishes and desires are. You have already been introduced to Gwen Verdon on page 32. Let's fill in some of the other facets of her life so you may intelligently judge how well suited she and Bob Fosse are to each other.

Verdon's parents were English-born and emigrated to California via Canada. Her mother was a former vaudeville dancer and her father, an erstwhile gardener, became a stage electrician for Metro-Gold-wyn-Mayer studios. You can see that with the Moon trine Mercury, Venus and Jupiter, Gwen most likely felt that her mother played an important and harmonious role in her childhood. Not only did she prevent the doctors from artificially straightening her legs, but it was she who started Gwen on a dancing career. By the time Verdon was four, she and Mom performed together and at age six she was billed as the "world's fastest tapper" at the Loew's theater in Los Angeles.

The Moon in Virgo in the 6th house suggests that "Mom" influenced her work and probably had much to do with her meticulous approach to dancing and habit patterns. Venus (the other feminine archetype) which also describes how Gwen views her mother, is in the 10th and confirms her role in Gwen's professional life; its trine to Neptune could hint at some overidealization on both sides.

Verdon's perception of her father seems a bit harsher. Her Sun quincunxes Neptune and suggests that with his irregular and often long hours at the studio, she felt he did not really know her, nor did she understand what he expected from her (Mars quincunx Saturn and square Pluto). On the other hand, he helped her with entree to the studios (Sun sextile Uranus and the Ascendant) and she gave him credit for helping her to perfect her dancing by paying for lessons and providing encouragement (Saturn trine Uranus and Pluto).

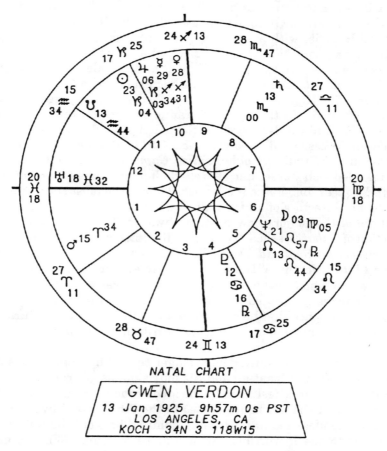

NATAL CHART

GWEN VERDON
13 Jan 1925   9h57m 0s PST
LOS ANGELES, CA
KOCH   34N 3  118W15

As a teenager Verdon posed for bathing suit pictures at Venice Beach in California and danced in night club chorus lines. In between she studied ballet. After a five-year hiatus to get married and have a son, she returned to work as assistant to dance director, Jack Cole. With chart ruler Neptune in the 6th house, work is Gwen's mainstay and with Venus and Jupiter in the 10th, a career is a given. She managed to get some small dance parts, but because she was so outstanding in everything she did, her performances were invariably cut or eliminated. Instead she taught new dance routines and correct movements to Hollywood stars.

Tired of the lack of recognition, in 1953 Verdon auditioned for the musical *Can-Can* on Broadway. She was accepted, but soon proved so good that she threatened to overshadow the show's star. Her role was whittled down to two dance numbers. First-nighters gave her an ovation with the audience chanting, "We want Verdon." A star was born.

The role earned Gwen a Tony award. So did *Damn Yankees* which followed in 1955, with every Broadway critic acclaiming her dancing and acting as Lola. "Vivacious, as sleek as a car on the showroom floor and as nice to look at, she gives brilliance and sparkle (Uranus conjunct the Ascendant) to the evening with her exuberant (Ascendant ruler Neptune in Leo) dancing (Pisces); her wicked, glistening green eyes and her sheer delight in the foolery (Uranus square the MC)." were just some of the kind words uttered by the usually caustic critics.

Other successes followed with *New Girl in Town* in 1957, *Redhead* in 1958 and the unforgettable *Pajama Game* in 1960. That same year she married Bob Fosse, her choreographer and dance partner since *Damn Yankees*. Bob Fosse is considered one of the most successful choreographer-directors of all time, and one of the few individuals to win all three of the major show business awards. Three "Oscars" for his direction of *Cabaret*, seven "Tonys" for directing and/or choreographing *Pajama Game, Redhead, Damn Yankees, Sweet Charity, Dancin, Pippin* and *Little Me*; three "Emmys" for the television special *Liza with a Z*. But as all who knew him said, the awards were not the important thing, what really counted was the man himself– the genius and dedication to excellence that he brought to everything he did. (Saturn conjunct the Midheaven in a grand trine with Jupiter, Uranus and Mercury.)

Fosse's father was a vaudeville singer-turned-insurance salesman; his mother saw to it that he and his four siblings got religion and an education. Mother is described by the Moon exactly trine Neptune, and Venus, ruler of the 4th house in Leo in the 7th, flanked by Mars and Neptune. He idealized her, probably admired her, but did not always know how to speak with her (Moon square Mercury). With so many creative aspects to Mars and Saturn (significators of the male parent), he probably learned from and looked up to his father. But he may not have known how to show Dad his feelings, or somehow felt ill-at-ease as is often the case when you have three quincunxes and two squares to the Sun.

Since Fosse was stagestruck at a very early age, his parents sent him to a neighborhood dancing school and then to a special ballet school where he was the only boy in the class. "I got a lot of jokes and I was whistled at a lot," he recalled. "But it tapered off after a while..." Just 13 when he and another young dancer teamed up to become the Riff Brothers, the innocent teenager successfully danced his way into burlesque. Pluto, ruler of his Midheaven is in the 6th house of work, intensifying his need to give his all. Saturn in the 10th has the reputation for being a tough taskmaster, demanding perfection in all professional and career matters. Saturn and the MC trine Mercury in the 6th and Jupiter conjunct Uranus in the 2nd of money earned (a grand fire trine) point to good timing...being in the right place at the right time.

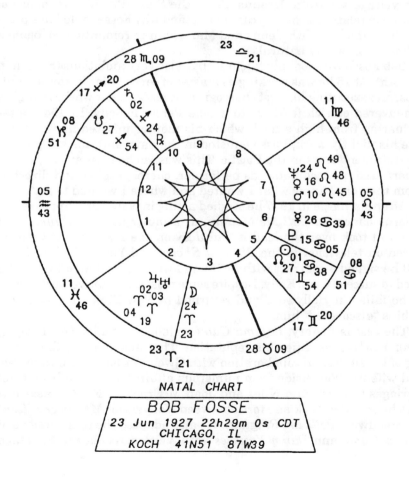

NATAL CHART

BOB FOSSE

23 Jun 1927 22h29m 0s CDT
CHICAGO, IL
KOCH 41N51 87W39

According to *All His Jazz, the Life and Death of Bob Fosse* by Martin Gottfried, this early exposure to a rather raunchy type of nightlife was not the best. Fosse recalled, "I was really unhappy and scared; it left certain impressions on me that weren't too good. I was too young to be exposed to naked ladies." Fosse never really outgrew that period according to Gottfried. In his work, sex became tinged with guilt and voyeurism. In private life, the permanent adolescent, doubtful about everything, including his talent, kept trying to reassure himself with nonstop affairs which persisted through three marriages.

Mercury, ruler of his 5th and 8th houses is in a grand trine with Jupiter (excesses), Saturn (overcompensation for imaginary shortcomings) and Uranus (need for stimulation for the new and untried). Some of these imaginary shortcomings are suggested by the 5th house Cancer Sun quincunx Saturn (both male prototypes) and the Ascendant (as he sees himself) exacerbated by a self-indulgent square to Jupiter and a high voltage square to Uranus. Since the Sun rules his 7th house of one-to-one relationships, you can understand why Fosse could have problems in that area. With Venus and Mars, both in romantic Leo, being a "ladies man" is only natural.

Bob Fosse was not only talented, but also very ambitious (Saturn in the 10th). At 15 he was working as master of ceremonies in small nightclubs, and executing his first choreographic assignment where four girls maneuvered ostrich feathers to a Cole Porter melody. In 1945, after graduating from high school, which his mother insisted he finish despite his nightly work, Fosse enlisted in the navy and was assigned to entertainment units in the Pacific. This was, as he later stated, where he perfected his techniques as performer, choreographer and director. "From then on, I knew what I wanted and where I wanted to go."

After discharge in 1947 he studied acting in New York, appeared as a chorus dancer in *Call Me Madam,* as a minor actor in *Dance Me a Song* and took over the lead in *Pal Joey* on the road. In between he danced on television in the *Show of Shows* and *Your Hit Parade.* In 1953 he signed a contract with MGM and went to Hollywood where he hoped to succeed Gene Kelly. Despite some most imaginative work, Fosse felt he failed in Hollywood and returned to New York where Jerome Robbins "discovered" him.

The rest is history. *Pajama Game* indelibly established his style; *Damn Yankees* solidified his reputation. That also marked the beginning of his successful collaboration with Gwen Verdon, who became his third wife in 1960. Aside from numerous affairs, there had been brief marriages to Mary-Ann Niles and Joan McCracken. For the next few years he shuttled back and forth between Hollywood (*My Sister Eileen*) and Broadway (*Bells are Ringing*). He also adapted the film versions of *Pajama Game* and *Damn Yankees* with Verdon recreating his stage choreography. The pair went east again for *Redhead* which was a major triumph for both.

With an unaspected Pluto ruling Fosse's Midheaven placed in his 6th house, he may have been even more work and career obsessed than Verdon. But they certainly made a terrific pair. Fosse had other difficulties to overcome in order to sustain an intimate union. He had no interplanetary oppositions, reflecting difficulty in understanding where others are coming from. He had no planets in earth signs, implying an often unrealistic view of life. This is great for a dancer who thrives on "head in the clouds" imagination and "feet off the ground" steps, but not so wonderful for comprehending what a down-to-earth marriage is all about. Yet Fosse and Verdon were attracted to each other like magnets. When you compare their charts, you can see many reasons why.

## 7TH HOUSE NEEDS

Fosse wants a dramatic (Leo on the 7th), active (Mars in the 7th) woman who is sensitive enough to understand and love him (ruler of the 7th, Sun in Cancer in the 5th). Since this is his third marriage, you should look to his 11th house for additional insights. Sagittarius on the cusp points to a free spirit and ruler, Jupiter in Aries, illustrates an active person, confirming the 7th house Mars.

Gwen Verdon fits these needs pretty well. With Mars in Aries in the 1st house, she is very active; her Moon trines her Venus/Mercury/Jupiter conjunction, suggesting a gentle soul, even a 'softie.' With Venus trining hardworking (6th house) Neptune, she has imagination galore. Add to that Pisces rising with Uranus conjunct the Ascendant and you see dramatic imagination and creativity. The Moon ruling the 5th trine Venus denotes that she is capable of much love if she finds the right person. With Mercury, ruler of her 4th and 7th houses in Sagittarius, as well as Uranus conjunct the Ascendant, you know that she is a free spirit at heart and seems to well fulfill all of Fosse's 7th house needs.

She on the other hand is looking for a man who is discriminating (Virgo on the 7th), career oriented (ruler Mercury in the 10th), also a free thinker (Sagittarius), warm (Mercury conjunct Venus) and generous (Mercury conjunct Jupiter). This is her second marriage; Scorpio on the 9th indicates that she is looking for an intense person, active (Mars in Aries in the 1st) yet sensitive and loving (Pluto in Cancer in the 4th).

Fosse surely filled that bill in all areas. He is very career oriented (Saturn in the 10th), free thinking (Aquarius rising), very warm-hearted toward others (Mars and Venus conjunct in Leo in the 7th) and generous to a fault (Jupiter conjunct Uranus in the 2nd). His intensity was legendary (Pluto unaspected and Scorpio on the Midheaven); he was hyperactive (seven planets in fire, three of them in Aries). These fire planets showed him to be a very loving man, as did his Cancer Sun in the 5th, exuding love and sensitivity. The only missing factor may be the discriminating Virgo quality, yet with Fosse's Mercury in the 6th house, he did incorporate some of those characteristics.

## AFFINITIES
Verdon's 11th house Sun attracts Fosse's Aquarian Ascendant. They can innately understand each other's innermost feelings and thoughts. She will not think of his personal behavior (Ascendant) as bizarre or different (Aquarius). Though her Sun is in proper and traditional Capricorn, its 11th house position shows enough Uranian traits to relate to his actions. His 10th house Saturn, on the other hand, helps him empathize with her Capricorn Sun needs.

## PLANET PLACEMENTS
By placing his planets around her horoscope, you can see that he can help her personal growth (his Jupiter in her 1st) in some unique fashion (his Uranus there) and that he'll put his full emotional nature into it (his Moon in her 1st). Fosse brings much of himself, his heart and soul (Sun) to their home (4th) and this was probably the only time and place he permitted himself to show another, softer side to his nature. It also confirms what all the biographies state, that he deeply and even intensely (his Pluto in her 4th trine her Saturn) loved Verdon. By bringing his sensitive Cancer Mercury, as well as his romantic and ardent Leo Mars into Verdon's empty 5th house, he probably opened her being to a deeper understanding of love...and maybe motherhood, since they had a daughter together.

They both bring Saturn to each other's empty 9th houses, enabling them to put their dreams and visions (9th) into form (Saturn) which they most certainly did with their, for those days, totally unique way of dancing. With Verdon's Mercury and Jupiter falling into Fosse's empty 11th house, she was able to show him what friendship, combined with deep love and true generosity of heart, was all about. Her wonderfully aspected Moon in his 7th, as well as his Sun in her 4th, both contributed to their serious commitment.

Of course, sex played a role. Her Mars is in a tight trine to his Venus, and more all encompassing, her Venus/MC/Mercury trine his Moon and Neptune forming a grand fire trine. This was also good for her professionally, since it involves her 1st, 6th and 10th houses. Though he was greatly attracted to her, his Mars and Venus squared her Saturn and she may have put an occasional damper on his sexual prowess or cramped his style when he felt like chasing damsels.

## FILLING LACKS
Verdon brought a lot of earthiness to the relationship with her Virgo Moon and her Sun and Jupiter in Capricorn. Her lack of air planets was

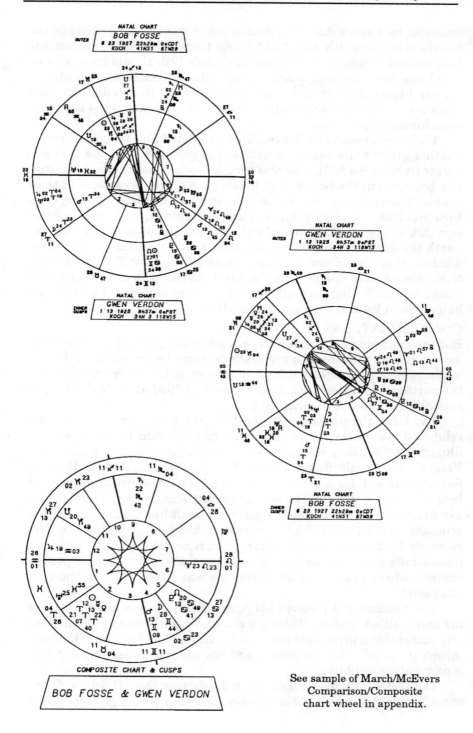

NATAL CHART
BOB FOSSE
6 23 1927 22h29m 0sCDT
KOCH 41N51 87W39

NATAL CHART
GWEN VERDON
1 13 1925 9h57m 0sPST
KOCH 34N 3 118W15

NATAL CHART
GWEN VERDON
1 13 1925 9h57m 0sPST
KOCH 34N 3 118W15

NATAL CHART
BOB FOSSE
6 23 1927 22h29m 0sCDT
KOCH 41N51 87W39

COMPOSITE CHART & CUSPS

BOB FOSSE & GWEN VERDON

See sample of March/McEvers
Comparison/Composite
chart wheel in appendix.

balanced by Fosse's Aquarius Ascendant. Fosse has no planets in the houses of endings (4th, 8th, 12th), a lack that alludes to a reluctance to look inward. Verdon's Sun falling in Fosse's 12th should have amelio- rated this. She also brings him four oppositions (her Sun to his Mercu- ry, her Venus, Jupiter and Mercury to his Sun) that could engender more awareness in his mind as to who he really is and what he wants from himself and others.

With her Uranus and Saturn, his unaspected Pluto becomes part of another grand trine auguring well for his work (Pluto in his 6th) and career (it rules his MC). This was good for both of them. His choreogra- phy brought out the best in her, leaving the critics breathless in their praise: "The amount of physical activity in which this frail-seeming crea- ture indulges is perfectly flabbergasting; spinning, prancing, leaping, curvetting, she is seldom out of sight and never out of breath. Yet be- neath the athletic ebullience is something more rarified– an unfailing delicacy of spirit," Kenneth Tynan wrote in the New Yorker. "Perfec- tion," some critics said of Fosse "A dance master who is batting 1000," stated others. Filling each other's lacks is very significant and indeed helped them learn more about themselves.

## CONFIGURATIONS
But the most binding facets of their relationship, aside from their Sat- urn aspects, are the many configurations formed when merging the two horoscopes. This integration from one person to the other explains why the partnership lasted until Fosse's death in 1987, despite their sepa- ration in 1972 and divorce in 1975.

You have already observed the two grand trines which show the relationship's pizzazz (fire) and depth (water). Add to that two yods illustrating that they had to make certain adjustments to each other. Verdon's Moon quincunxes Fosse's Ascendant sextile Jupiter/Uranus, forming one yod. He had to learn to curb his exuberance (Jupiter) and love of the outré (Uranus) as well as his ceaseless energy, (both sextile his Ascendant) if he wanted to get along with her much calmer, dis- criminating nature. She had to reorganize her feelings and not be hurt so easily by his occasionally bizarre behavior. Though they may not have totally succeeded in their private lives, they certainly did profes- sionally where in the eyes of others, she was considered his "dancing alter ego."

Their second yod involves his Ascendant quincunx her Moon, and his Sun sextile her Moon. This may show how she became less emotion- ally vulnerable and he more contained...through the balance of the fem- inine/masculine spirit expressed and the mutual understanding this configuration can bring.

The two T-squares formed when combining their charts indicate some wonderful exchanges of energy, but they also signify possible problems, especially with a man like Fosse whom one of his friends describes as: "Full of an inexhaustible appetite for success and self-annihilation" and who describes himself as: "Eager, pushy, needy, scared, hungry and confident." One T-square encompasses Fosse's Jupiter/Uranus conjunction square his Sun and square Verdon's Jupiter. She is used to an opposition to her Jupiter...in her chart Pluto opposes it; but she needed time to get used to the enormous verve and vigor a square to Jupiter and Uranus in Aries represents, especially since these planets fall into her 1st house of the physical self.

Fosse, on the other hand, has the square from the 2nd to the 5th house natally. What is totally new to him, since he has no natal inter-planetary oppositions, is sensing Verdon's Jupiter in his 11th house. Did the special feeling of love given (5th) and love received (11th) make this marriage different from his earlier ones? Friends say he idolized and loved her, in spite of his womanizing, and their continuing friendship (11th) and shared child, daughter Nicole (5th) made his life worth living.

The second T-square is formed by his Moon square his Mercury and her Sun, bringing him another opposition from his 6th house industrious Mercury to her Sun in his 12th. Did this enable him to gain better insight into the "dark" side of his nature? As his friend, composer Cy Coleman says: "Fosse was almost always dressed in black. He was self-mocking and he never believed that anything would turn out right. He's dark, but out of the dark he lights a candle...every time!"

Verdon with her Sun sextile Uranus and her Ascendant, probably enjoyed the opposition to Fosse's Mercury in her 5th house. Perhaps she became more aware of what she wanted from a lover, what she had to give to her children and what her creativity was all about. The square to his Moon in her 1st house may have been a bit harder to absorb and react to. Sun square Moon in a male/female relationship usually indicates a certain tension within and between the two people. Though they have a Moon (hers) sextile Sun (his) aspect which is most helpful, it does not eliminate or nullify the issues of the square. Despite a mutual infatuation with each other and even though they stimulated each other creatively, this square could have represented sexual as well as psychological problems.

## NODAL CONTACTS

For those of you who believe in reincarnation and karmic reasons for getting together, please note that Verdon's North Node conjuncts Fosse's Mars/Venus in the 7th house, symbolizing that through marriage, she could help him better understand how to use these two planets in the most fulfilling way. Fosse's South Node conjuncts her Venus/Mercury in her 10th house of status and career. The South Node is considered more of a "taker" so karmically it looks as though Fosse had a lot to gain through their marriage.

Though very successful professionally, the pair separated and according to Gottfried: "By then he was living on Dexamil, and no sexual or professional triumph could last." He had several glamorous girl friends, including Ann Reinking and Jessica Lange, but Fosse claimed that after his divorce, "That area of life had slowed down. I certainly don't pursue ladies as much as I used to, I'm afraid I'll catch them and then have to do something. But I am a little more charming and funnier when ladies are around, I seem to strut more. Some inferiority complex when I was a little boy, I suppose. Some need to prove myself."

Though this gives you a very good idea of the kind of marriage Verdon and Fosse experienced - the applause and heartaches, the difficulties and the glory - the composite chart will show you even more aspects of the relationship and the way they conducted themselves as a couple.

# VERDON/FOSSE COMPOSITE CHART

As we explained in Lesson 13, the composite chart mirrors the relationship of, in this case, a pair of people operating as one. This kind of chart does not describe each individual relating to the other as we have just done in the comparison. It interprets how this couple, Gwen Verdon and Bob Fosse, relate to the world as a compound unit. Separate them from each other and their personalities change and modify, but when you view them through the lens of the composite chart, they appear as a single soul coping as one with the world around them.

In Gwen Verdon's and Bob Fosse's composite chart, friendship reveals itself as the basis of their relationship. Aquarius rises and with Uranus in the 1st house, theirs was a doubly unique pairing, one of two very strong individualists blending their talents, but perhaps not always seeing eye-to-eye since Uranus quincunxes Neptune, the ruler of the 1st house interception. With Neptune in the 6th house, they may have differed in their work regimen and daily habit patterns. Naturally, there were adjustments and reorganization necessary— two strongly individualistic people, temperamental and artistic often find it necessary to accommodate each other.

As mentioned earlier in Lesson 15, aside from the traditional astrological meanings, the Sun and Mars represent the man in the composite and the woman is portrayed by the Moon and Venus. The interaction of these planets in the Verdon/Fosse composite is most intriguing. The Moon in Gemini is in the 4th house and Venus is in the 2nd in Aries picturing Gwen as impatient, energetic, somewhat emotionally detached, but value conscious and home-loving. The Sun is in Aries in

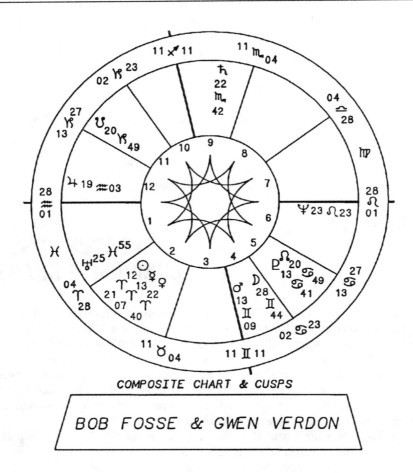

COMPOSITE CHART & CUSPS

BOB FOSSE & GWEN VERDON

the 2nd house and Mars is in the 4th in Gemini representing Bob as having the similar reactions, needs and traits to Gwen's.

Uranus trines Saturn in the 9th, ruling the 11th and 12th houses, reinforcing the true friendliness they felt toward each other as well as their ability to encourage and support each other. Uranus also squares the Moon in Gemini, ruler of the 6th house, undoubtedly reinforcing the differences in their outlook toward work, especially since Verdon (Moon) appears to be more emotional than Fosse (Sun) who is more intense about life (Sun square Pluto).

With the Sun in the 2nd house, values, self-worth and earning ability become the focus of the relationship. The Sun square Pluto in the 5th house heightens their mutual creative ability. They each provided a sounding board, critiquing each other's work as well as being each other's best audience. When asked if he had created Gwen, Fosse replied, "She was hot when I met her. Her in a leotard I will never forget. That alabaster skin, the bantam rooster walk...."

With eight planets below the horizon, as a couple, they are analytical and deeply absorbed in their relationship and though they lack planets in earth signs, they have four in the substance houses. Thus, though there may occasionally be a lack of stability and endurance in their partnership, financially they succeeded and found recognition and daily accord. They lack planets in the relationship houses, but again there is compensation because of three planets and Ascendant in air signs. The Mercury/Mars exact sextile enhances their conversational ability and the ruler of the 3rd house, Venus sextile Jupiter and closely trine Neptune verifies their communication skills, as well as their ability to stimulate each other creatively. It's doubtful they ever lacked subjects for discussion.

The composite signature is Aries (four planets in cardinal, four in fire) indicating the strong physical activity they engaged in, not just in their careers, but also in their personal affairs. Together, they come across as dynamic, energetic and fiery. The chart pattern is a Bucket, with Saturn in Scorpio in the 9th functioning as the handle. As an outlet for the Bowl, Saturn focuses its energies into disciplined action in 9th house areas: aspirations, travel, philosophy, ethics, legal matters; and through its rulership of the 11th– friendship, mutual goals and group activities; and of the 12th– the dance, the all-encompassing world of dance and choreography, as well as backing and abetting each other's strengths.

The major configuration in their composite chart is 12th house Jupiter opposed 6th house Neptune, both square Saturn in the 9th, already significant because it is the Bucket Pattern handle, now again in the spotlight as the focusing planet of the T-Square. Since Jupiter in the 12th rules the composite Midheaven, its opposition to Neptune suggests their ability to balance each other when it came to career issues. Both planets square Saturn suggests, that though disciplined in the work arena, problems arose in their everyday environment (the empty house of the T-square is the 3rd).

Others obviously viewed them as a totally working unit with Saturn trine the Ascendant ruler Uranus, but what of its square to Neptune the other ruler of the 1st house? Were they kidding each other about their relationship? Surely, at times they were. Uranus quincunx Neptune verifies that. When they could make the necessary adjustments, it was in connection with their work; when they couldn't see eye to eye, it reflected in their personal lives.

The emphasized 2nd house implies that their relationship focussed on issues of finance, values and the struggle to be top dog (who was worthier?). The Sun and Mercury both square Pluto and from the composite chart it would seem that they did not always agree on creative themes, or possibly how to raise their daughter. Natally, Fosse has an unaspected Pluto, and the challenging aspects here do not make Pluto integration any easier for him. Mars, the ruler of the 2nd house, trines Jupiter in the 12th so it was relatively easy for them to intuitively sense each other's needs and modes of action. Mars (energy) trine Jupiter (expansion) most likely eased the path of fame and recognition for them (Jupiter ruling the 10th).

Venus, ruler of the 3rd and 8th, trine Neptune certainly presents an image of accord in communication and sexual areas; this aspect also confirms the backing and support (8th) they provided for each other. He made her look good with his choreography, she in turn made him look good with her performance of it and as a couple in the limelight, they were unbeatable.

As we remarked in the comparison, the home comfort and security they set up for each other was most significant and is verified in the composite chart. Mercury, ruler of the 4th is in the 2nd and sextiles Mars in the 4th, as does the Sun. These aspects imply flow and harmony in their, at times, tumultuous home life (Mercury square Pluto).

Since, in the composite chart the 5th and 6th houses are linked (Cancer on both cusps), it is hardly surprising that they worked so well and so creatively together. The square of the Moon to Uranus only heightened their unique collaboration, while its trine to the Ascendant mirrored their excellent physical coordination, and the sextile to Neptune, their grace and beauty of performance.

Others undoubtedly viewed them as financially successful (Sun, ruler of the 7th in the 2nd), able to communicate (Mercury conjunct the Sun), lively and energetic (Sun/Mercury sextile Mars). But the troublesome square of the Sun/Mercury to Pluto, more than likely caught the attention of those who knew them well and could hear the rumblings of discontent.

We suggested that you put each one's natal planets and angles around the composite chart for more information about how each person relates to the partnership. In this case Fosse's natal Moon conjuncts composite Venus; his Sun conjuncts the composite Moon and trines the composite Ascendant. Verdon's natal Ascendant trines composite Saturn and her Mars conjuncts the composite Sun and Mercury. Besides reinforcing much of what we have discussed, these positions also verify the fact, that Fosse benefitted more through the relationship than Verdon did.

In the comparison charts, each brought Saturn to the other's 9th house. Natally his is in the 10th; hers in her 8th. Saturn is usually quite comfortable in the 9th and its trine to Uranus in the composite suggests that they often shared the same aspirations. But, its quincunx to Venus, ruler of the 3rd and the 8th confirms difficulties in communicating (Venus rules the 3rd) as well as sexually (Venus rules the 8th) and psychologically (Saturn rules the 12th). If their difficulties in these areas could have been smoothed, the marriage might have lasted as long as the friendship.

## Directing the Composite Chart

We have told you that you can move the composite chart forward by Solar Arc direction and would like to give an example here. Beginning in 1960, the year they married, we will project it forward to 1987, the year Fosse died. Since this took place 27 years after the marriage, add that increment to each planet and angle. By then the Ascendant at 25 Pisces conjuncted Uranus, its ruler; the 4th house (end of the relationship) Moon at 25 Cancer trined Uranus; Uranus at 22 Aries conjuncted Venus, setting off the quincunx to Saturn and the trine to Neptune. Venus at 19 Taurus squared Jupiter, ruler of the 10th (the end of the professional partnership). Saturn at 19 Sagittarius sextiled Jupiter (the memories linger on).

Verdon and Fosse had stayed friends through thick and thin (her Saturn trine his Pluto; the composite Saturn ruler of the 11th trine Uranus in the 1st, ruler of the composite Ascendant). In 1985 Gwen got on a rehearsal stage and danced a complete number from *Sweet Charity,* for Fosse's eyes only. Both of them nearly 60 years of age and yet both of them "owning" that stage. Two years later, they had both been working all day on a revival of *Sweet Charity*, when he was stricken in his hotel room after a full day of dress rehearsal. They rushed him to George Washington University hospital where doctors tried to revive him and couldn't. He was pronounced dead of cardiac arrest on September 23, 1987 at 7:23 PM EDT. Gwen Verdon was at his side. His entire estate was left to her and their daughter, Nicole.

## Concluding Thoughts

Relationships are what life is all about. If we cannot share our joys or sorrows, life can seem lonely and unfulfilled. As you read this book, we hope you realize that all relationships are workable. Your wish to make them work will make the difference. Your ability through astrology to find the areas of tension or hardship to overcome and those of warmth and harmony to benefit from can also make a difference.

We started this book with John Donne's quote that "No man is an island." We'll end it with Jacques Delille's axiom that "Fate makes our relatives, choice makes our friends and lovers" and add the March/McEvers adage "and astrology makes possible the discernment to handle whatever relationship comes your way."

# APPENDIX

## FOOTNOTE DATA

Warren Beatty                                                            73
   Mar 30, 1937 5:30 PM EST Richmond, VA 37N33 77W27
   BC Holliday confirmed by *CAH* **AA**
Marlene Dietrich                                                         73
   Dec 27,1901 9:15 PM CET (-1) Berlin, Germany 52N28 13E22
   BC Rodden **AA**
Burt Reynolds                                                           95
   Feb 11, 1936 12:10 PM EST Lansing, MI 42N44 84W33
   BC Steinbrecher **AA**
Prince Albert of Monaco                                                 96
   Mar 14, 1958 10:50 AM CET (-1) Monte Carlo, Monaco 43N45 7E25
   Recorded **A**
Claretta Petacci                                                        98
   Feb 28, 1912 10:15 AM CET (-1) Rome Italy 41N54 12E29
   BC Bordoni **AA**
Rebecca West                                                        47, 108
   Dec 21, 1892 8:15 AM WET (0) Edinburgh, Scotland 55N57 3W13
   Letter from her to A. MacKenzie **A**
H.G. Wells                                                          47, 108
   Sep 21, 1866 4:30 PM LMT Bromley, England 51N24 0E02
   1963 Bio by MacKenziepage 3 **B**
Cary Grant                                                          41, 110
   Jan 18, 1904 1:07 AM WET (0) Bristol, England 51N27 2W35
   Bio by Albert Cavoni 1971 page 16 "1st morning hour" **B**
Rosalynn Carter                                                        115
   Aug 18, 1927 6:00 AM CST Plains, GA 32N02 84W24
   *Family Circle Magazine* 1/76 quotes BC **A**
Erwin Rommel                                                           166
   Nov 15, 1891 12:00 PM LMT Heidenheim, Germany 49N01 10E44
   *Gauquelin #2098 Vol III* **AA**
Margaret Thatcher                                                      170
   Oct 13, 1925 9:00 AM WET (0) Grantham, England 52N55 0W39
   C. Harvey quotes her personally **A**
John Major                                                            170
   Mar 29, 1943 2:45 AM WEWT (-1) Brixton, England 51N28 0W06
   R. Grant quotes him between 2 & 4:30 AM **C**
Max Perkins                                                           173
   Sep 20, 1884 7:00 AM EST Manhattan, NY 40N46 73W59
   Rodden from Yoe Stein **C**
Arthur Miller                                                         180
   Oct 17, 1915 5:12 AM EST New York, NY 40N45 73W57
   Church of Light quotes Drew **C**

# March/McEvers
# COMPARISON/COMPOSITE CHART

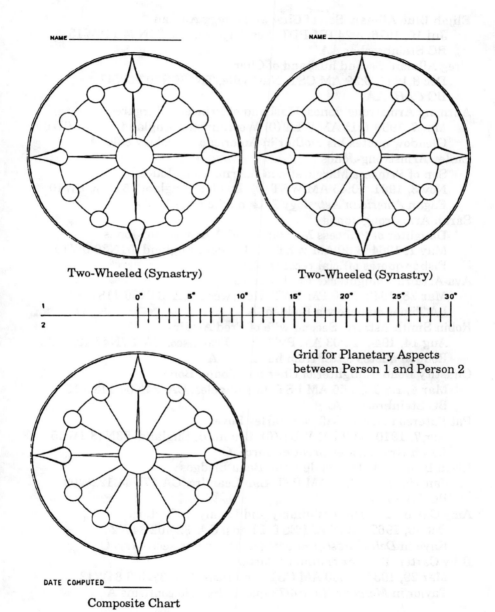

NAME _____

NAME _____

Two-Wheeled (Synastry)

Two-Wheeled (Synastry)

0°     5°     10°     15°     20°     25°     30°

1
2

Grid for Planetary Aspects
between Person 1 and Person 2

DATE COMPUTED_____

Composite Chart

# CHART DATA FOR YOUR FURTHER STUDY
## (People related to examples used in this book)

Elijah Blue Allman  Son of Cher and Gregg Allman
   Jul 10, 1976  3:24 PM PDT  Los Angeles, CA  34N04 118W15
   BC Steinbrecher **AA**
Greg Allman  Second husband of Cher
   Dec 8,1947  3:39 AM CST  Nashville, TN  36N10 86W47
   BC *CAH* **AA**
Anthony Armstrong-Jones  Husband of Princess Margaret
   Mar 7, 1930  6:15 AM WET (0)  Westminster, England  51N30 0W09
   Gleadow quotes his mother in American Astrology 8/60  **A**
Linley Armstrong-Jones
   Son of Princess Margaret and A.Armstrong-Jones
   Nov 3, 1961  10:45 AM WET (0)  London, England  51N30 0W10
   Fagan *American Astrology* 2/62  public records  **AA**
Sarah Armstrong-Jones
   Daughter of Princess Margaret and A.Armstrong-Jones
   May 1, 1964  8:30 AM WET (0)  London, England  51N30 0W10
   Fisher quotes official records  **AA**
Ava Astaire  Daughter of Fred Astaire
   Mar 28, 1942  5:00 PM PWT  Hollywood, CA  34N06 118W20
   LA Times on date via Rodden  **A**
Robin Smith Astaire  Second wife of Fred Astaire
   Aug 14, 1944  12:03 AM PWT  San Francisco, CA  37N47 122W25
   Rodden quotes letter from her 11/77  **A**
Chastity Bono  Daughter of Cher and Sonny Bono
   Mar 4, 1969  12:55 AM PST  Los Angeles, CA  34N04 118W15
   BC Steinbrecher **AA**
Pat Paterson Boyer  Wife of Charles Boyer
   Apr 7, 1910  5:00 PM WET (0)  Bradford, England  53N48 1W45
   Ralph Kraum cites private source  **C**
Lloyd Bridges  Father of Jeff and Beau Bridges
   Jan 15,1913  10:45 AM PST  San Leandro, CA 37N44 122W09
   BC *CAH* **AA**
Amy Carter  Daughter of Jimmy and Rosalynn Carter
   Oct 19, 1967  12:26 AM EST  Plains, GA  32N02 84W24
   Kaye in *Dell Horoscope* quotes Carter press secretary  **C**
Billy Carter  Brother of Jimmy Carter
   Mar 29, 1937  12:30 AM CST  Americus, GA  32N03 84W13
   Taylor in *Mercury Hour* 4/79 quotes BC  bio confirms  **A**

Lillian Carter  Mother of Jimmy Carter
Aug 15, 1898  2:00 PM LMT  Richland, GA  32N06 84W40
*Horoscope Magazine* 8/77 quotes her **A**
Andreas Casiraghi  Son of Princess Caroline and Stefano Casiraghi
Jun 8, 1984 10:50 PM CEDT (-2) Monte Carlo, Monaco  43N45 7E25
*People Magazine* quotes Prince Rainier's telegram **A**
Charlotte Casiraghi
Daughter of Princess Caroline and Stefano Casiraghi
Aug 3, 1986  7:00 PM CEDT (-2) Monte Carlo, Monaco  43N45 7E25
Rodden quotes news on date **A**
Stefano Casiraghi  Second husband of Princess Caroline of Monaco
Sep 8,1960  10:30 PM CET  Milan, Italy  45N28 9E12
Bordoni  BC **AA**
Joe Dimaggio  Second husband of Marilyn Monroe
Nov 25, 1914  7:00 PST  Martinez, CA  38N01 122W08
Steinbrecher has BC no AM or PM
John Paul Densmore (The Doors)
Dec 1, 1944  4:27 AM PWT  Santa Monica, CA  34N01 118W27
Steinbrecher quotes BC from Garner **AA**
Robbie Krieger (The Doors)
Jan 8, 1946  10:54 PM  Los Angeles, CA  34N04 118W15
Steinbrecher quotes Garner from him **A**
Ray Manzarek (The Doors)
Feb 12, 1939  3:30 AM CST  Chicago, IL  41N52 87W39
Steinbrecher quotes Garner from him **A**
Jack Ford  Son of Gerald and Betty Ford
Mar 16, 1952  1:40 AM EST  Washington, DC  38N53 77W01
Rodden quotes public records BC **AA**
Michael Ford  Son of Gerald and Betty Ford
March 14, 1950  6:14 AM EST  Washington, DC  38N53 77W01
Rodden quotes public records BC **AA**
Susan Ford  Daughter of Gerald and Betty Ford
Jul 6, 1957  3:53 PM EDT  Washington, DC  38N53 77W01
N. How quotes Mrs Ford's personal secretary via R Dewey **A**
Jennifer Grant  Daughter of Cary Grant and Dyan Cannon
Feb 26, 1966  7:41 PM PST  Burbank, CA  34N11 118W19
Steinbrecher  BC **AA**
John Kennedy, Jr.  Son of JFK and Jacqueline Onassis
Nov 25, 1960  12:22 AM EST  Washington, DC  38N53  77W01
*Kennedy's Children* by Bill Adler **B**
Joseph Patrick Kennedy III  Son of Ethel and RF Kennedy
Sep 24, 1952  12:15 PM EDT  Brighton, MA  42N21 71W08
McEvoy quotes *Boston Globe* 9/25/52 **A**

Mary Courtney Kennedy  Daughter of Ethel and Robert Kennedy
Sep 9, 1956  7:48 PM EDT  Boston, MA  42N22 71W04
McEvoy quotes Boston papers for BC  **AA**

Mary Kerry Kennedy  Third daughter, 7th child of RF
and Ethel Kennedy
Sep 8, 1959  12:55 PM EDT  Boston, MA  42n22 71W04
McEvoy quotes BC  **AA**

Ted Kennedy  Senator from Massachusetts/brother of JFK RFK
Feb 22, 1932  3:58 AM EST  Dorchester, MA  42N22 71W04
J. Hill quotes hospital records **A**

Joey Luft  Son of Judy Garland, brother Lorna Luft, half brother Liza
Mar 29, 1955  2:16 AM PST  Los Angeles, CA  34N04 118W15
Smyth/Wilson BC  **AA**

Shirley MacLaine  Sister of Warren Beatty
Apr 24, 1934  3:57 PM EST  Richmond, VA  37N33 77W27
BC  Steinbrecher **AA**

Romano Mussolini  Son of Benito and Rachele Mussolini
Sep 26, 1927  11:05 PM CET (-1)  Forli, Italy  44N13 12E03
Steinbrecher Birth registration **AA**

Patricia Nixon  Grandmother of Alex Eisenhower
Mar 16, 1912  11:45 PM PST  Ely, NV  39N15 114W54
McEvoy quotes her daughter Julie "just before midnight" **A**

Jackie Onassis  Mother of Caroline, wife of JFK
Jul 28, 1929  2:30 PM EDT  Southhampton, NY  40N54 72W23
Tyl in *The Principles and Practice of Astrology* **C**

Mark Phillips  Ex-husband of Princess Anne
Sep 22, 1948  1:45 AM WEDT (-1)  Tetsbury, England  51N59 2W09
Letter from press secretary to the Queen **A**

Pablo Picasso  Father of Paloma
Oct 25, 1881  11:15 PM Madrid time  Malaga, Spain  36N43 4W25
Biography by P. Cabanne **B**

Carlo Ponti, Jr.  Son of Sophia Loren and Carlo Ponti
Dec 29, 1968  8:53 AM CET (-1)  Ginevra, Italy  46N12 6E09
Bordoni quotes *Oggi* **B**

Edoardo Ponti  Son of Sophia Loren and Carlo Ponti
Jan 6, 1973  8:30 AM CET (-1)  Ginevra, Italy  46N12 6E09
Bordoni quotes *Corriere* **B**

Prince Edward of England  Son of Queen Elizabeth and Prince Philip
Mar 10, 1964  8:20 PM WET (0)  London, England  51n30 0W10
BR  Steinbrecher **AA**

Prince Harry of England  Second son of Prince Charles
and Princess Diana
Sep 15, 1984  4:20 PM WEWT (-1)  London, England  51N30 0W10
Official records **A**

Prince Rainier of Monaco  Father of Princess Caroline
    May 31, 1923  6:00 AM CET (-1) Monte Carlo, Monaco  43N45 7E25
    Official records  **A**
Prince William of England  First son of Prince Charles & Princess Diana
    June 21, 1982  9:03 PM  WEWT (-1)  London, England  51N30 0W10
    Notice from Buckingham Palace **A**
Princess Grace of Monaco  Mother of Princess Caroline
    Nov 12, 1929  5:31 AM EST  Philadelphia, PA  39N57 75W10
    Garner quotes BC  **AA**
Princess Stephanie of Monaco  Sister of Princess Caroline
    Feb 1, 1965  6:25 PM CET (-1)  Monte Carlo, Monaco  43N45 7E25
    Royal Archives of Monaco **AA**
Isabella Rossellini  Twin daughter of Bergman and Rossellini
    Jun 18, 1952  6:30 PM CET (-1)  Rome, Italy  41N54 12E29
    Bordoni quotes BC  **AA**
Isotta Rossellini  Twin daughter of Bergman and Rossellini
    Jun 18, 1952  6:41 PM CET (-1)  Rome. Italy  41N54 12E29
    Bordoni quotes *Oggi*  **B**
Robertino Rossellini  Son of Bergman and Rossellini
    Feb 2, 1950  7:00 PM CET (-1)  Rome, Italy  41N54 12E29
    Bordoni BC  **AA**
Athina Onassis Roussel  Grandaughter Aristotle Onassis
    Jan 29, 1985 2:50 AM CET (-1) Neuilly Sur Seine, France 48N53 2E16
    Steinbrecher  BC **AA**
Robert Schumann  Husband of Clara Schumann
    Jun 8, 1810  9:10 PM LMT  Zwickau, Germany  50N44 12E29
    Parish records  **AA**
Maria Scicolone  Sister of Sophia Loren/wife of Romano Mussolini
    May 11, 1938  3:00 AM CET (-1) Naples, Italy  40N51 14E17
    Bordoni quotes BC  **AA**
Vanessa Vadim  Daughter of Jane Fonda and Roger Vadim
    Sep 28, 1968  8:30 AM CET (-1)  Paris, France  48N52 2E20
    Bordoni quotes *Oggi*  **B**

# Especially for the TWO of YOU

## COMPATIBILITY PROFILE

### Do you REALLY know your relationships?

Everyone knows how important understanding is in making a relationship work! This report compares your chart with another, discusses what each of you wants and needs from the relationship and how you impact one another. Select your profile for a specific type of relationship:

| | | |
|---|---|---|
| **CPL**—Romantic Partners | **CPF**—Friends | **CPC**—Business Colleague |
| **CPM**—Mother/Child | **CPD**—Father/Child | **CPG**—Grandparent/Child |
| **CPR**—Other Relatives | | |

**Compatibility Profile** is bound; includes 15-22 pages of text and a 2-Wheel Concentric Color Chart. When ordering you must be prepared to give places, dates and times for TWO people.
**CP** (use complete codes as above) **Compatibility Profile...$21.95**

## ROMANCE REPORT

Here's a report especially designed for romantic relationships! Using the method called synastry, it considers all of the astrological factors that apply to relationships in the charts of two lovers. Special emphasis is given to certain houses, and to planetary aspects between the two charts. Discusses mental compatibility, sexual interests, emotional needs, complements and conflicts, and much more. **Romance Report** is bound, about 15 pages, and includes a 2-Wheel Chart. A Chart Comparison is included in the price (but not bound in). This report is available either by itself or as a part of the Romance Package (see below). **CP2I Romance Report...$21.95**

## THEMES FOR TWO

Especially written to interpret a Composite Chart (a chart formed by the mid-points of the planets in two individual charts.) It looks at all house placements, signs and planetary aspects in the Composite Chart. The text is written to focus primarily on romantic associations, but is applicable for business and other relationships as well. The report is bound, approximately 7 to 10 pages long and includes a color Composite Chart. This report is available either by itself or as a part of the Romance Package (see below). **CP3I Themes for Two...$21.95**

# Also by ACS Publications

All About Astrology Series
The American Atlas: US Latitudes and Longitudes,
    Time Changes and Time Zones (Shanks)
The American Book of Tables
The American Ephemeris Series 1901-2000
The American Ephemeris for the 20th Century [Midnight] 1900 to 2000
The American Ephemeris for the 20th Century [Noon] 1900 to 2000
The American Ephemeris for the 21st Century 2001-2050
The American Heliocentric Ephemeris 1901-2000
The American Midpoint Ephemeris 1991-1995 (Michelsen)
The American Sidereal Ephemeris 1976-2000
Asteroid Goddesses (George & Bloch)
Astro Alchemy: Making the Most of Your Transits (Negus)
Astro Essentials: Planets in Signs, Houses & Aspects (Pottenger)
Astrological Games People Play (Ashman)
Astrological Insights into Personality (Lundsted)
Basic Astrology: A Guide for Teachers & Students (Negus)
Basic Astrology: A Workbook for Students (Negus)
The Book of Neptune (Waram)
The Changing Sky (Forrest)
Complete Horoscope Interpretation: Putting Together Your Planetary Profile
    (Pottenger)
Cosmic Combinations: A Book of Astrological Exercises (Negus)
Dial Detective (Simms)
Easy Tarot Guide (Masino)
Expanding Astrology's Universe (Dobyns)
Hands That Heal (Burns)
Healing with the Horoscope: A Guide to Counseling (Pottenger)
Houses of the Horoscope (Herbst)
The Inner Sky (Forrest)
The International Atlas: World Latitudes, Longitudes and Time Changes (Shanks)
The Koch Book of Tables
Midpoints: Unleashing the Power of the Planets (Munkasey)
The Only Way to. . . Learn Astrology, Vol. I-III (March & McEvers)
    Volume I - Basic Principles
    Volume II - Math & Interpretation Techniques
    Volume III - Horoscope Analysis
    Volume IV- The Only Way to... Learn About Tomorrow
Planetary Heredity (M. Gauquelin)
Planetary Planting (Riotte)
Planets in Solar Returns (Shea)
Planets in Work (Binder)
Psychology of the Planets (F. Gauquelin)
Skymates: The Astrology of Love, Sex & Intimacy (Forrest & Forrest)
Spirit Guides: We Are Not Alone (Belhayes)
Tables of Planetary Phenomenon (Michelsen)
Twelve Wings of the Eagle (Simms)
The Way of the Spirit: The Wisdom of the Ancient Nanina (Whiskers)